D1195479

LINCOLN'S QUEST FOR EQUALITY

LINCOLN'S QUEST FOR EQUALITY

The Road to Gettysburg

CARL F. WIECK

NORTHERN
ILLINOIS
UNIVERSITY
PRESS
DeKalb

2002

Published by the Northern Illinois University Press, DeKalb, Illinois 60115

Manufactured in the United States using acid-free paper

Designed by Julia Fauci

Library of Congress Cataloging-in-Publication Data

Wieck, Carl F., 1937–

Lincoln's quest for equality : the road to Gettysburg / Carl F. Wieck.

p. cm.

Includes bibliographical references (p.) and index.

ISBN 0-87580-299-0 (alk. paper)

1. Lincoln, Abraham, 1809–1865—Views on slavery. 2. Lincoln, Abraham, 1809–1865—Views on African Americans. 3. Lincoln, Abraham, 1809–1865—Gettysburg address. 4. Slaves—Emancipation—United States. I. Title.

E457.2.W64 2002

973.7'092—dc21

2002023012

To my sister and brothers,

Grace, Clifford, and Randolph,

in recognition of their generosity of spirit.

Contents

Acknowledgments ix

Introduction 3

1 Lincoln, Parker, and Abolitionism 12

2 Concealing Lincoln's Abolitionism 41

3 Parker and Politicians 72

4 Lincoln's "House Divided" Revisited 91

5 What Lincoln Took to Gettysburg 124

6 The Gettysburg Phrase 150

Conclusion 174

Notes 179

Bibliography 201

Index 207

Acknowledgments

❧ One can never adequately acknowledge the support and acts of kindness that make possible a work such as that which follows. One can only imperfectly describe the lightened step produced by the librarian who has gone the extra mile to resolve a question, or to uncover and send along a copy of a document, which arrives in the mail "with the compliments of. . . ." It is impossible to express the elation provided by the reader of the manuscript whose laser-eyed criticism has unerringly identified soft spots, sharpened arguments, or spared you embarrassment. Never can the friend or relative who quietly shores you up in unstinting fashion know how much that means in the moment.

The following persons fit into one or more of the categories just mentioned, and they and I know which. I believe that is enough, for this public acknowledgment still has a private dimension I wish to preserve. I recall their names, therefore, in no particular order, as each in some unique way has contributed to improving my work. I am proud to have had their help, and I owe each of those mentioned sincere gratitude for the gift of time and attention bestowed on my effort: Martin P. Johnson, David Zarefsky, Deba P. Patnaik, Philippa Letsky, Kathleen C. McDonough, Winifred Collins, Carmen Embry, Joseph F. Fullum, Eeva Väyrynen, Roberta Zonghi, Claudia Engler, Grace Wilson, Anne M. Decker, Betsy Martin, E. Cheryl Schnirring, Olga Tsapina, Clark Evans, James H. Hutson, Leslie A. Morris, Susan Bean, Nicholas Graham, Connie Butts, Mary Michals, Kim Bauer, Carrie Foley, Burwell Hardy, Ralf Norrman, Maurice LeBreton, Bernard Poli, Clifford Wieck, Randolph Wieck, and Herman and Jean Wieck.

An institution is at best a collection of the kinds of individuals just mentioned. And the following institutions, several of which have one or more of those individuals in their service, have buttressed my efforts in every useful way: the Massachusetts Historical

Society; the Houghton and Widener Libraries of Harvard University; the Boston Public Library; the Library of Congress; the Huntington Library; the Illinois State Historical Library; the Unitarian-Universalist Association Library; Mr. Williams Library, London; the Cornell University Library; the University of Louisville Library; the British Library, London; the Southern Baptist Theological Seminary Library, Louisville; the University of Iowa Library; the Sorbonne Library of the University of Paris; the Benjamin Franklin Library, Paris; the Louisville Free Public Library; the Bodleian Library, Oxford; the Bibliothèque Nationale, Paris; the University of Tampere Library, Finland; the American Studies Library of the University of Tampere; Northern Illinois University Press.

To those whose names and institutions should figure here but do not, I wish to apologize. I can assure them that their help has been appreciated even if my memory does not at present accord them their due, if I have been unaware of their aid, or if for any other reason they are not named. Although they go unsung, their contribution can be traced somewhere in the pages of this work, and I hope they may take satisfaction from the results they have helped generate.

LINCOLN'S QUEST FOR EQUALITY

Introduction

❧ Abraham Lincoln is revered as one of America's greatest presidents, and his Gettysburg Address has been praised as "the best modern speech in English," an "intellectual revolution [that] remade America."[1] Yet up until now the intellectual, philosophical, and linguistic roots of Lincoln's clarion call for full equality and democracy, though often matter for discussion and debate, have remained less than clear. In the pages that follow I suggest that the Unitarian minister and prominent abolitionist Theodore Parker (1810–1860) exerted pivotal but almost unperceived influence on Lincoln's thought and moral development, culminating with the Gettysburg Address and revealing that Lincoln had considerably stronger ties to abolitionism than has previously been suggested. This insight—with its far-reaching consequences for understanding the Great Emancipator's intellectual journey to Gettysburg—can considerably increase our appreciation of the intricate workings and development of the mind of a man whose understanding of the founders' concepts has fundamentally shaped American society.

Although Lincoln cautiously preserved discreet public distance from avowed abolitionists like Parker, his private links to such men prove to have been closer than has generally been presumed, owing primarily to the vigilance he exercised in keeping the extent of his connections concealed. Lincoln's silence on matters that might endanger his political career was so thoroughgoing that Parker goes unmentioned by the future president—despite the fact that his law partner, William H. Herndon, maintained a steady correspondence with Parker between 1854 and 1859;[2] despite the fact that the minister's works were present in the Lincoln-Herndon law office; and despite extended discussions between Lincoln and Herndon concerning much of what they read.[3] Lincoln was nonetheless aware of the preacher's thinking on the need for direct action against slavery, was also possibly more sympathetic to it than he gave voice to in public, and, for reasons soon to be explored, would not have been taken aback to learn that Parker was an ardent secret supporter of the militant abolitionist John Brown, fully cognizant of the combustible potential connected with the revolutionary's plans.

In that instance, Parker's strategic silence concerning his tie to Brown, together with Lincoln's precarious but conscious distancing tactics, served to safeguard the political virginity essential to preserving the Republican party's respectability in the eyes of voters of differing persuasions. Following Brown's failed raid on the government arsenal at Harpers Ferry, Virginia, in 1859, Lincoln could deny with a clear conscience that any member of the Republican party was linked to the debacle.[4] Nor were the stakes inconsequential; for had Parker apprised Herndon of his involvement with Brown, Lincoln almost certainly would have become privy to the information and would have had difficulty countering the assertions of his adversaries. However, despite Parker's diplomatic reserve on this occasion, it should be realized that this was an exception, and that the minister shared other private political views as well as all his published writings with Herndon, writings and views incorporating more than enough incendiary material to which Lincoln would not have wished to see his name openly connected.

To understand that Parker strongly influenced Lincoln can therefore allow us to perceive much more of the politician's political astuteness than previously has been evident. And because Lincoln's words represent enduring moral milestones in the struggle for justice and equality for all of America's citizens, and because they constitute a fundamental interpretation of democracy for subsequent generations of Americans, a realization of the key sources from which he drew in developing his principal concepts is indispensable to understanding the manner in which his powerful and creative mind integrated, adapted, and transformed the ideas at his disposal. Theodore Parker was just such a key source, but although he is generally credited with providing Lincoln with the words "government of the people, by the people, for the people" (usually known as the Gettysburg Phrase, having been made famous in the Gettysburg Address), Lincoln's greater debt to the preacher has never been fully comprehended.

Over the years only one historian, Garry Wills, has ventured much beyond the confident claim concerning Parker's role with respect to the Gettysburg Phrase that was put forward by Herndon in the 1889 biography of Lincoln he coauthored with Jesse W. Weik. And because of Herndon's close ties to his law partner, subsequent biographers have commonly left unquestioned his account concerning Parker's possible influence on Lincoln. Nevertheless, in *Lincoln at Gettysburg: The Words that Remade America,* Wills does yeoman service in elegantly analyzing and shedding light on the importance to Lincoln of Parker and his transcendental thinking.[5] Yet much of vital significance is left undiscovered and, as a result, untold. In the present study I shall examine grounds for this, while undertaking to illustrate the critical influence exerted—not only on Lincoln's Gettysburg Address but also on his House Divided speech—by Theodore Parker's extraordinary "Sermon of the Dangers which Threaten the Rights of Man in America," delivered on July 2, 1854.[6]

❧ Parker's sermon (even measured by the minister's own prolific standards) is a long one and has never before given rise to the claim I advance here. However, when we realize that it was first delivered shortly after Herndon began corresponding with Parker and shortly after he first received Parker's published works, it begins to take on increased luster. Herndon held Parker in high esteem and he shared what he read with his partner, which meant that Lincoln, at just this period, came within range of the preacher's fiery pen, a pen deeply dipped in the ink of abolitionism. Parker's sermon is a wide-ranging and imposing effort. It covers a broad spectrum of his thinking, a critical feature of which was his conception of the weight the issue of slavery bore for the nation. With America's Independence Day celebration only two days off, Parker, who considered slavery the greatest threat then being posed to the young republic, took advantage of the occasion to awaken his listeners to the gravity of the peril. The question was nothing less than whether "America is to live or die?" (Rights of Man, 342). Nine years later at Gettysburg, Pennsylvania, Abraham Lincoln would also contemplate "whether that nation or any nation so conceived and so dedicated can long endure."[7] And this would not be the only instance where a parallel could be drawn between the utterances of the two men.

Up until now, aside from the Declaration of Independence (to which Lincoln directly refers), Daniel Webster's celebrated Reply to Hayne—in which the senator argued powerfully in defense of the

Union and against the rights of states to reject or "nullify" federal laws they happened to disagree with—has been considered the major influence on Lincoln's speeches.[8] The nullification question bears directly on the right of a state to secede from the Union, a problem facing Lincoln while he was writing his First Inaugural Address, so there are clear grounds for his interest in, respect for, and obvious application of Webster's speech on that occasion. Wills follows Herndon in affirming that Lincoln thought Webster's Reply to Hayne "the greatest American speech, and consulted it in composing his House Divided Speech and the First Inaugural."[9] Wills further contends that "Echoes of it can be found in other Lincoln speeches, including the Gettysburg Address. It would be hard to find any other text, except the Declaration of Independence, which Lincoln used with such familiarity and respect."[10] Nor have other scholars strayed from this path when tracing the roots of Lincoln's thinking—in particular on the subject of slavery.

Despite such unanimity, I shall argue with respect to the House Divided speech and the Gettysburg Address that Abraham Lincoln used Theodore Parker's "Sermon of the Dangers which Threaten the Rights of Man in America" in a far wider and more profound fashion than Daniel Webster's Reply to Hayne. A fundamental reason for this is that in neither the House Divided speech nor the Gettysburg Address was the nullification concept Lincoln's central focus, as it was with the First Inaugural. Webster's Reply to Hayne, while important to Lincoln, was thus of less immediate use to him on those occasions as he formulated his arguments, philosophy, and phrasing. On the other hand, Parker's "Rights of Man" sermon dealt with the Kansas-Nebraska question raised in Stephen Douglas's 1854 bill concerning the rights of territories with regard to the introduction of slavery, and this question would be at the core of Lincoln's House Divided speech of 1858. Moreover, Parker's philosophical exposition in his sermon of "the idea of freedom" he saw embodied in the Declaration of Independence would provide Lincoln with matter for reflection when, five years further on, in 1863, prior to Gettysburg, he turned for inspiration to "the proposition that all men are created equal." It was therefore possible for Lincoln to draw heavily in 1858 and again in 1863 on a sermon first delivered in 1854. The regard in which he held the sermon, as was also the case with Webster's 1830 Reply to Hayne, is illustrated by the fact that he placed no statute of limitations on the pertinence of its concepts. And it would appear that Lincoln considered the wisdom contained in the sermon of a nature sufficiently grand to accompany and sustain him as he grew from frustrated politician in 1854, to candidate for the U.S. Senate in 1858, to war-weary president honoring the Union dead at Gettysburg in 1863.

❧ Seldom is it simple to come to categorical conclusions concerning questions touching on the often-enigmatic subject of "influence," and the task can be daunting in connection with hallowed figures or the well-nigh sacred documents we have inherited from them. We often seem to wish to have our idols spring fully formed into the world without dependence on the past, and Abraham Lincoln is one of those figures who fits easily into such a category. It may therefore appear far-fetched to suggest that a man so imbued with respect for law and rationality might be beholden in a significant way to a radical preacher he seems never to have met.[11] Grounds for such a claim would appear even less substantial when it is realized that Parker, though considered an intellectual of the first order who, according to one contemporary, "belonged to the true race of the giants of learning," was rejected by many of his Unitarian brethren for questioning the importance of Christ's divinity.[12] He also enjoyed a reputation as an acknowledged abolitionist actively participating in the Underground Railroad. With flagrant disregard for the law, and undisguised bravado, the minister once joined two fugitive slaves in marriage, gave the husband a Bible and a sword, together with instructions "in the use of both," then wrote a letter to the president of the United States flaunting his illegal act.[13]

Notwithstanding such apparently frail underpinning for an assertion of Parker's influence on Lincoln, I intend to demonstrate that the minister consciously strove to sway the thinking of leading political figures of his era; that Lincoln was not averse to borrowing ideas and phrasing from other writers; that key elements of both the Gettysburg Address and the House Divided speech are directly traceable to philosophy, rhetoric, logic, and ideas found in "A Sermon of the Dangers which Threaten the Rights of Man in America"; and that the sermon incorporates specific phrases such as "a house divided against itself," "we shall not fail," and two instances of "government of all, by all, for all," which are the same as or similar to those used by Lincoln.[14] In addition, I propose to illustrate how, although the Illinois lawyer took pains to conceal his links to abolitionists such as Parker, William Herndon served as the direct channel between the two men that made possible the effective operation of the minister's influence. Central to this discussion is my disclosure of the hitherto unremarked manner in which both Herndon and Joseph Fort Newton, editor of the Herndon-Parker correspondence, have unintentionally contributed to obscuring Parker's importance to Lincoln.

Few questions pertaining to influence are single-faceted, however, and one feature of the current work concerns the manner in which the writings of Daniel Webster interweave with Parker's own to affect Lincoln's. At times Webster's work seems dominant, but more often it is Parker's. There is nevertheless little doubt that the work of both thinkers often combined or interacted to aid Lincoln in crystallizing thought and expression appropriate to the condition of the country on more than one critical occasion when he seems to have most needed silent support. A key reason for this is that Parker as well as Lincoln owed a clear—if unconscious—debt to Webster, the senior member of the trio, a debt that becomes manifest in comparing the works of the three men. But Webster died in 1852, and although thereafter his notions and locutions could still offer color, still contribute in spirit and counsel continuance of the Union, by 1858 the senator had been absent from the political stage for too long to provide the contemporary philosophical and pragmatic guidance Lincoln sorely needed when looking within and around himself for tools with which to tackle the nation's more recent problems. This role seems to have been filled by Theodore Parker.

For as Lincoln was gradually driven into ever tighter corners, with less and less room to maneuver on the slavery issue, he seems to have regarded ever more features of Parker's abolitionist attitudes as at least partially admissible. Although in 1854 Lincoln would not have been inclined to publicly adopt Parker's fundamental philosophy concerning the potential fate of a "house divided against itself," by 1858 the views being openly embraced by the senatorial candidate from Illinois had moved much nearer to those expounded by the Boston preacher. Lincoln realized that the situation was out of balance and that, as Parker had put it, "Equilibrium must come" (Rights of Man, 368).

In time Lincoln also came to understand that removal of America's slaves to another country, through the creation of new colonies, was not going to prove a feasible way of resolving the problem. This solution—which he appears to have adopted from Thomas Jefferson and its later proponent, the Kentucky statesman Henry Clay—revealed itself decreasingly viable within the reality the Illinois politician was obliged to confront.[15] Lincoln had displayed his support of and respect for that position when he meticulously set forth Clay's views in his eulogy for the great man in 1852.[16] But the program of the American Colonization Society, an organization Clay still headed at his death, was hampered by being aimed only at free blacks.

Such a limitation created a considerable obstacle for those intent on resolving the larger problem of slavery itself. Equilibrium within the country desperately needed to be achieved, but, as Lincoln continued to wrestle with finding a reasonable means of bringing it about through some form of resettlement, developments in America were outpacing him. The country's options were swiftly being reduced to a single one. Parker, as did other abolitionists, resolutely took this position much earlier than Lincoln, but when the lawyer finally settled on a similar solution, he knew where to look for support: Webster could aid in maintaining the Union; Parker with defining the problem of slavery and drawing the ineluctable conclusions inherent in the logic of the contemporary situation.

Lincoln himself had never approved of slavery, once stating unequivocally: "I am naturally anti-slavery. If slavery is not wrong, nothing is wrong. I can not remember when I did not so think."[17] He knew that its continuation could have a pernicious effect on the nation's underlying morality. Yet, even after acquiring the powers of president, Lincoln "never understood that the Presidency conferred upon me an unrestricted right to act officially upon this judgment and feeling. . . . I understood, too, that in ordinary civil administration this oath [to safeguard the Constitution] even forbade me to practically indulge my primary abstract judgment on the moral question of slavery."[18] By 1862, however, he found himself compelled by circumstances to take a position more closely approximating Parker's; and the liberation of the slaves in the states in open rebellion, through the Emancipation Proclamation of January 1, 1863, was one of the results.[19] It thus seems only fitting that the minister's ideas and formulations should find their way into the address Lincoln presented at Gettysburg, in November of the same year, enunciating the importance of "a new birth of Freedom." This speech would go far toward redrafting the philosophical and political foundation of the United States of America.[20] And that Lincoln could manage to do so in only 272 words is in many ways thanks to Theodore Parker's long, careful 1854 exposition of the "Dangers which Threaten the Rights of Man in America."[21]

Acknowledging the influence of Parker's sermon on the Gettysburg Address and House Divided speech can consequently reorient a number of received ideas concerning the originality of concepts and language that in Lincoln's capable hands became endowed with near-mystic power. Realizing the probable source of these concepts and this language will not diminish the magnitude of Lincoln's accomplishments, but it can enable us to better penetrate the motives behind many of his actions and so acquire broader insight into the workings of the mind of this major figure. Allowing Parker to join Jefferson and Webster on Lincoln's stage, for example, permits more precise tracing than has previously seemed possible of the connection between Lincoln's antislavery leanings and the congruence of rationalist, religious perceptions that united the politician and the preacher. This affinity, in J. David Greenstone's view, could conceivably have stemmed from the fact that Lincoln's "political ethic can be traced, even if only indirectly, to the same New England Protestant tradition that spawned abolitionism," a "religious tradition common to both Whigs and abolitionists [which] constituted a family of related belief systems."[22] Such an identity of outlook could allow the logical, self-taught Illinois lawyer to relate to and retain the moral lessons contained within Parker's antislavery rhetoric, and in turn may have contributed to easier acknowledgment of the minister's basic political convictions as reasonable, despite his radical stance.

Recognizing Parker's importance can also permit a wider awareness of the kinds of ideas and guidance he could offer as Lincoln grappled with making decisions and adopting measures Webster had never had to contemplate. Parker lived eight years longer than Webster, and those years were marked by increasing threats to the Union Webster had so admired and defended. There were, in addition, developments during those years of which Webster had had no notion, such as the effective repeal of Henry Clay's 1820 Missouri Compromise by the Kansas-Nebraska Act of 1854. In this study I intend to establish that Parker's understanding and analysis of the probable repercussions of this development, as presented in his "Rights of Man" sermon, became of key importance to Lincoln as he lived through the demands placed upon him by the political upheavals of his day.

❧ Gifted with a talent for seizing on and shaping pertinent thoughts and words of others in responding to his and the nation's needs, and skilled in the lawyer's art of uncovering precedents, Abraham Lincoln was not averse to borrowing what he needed from any promising source. The importance to him of the Declaration of Independence—whose deceptively simple contention that "all men are created equal" would not permit him to sleep easy—has long been known; and his familiarity with Webster's Reply to Hayne is well documented.[23] But Theodore Parker has most often been relegated to the shadows, with only a modicum of attention paid to his link to the Gettysburg Phrase. Parker has occupied little space in the story of Lincoln's conception of two of America's most memorable speeches, and not even Wills accords the minister's influence the importance it merits. The time has come for this to change. It is essential to understand that Lincoln was not creating his speeches in a vacuum; he was building with bricks that had already been fired and were ready to hand, not all of which had come from the kilns of Jefferson and Webster.

For this reason, the following pages undertake to unlock a door that has effectively been sealed for almost a century and a half, in order to bring the reader face-to-face with a heretofore hidden Lincoln. To open this door can oblige a reconsideration of earlier interpretations of the great man and can mandate reexamination of notions regarding the labyrinthine path he was constrained to follow in his lonely, often agonizing efforts to preserve in a principled and humane fashion the ideals inherited from his predecessors. But beyond this door we may discover a far more complex mortal than has commonly been assumed, and find ourselves once again vouchsafed cause for esteem as well as awe.

CHAPTER ONE

Lincoln, Parker, and Abolitionism

❧ Abraham Lincoln's earliest initiatives as a member of the U.S. House of Representatives were connected directly with war and indirectly with slavery, two forces destined to leave indelible marks on his career. On December 22, 1847, the recently elected Whig politician offered resolutions designed to force President James K. Polk to commit himself as to whether the war between the United States and Mexico—a conflict with the potential of advancing the cause of slavery by providing territory that might be carved up into additional slave states—had begun on "a particular spot" of American soil and could therefore be considered justified by Mexican aggression.[1] Attempting to embarrass the president and to cast the Democrats in an unfavorable light, Lincoln followed up his "Spot" resolutions by voting on January 3, 1848, for George Ashmun's amendment censuring the president. He expanded his challenge in a carefully prepared speech before the House on January 12.[2] These moves took place nearly two years after the Mexican War had begun, when all the military battles had already been fought and as the clash between the two nations was actually drawing to an end. Lincoln's long-range goal in attacking Polk was to see Mexican War hero Zachary Taylor replace the president, but considering the heated feelings to which the war had given rise, the fledgling congressman's speech, though often colorful, seems relatively restrained, one possible reason being the limits to which he was subject.

Lincoln realized only too well that a mistake in strategy could result in having to live down caustic criticism for years afterward. Yet, believing the political hay to be made at Polk's expense worth the risk of appearing to refuse support to his countrymen in time of war (a charge that might be blunted by backing General Taylor for the nation's highest office), he repeated in his speech the challenge to the president he had issued a few weeks earlier. Lincoln raised a banner he knew might well draw enemy fire, and it did, apparently even more than he expected. In later years his former law partner William H. Herndon, though perhaps somewhat overdramatizing, recalled, "By Mr. Lincoln's course in Congress in the Mexican War he politically killed himself here [in Illinois]: he offered some resolutions in Congress calling for the 'spot' where the first blood was shed by the Mexicans."[3] This swiftly earned Lincoln the demeaning nickname "Spotty," and even ten years afterward, in his debates with Stephen A. Douglas, the "spot" would return to haunt him when Douglas used it to impugn his patriotism.[4]

Lincoln was aware that the game was not without hazards, and although the speech he made, the resolutions he offered, and the votes he cast against the Mexican War occurred at a point when the war had all but ended, he was not insensitive to the fact that the position he had adopted might have negative effects on his political career. He fretted that his fence-straddling posture ("voting supplies" without supporting the war for which those supplies were intended) might be misunderstood. And the qualms he felt about the potential implications of his actions are sharply delineated in a letter he sent Herndon shortly after delivering his speech:

> because of my vote for Mr. Ashmun's amendment, you fear that you and I disagree about the war. I regret this, not because of any fear we shall remain disagreed, after you shall have read this letter, but because if *you* misunderstand, I fear other good friends will also. . . . I do not mean this letter for the public, but for you. Before it reaches you, you will have seen and read my pamphlet speech, and perhaps, scared anew, by it. After you get over your scare read it over again, sentence by sentence, and tell me honestly what you think of it.[5]

Through his repetition of words such as "fear" and "scare," Lincoln betrays definite uneasiness, and considering his obvious apprehension, it is not surprising that he constantly felt compelled to exercise caution when adopting political positions at the edge of acceptability. Despite his understanding of the necessity for prudence, however, the man who in later years would hold steady the tiller of the ship of state during the storm of civil war showed true daring where others preferred to protect their flanks.

On the other hand, the potentially critical link between the Mexican War and the slavery issue appears to have caused the congressman less concern. That it was not paramount on his list of priorities is apparent in the fact that he championed Taylor, although the general was a Southern slaveholder. Two years earlier, moreover, Lincoln had shared with a friend his considered doubt that the annexation of Texas "would augment the evil of slavery."[6] But as the Mexican War neared its close, there were nonetheless elements in the Illinois politician's approach from which antislavery forces could draw comfort, since he expressed the clear "desire that we shall not acquire any [territory] extending so far South, as to enlarge and agrivate [*sic*] the distracting question of slavery."[7] He also regularly endorsed the Wilmot Proviso, which was aimed at prohibiting the introduction of slavery into territory acquired either peaceably or militarily from Mexico. And in a speech before the House on July 27, 1848, Lincoln expressed the hope and belief that Taylor as president would not veto the proviso in the event of its passage, nevertheless pledging to vote for the general in any case, since he felt that the alternative, General Lewis Cass, would only prove worse.[8]

Lincoln's balanced wariness thus dictated that his tactics and timing with respect to the slavery issue would often and of necessity be at variance with the wishes of advocates of immediate abolition. And he studiously guarded his distance from openly avowed abolitionists, since a proven connection could impair if not completely undo his efforts to maintain indispensable local political support. As one historian points out, "To be branded as an abolitionist in central Illinois—his constituency as a legislator and a U.S. congressman—would have been certain political suicide."[9] At a late stage in his presidency, moreover, Lincoln frankly admitted that in his actions regarding emancipation, "I claim not to have controlled events, but confess plainly that events have controlled me."[10] In striving to conscientiously serve and speak for the majority of the people, Abraham Lincoln clearly needed to be certain he heard their combined voice—not just that of the most vociferous fraction—before deciding on an approach that would best serve their welfare.

The Unitarian preacher Theodore Parker, on the other hand, experienced no such need to appeal to a plurality of voters, and no such reservations about adopting a radical stance on either the Mexican War or the subject of abolition. Although the Boston minister realized, as with Lincoln, that his public position placed certain restrictions on him, his actions often seemed to fly in the face of those restrictions. And this had begun early.

THEODORE PARKER

(Courtesy of the Unitarian Universalist Association)

On May 19, 1841 (only four years following his ordination as a minister on June 1, 1837), Parker preached "A Discourse of the Transient and Permanent in Christianity," a sermon that would ultimately revolutionize Unitarianism. At the time, it meant that for Parker "Most of my clerical friends fell off; some would not speak to me in the street and refused to take me by the hand; in their public meetings they left the sofas or benches when I sat down, and withdrew from me as Jews from contact with a leper."[11] While barely avoiding excommunication by his fellow Unitarian clergymen, Parker nevertheless persisted in committing himself to social causes that risked irritating political and religious sensibilities. In the field of women's rights, for instance, he was both vocal and active, flouting convention by referring to God as "Father and Mother of us all," and by inviting leading activists such as Lucretia Mott and Seba Smith to his pulpit. When Antoinette L. Brown, the first woman minister ordained in the United States, visited Boston, she too was invited to address Parker's Twenty-Eighth Congregational Society.[12]

Parker also agitated for reform in the area of education as well as in the treatment of criminals, the poor, immigrants, and other underdogs of society. There was nothing out of the ordinary, therefore, when the dynamic preacher with the same unfettered dedication set his hand and mind to reversing the direction of the juggernaut of slavery. Although the optimism of the nineteenth century led Parker and his fellow reformers to consider progress inevitable, and to be convinced their efforts could not fail to meet with ultimate success, one of the paradoxes of the period is that belief in the inevitability of progress did not diminish to any discernible degree the puritan sense of personal responsibility necessary to effecting that progress. As a consequence, Parker did not shrink from expending enormous amounts of energy in order to bring about results often viewed as preordained. And since he was habitually in the vanguard of those calling for what he termed "fair-play" for the less favored of the world, it is not surprising to find him early on castigating President Polk for pursuing an unjust American war against Mexico.

For Parker the Mexican War amounted to rape. Only one month after its beginning in April 1846 he condemned it outright: "We are wholly in the wrong," he proclaimed, "abroad we are looked on as a nation of swindlers and men-stealers: What can we say in our defense? Alas! the nation is a traitor to this great idea,—

that all men are born equal, each with the same unalienable rights."[13] Nine months later, on February 4, 1847, in a meeting called to protest the war, Parker found that soldiers with bayonets had been sent to dampen the spirit of the gathering. Rather than temper his words, however, the minister used the presence of the soldiers to drive home to his listeners the moral decadence into which he felt the administration had fallen: "Never since the Boston Massacre on the 5th of March, 1770," had Americans seen "a body of armed soldiers attempting to overawe the majesty of the people, when met to deliberate on the people's affairs," he declared. Terming the armed men "the hireling soldiers of President Polk," Parker then dismissed them from his mind as he told his audience, "It is a mean and infamous war we are fighting. It is a great boy fighting a little one, and that little one feeble and sick. What makes it worse is, the little boy is in the right, and the big boy is in the wrong, and tells solemn lies to make his side seem right"; better say straight out, "Mexico has land, and we want to steal it." When there were cries of "Kill him, kill him," accompanied by a flourish of bayonets, Parker cowed the toughs with "Kill him! I shall walk home unarmed and unattended, and not a man of you will hurt one hair of my head."[14] No one bothered Theodore Parker as he walked home alone and unarmed that night.

Theodore Parker's public response to the Mexican War was thus much earlier and much more militant than Abraham Lincoln's. And his exertions in the civic sphere posed a threat to the government that was of a nature quite different from Lincoln's more moderate posture on the floor of the House of Representatives. It would appear, in addition, that whereas Parker was frequently to be found running at the front of the pack, snapping at the heels of those weakly supporting, compromising with, or simply dodging issues to which he was committed, Lincoln allowed the dynamics of developing situations to help him shape effective responses to problems. But if Lincoln often elected not to lead the pack, it seems to have been because he preferred to take time to conscientiously weigh the conceivable impact of potential possibilities for the betterment of its members.

❧ There was nonetheless a quality shared by these two disparate but dedicated men, which served to create a bond between them: both were imbued with an uncompromising sense of moral justice, which surfaced strongly in connection with a parallel perspective on the wrong being done American slaves. Both men endorsed Thomas Jefferson's concept of human equality; both embraced the Christian principal of equality for all in the eyes of an all-seeing, all-knowing God; and both denied that blacks were less than human and could be considered property. When the problem of slavery caused Jefferson to "tremble for my country when I reflect that God is just,"[15] he therefore articulated a worry that would later torment Theodore Parker. And it appears to have been this specific worry of Parker's, communicated by Herndon to Lincoln, that planted the seed that would flower only many years afterward in several lines of the Second Inaugural Address (see Chapter 2).

Hence, when Lincoln's optimism concerning Henry Clay's 1850 compromise measures on slavery was shattered in 1854 by Stephen A. Douglas's Kansas-Nebraska bill, which effectively repealed Clay's earlier Missouri Compromise of 1820 (devised to keep slavery from spreading indiscriminately), Lincoln was no doubt quick to recognize a potential spiritual ally in Theodore Parker, a man who had attacked the bill with swift, fierce fervor. Making this possible was the link that had recently been established between the outspoken Boston preacher and Lincoln's law partner. For it was in May 1854 that William Herndon first wrote to Parker, expressing his admiration for the minister and indicating a desire to acquire and read anything he might either write or recommend. The importance Herndon attributed to Parker's views is clearly revealed in the Illinois lawyer's first two letters:

> Springfield Ill. May 13, 1854
>
> Mr. Parker
>
> Sir
>
> I wrote to you once when I first became acquainted with your writings. I then had but a few of them, I now have them all. My attatchment [*sic*] to the sentiments is stronger. I may say I am *pulled* to them.
>
> A few days since I wrote to Messrs. Crosby & Nichols to send me two books—one on spiritualism and one on materialism and knowing your tastes, I preferred your judgment to others. I hope you will choose me the two best books, and tell Messrs. Nichols and Crosby and they will send.
>
> If you will send me a list of a few books of your taste—known for

deep rich benevolence, strong, energetic and massive language, I will send and get. I love this peculiar kind of eloquence. May I say you are my ideal—strong, direct, energetic and charitable.

Your attention to this will much oblige me. Yet, if too much trouble, do not do so.

I did not in my letter to you give the proper direction—superscription—and for which I now offer you my apology.

Yours. truly

W. H. Herndon

Springfield Ill. June 11, 1854

Mr. Parker

Dear Sir

I rec[eive]d yours of May 22[n]d and your sermon on old age. I am under many obligations to you for both letter and sermon.

Let me say to you that I do you and Emmerson [*sic*], or rather *truth*, some good here. I have made presents of your sermons and some of Emmerson's rather than not have them read.

I hope you will write out your New York speech and your late Boston sermon. The country needs moving with an eloquent and *enthusiastic* power.

If you write out and publish please send me a copy.

Yours. truly

W.H. Herndon[16]

Herndon's second letter to Parker indicates not only that the preacher had replied to the letter of May 13, but that he had already forwarded a sermon "on old age." And since Herndon had also expressed the wish to receive the minister's "New York speech" as well as his "late Boston sermon," it warrants noting that of the eight sermons and speeches Parker published in 1854 five were on the subject of slavery, the "New York speech" being one he had delivered before the New York Anti-Slavery Society on May 12, only one day before Herndon mailed his first letter.

The "Sermon of Old Age" that Parker sent Herndon had been given on January 29, 1854, so it can reasonably be assumed—in view of the fact that Parker had an express interest in having as extensive an audience as possible for his ideas—that Lincoln's law partner received all of the preacher's efforts published subsequent to that date, and certainly all those published after the earliest written contact between the two men. Herndon's first letter to

Parker evidently resulted in having his name added to the list of those to whom the Boston clergyman regularly sent his speeches and sermons as soon as they were printed. It would thus seem safe to conclude, since Herndon indicates in the Lincoln biography he co-authored with Jesse W. Weik that there was extensive sharing of material between him and Lincoln, that from this period onward newly arrived sermons and speeches were soon brought to his partner's attention.[17] William Herndon therefore deserves a tip of the hat for understanding early the merit of Parker's work and for making his colleague aware of it at precisely the moment when, for Lincoln, the battle was truly joined.

Lincoln committed himself to that battle in the spring of 1854, in the midst of the furor engendered by Douglas's Kansas-Nebraska initiative; and Herndon's recently established link to Parker allowed him to make certain that Lincoln had easy access to the minister's freshest views on the topic that was to entice the lawyer back onto the political stage. Lincoln had withdrawn from that stage after the conclusion of his term in Congress, which roughly coincided with the end of the Mexican War, and had returned to his Illinois law practice. As Herndon later explained to Weik: "At this time [Lincoln] despaired of ever rising again in the political world: he was very sad and terribly gloomy—was unsocial and abstracted."[18] With the passage of time, Lincoln also noticed his interest in the political scene waning, once confiding to his friend Jesse W. Fell that "From 1849 to 1854, both inclusive, practiced law more assiduously than ever before. Always a whig in politics, and generally on the whig electoral tickets, making active canvasses. I was losing interest in politics, when the repeal of the Missouri Compromise aroused me again."[19]

This took place in 1854, and for both Lincoln and Parker this watershed year would turn out to be marked indelibly by crises connected with the slavery issue. The first of these began on January 4 when Stephen Douglas, the senator from Abraham Lincoln's home state of Illinois, introduced a bill in Congress that would subsequently be modified to revoke Henry Clay's Missouri Compromise of 1820, a measure that up until then had prohibited the expansion of slavery into certain territory. Douglas—who in 1850 had come to the aid of Clay, a man Lincoln greatly admired, in order to shepherd Union-saving, compromise measures on slavery through Congress—now, two years after the death of the "Great Pacificator," was seen by some as having betrayed the cause. Douglas's bill immediately stirred the wrath of opponents of the extension of the "peculiar institution."

The wrath was exacerbated when the bill passed in March by the Senate was confirmed in May by the House. But this was not the only event that aroused passions during the month of May. In Missouri a slave by the name of Dred Scott, who for years had been struggling in the courts to legally obtain his freedom, on the basis of having resided for a time in a free state and in a free territory within the United States, sued once again.[20] Scott would fail in his bid to gain either his point or his freedom, but his case was ultimately sent to the U.S. Supreme Court, where a final decision would strategically be delayed until after the 1856 presidential elections had safely come and gone, until only two days after the new president had taken office. Lincoln and many others would come to see the Dred Scott decision, with its suspiciously convenient timing, as one of the most significant legal and political developments of the years leading up to the Civil War.

Also during May, many miles distant from Missouri, a fugitive slave by the name of Anthony Burns was arrested in Boston and condemned to be returned to slavery on the basis of the Fugitive Slave Law of 1850, a law making it a legal duty to restore runaway slaves to their owners. As Oscar Sherwin points out, the provisions of the law were harsh: "a Negro might be identified through a mere affidavit of the slaveholder agent; the slave could not testify himself; there was no trial by jury; the commissioner's fee was doubled if the slaveholder prevailed; the bystanders could be summoned to aid in preventing an escape, and in case any person assisted the escape, such a person was to be fined a thousand dollars or imprisoned for six months."[21] In defiance of the law, however, Theodore Parker and other members of a group calling itself the "Vigilance Committee" undertook to block the return of the slave—peacefully if possible, by violence if necessary. But when the group's signals became confused, the effort fizzled. Soon afterward Burns was remanded to his owner and on June 2 was placed in irons aboard a ship bound for the South.

For Parker the Burns affair did not end with the slave's return to bondage. By November 1854, the minister was under arrest for the part he had played in the botched rescue attempt and was preparing to do battle against slavery through the court system. In anticipation of this new bully pulpit, and believing he would have a wider audience for the abolitionist message he had been trumpeting, Parker almost gleefully began writing his "Defense," a document that would ultimately run to over five hundred pages.

Abraham Lincoln, meanwhile, was stumping Illinois, giving speeches against the Kansas-Nebraska Act and sharply denouncing Stephen Douglas for proposing and supporting the original bill. When "The Kansas Nebraska bill was introduced into Congress in 1854 by Sen. Douglas," Herndon affirms, "Lincoln saw his opportunity and Douglas' downfall: he instantly on the introduction of that bill entered into the political field and by force of his character—mind eloquence he became our abolition leader: he was too conservative for some of us—and I among them and yet I stuck to Lincoln in the hopes of his sense of justice and the eternal right. I was the abolitionist and kept on my table such speeches as Theo Parker's—Gidding's, Phillips', Sumners—Sewards etc. [*sic*]."[22]

How much should be made of Herndon's assertion that Lincoln was an "abolition leader" is open to question, but Herndon's words reveal that although Lincoln was antislavery, and although Lincoln's sympathies clearly leaned in that direction, in his role as a politician he needed to make haste slowly. This accords with the approach he seems to have adopted from Thomas Jefferson and Henry Clay, that of seeking gradual repatriation to Africa of liberated black slaves.[23] Though Clay had died in 1852, this solution still seemed plausible to Lincoln in 1854 and for many years after that, allowing him to maintain a "conservative," gradual-emancipation position, while leaving the more aggressive demands for immediate action to his law partner and to more openly avowed abolitionists. From their discussions, Herndon obviously was aware of Lincoln's thinking in this area and apparently saw no reason to question his partner's commitment concerning the slavery issue, or to abandon him, despite the slower approach. But Herndon's letters to Theodore Parker reveal that his energetic and passionate personality felt *"pulled"* to the enthusiastic abolitionism of the minister and those of like mind, all the while making his own strong views on the issue of slavery known to Lincoln. Hence, early traces of Parker's influence might conceivably be found in speeches given by the future president as early as the fall of 1854, and there is in this regard a particular parallel in subject matter that merits closer attention.

In the "New York speech" Herndon specifically requested of Parker on June 11, 1854, the minister takes issue with then-current efforts at justifying slavery "scientifically" by "proving" that blacks were less than human, could thus be treated as personal property equivalent to domestic animals, and might not even possess souls. Parker quotes Louis Agassiz, the widely acclaimed Swiss-born Harvard University scientist, who "tells us this: '*The Mandingo and the Guinea negro "together" do not differ more from the orang outang than the Malay or white man differs from the negro.*' So, according to Mr. Agassiz, the negro is a sort of arithmetic mean proportional between a man and a monkey." In the preacher's estimation, Agassiz "comes to America; he is subdued to the temper of our atmosphere; and, from a great man of science, he becomes the *Swiss of slavery.* Southern journals rejoice at the confirmation of their opinion." Parker further suggests that the following extracts, taken from the Richmond *Examiner,* should be understood as an extension of Agassiz's notions: "The negro is not the white man. Not with more safety do we assert *that a horse is not a hog.* Hay is good for horses—but not for hogs; liberty is good for *white men,* but not for *negroes,*" and "They ['negroes'] may have souls for aught I know to the contrary; *so may horses and hogs.*"[24]

Not quite four months after this, in a speech delivered on October 4 at Springfield, Illinois, Lincoln too takes issue with the "horses and hogs" comparison, and also in connection with souls:

> It is said that the slaveholder has the same . . . right to take his negroes to Kansas that a freeman has to take his hogs or his horses. This would be true if negroes were property in the same sense that hogs and horses are. But is this the case? It is notoriously not so. Southern men do not treat their negroes as they do their horses. There are 400,000 free negroes in the United States. All the race came to this country as slaves. How came these negroes free? At $500 each, their value is $2,000,000. Can you find *two million dollars worth* of any other kind of property running about without an owner? These negroes are free because their owners, in some way and at some time, felt satisfied that the creatures had mind, feeling, souls, family affections, hopes, joys, sorrows—something that made them more than *hogs or horses.* Shall the Slaveholders require us to be more heartless and mean than they, and treat those beings as *property* which they themselves have never been able to treat so?[25]

By the time he reaches Peoria, on October 16, Lincoln has quietly improved his mathematics ("two million" has become "two hundred million"), but he employs the same analogy, if no longer with reference to souls:

> there are in the United States and territories, including the District of Columbia, 433,643 free blacks. At $500 per head they are worth over two hundred millions of dollars. How comes this vast amount of property to be running about without owners? We do not see free horses or free cattle running at large. How is this? All these free blacks are the descendants of slaves, or have been slaves themselves, and they would be slaves now, but for SOMETHING which has operated on their white owners, inducing them, at vast pecuniary sacrifices, to liberate them. What is that SOMETHING? Is there any mistaking it? In all these cases it is your sense of justice, and human sympathy, continually telling you, that the poor negro has some natural right to himself—that those who deny it, and make mere merchandise of him, deserve kickings, contempt and death.
>
> And now, why will you ask us to deny the humanity of the slave? and estimate him only as the equal of the hog? Why ask us to do what you will not do yourselves? Why ask us to do for *nothing,* what two hundred million of dollars could not induce you to do?[26]

No conclusive evidence has yet been uncovered to prove that Lincoln drew his horses and hogs imagery in these instances directly from Parker's speech. In fact, he might easily have picked it up from Southern newspapers or other publications just as Parker did, since Herndon once informed Weik that "Lincoln and I took from 1853 to 1861 such papers as the Chicago *Tribune,* New York *Tribune, The Anti-Slavery Standard,* Charleston *Mercury,* Richmond *Enquirer, National Era.*"[27] It should nevertheless be noted that Parker quoted from the Richmond *Examiner,* not from the Richmond *Enquirer* taken by Herndon and Lincoln.

The circumstances and dates surrounding Herndon's request for Parker's "New York speech" therefore indicate that he was probably in possession of it prior to Lincoln's fall onslaught on Douglas and the Kansas-Nebraska Act, and that Lincoln could well have had access to the minister's words and thoughts. This would be of only nominal importance if parallels between the writings of the two men were limited to only one or two. But there are more. It is therefore important to understand why and how they came to be there.

❧ As Herndon noted, he considered himself "the abolitionist" in the law office he shared with Lincoln, and he kept abolitionist material on his desk. It is consequently not surprising that during the unrest sparked by the Kansas-Nebraska Act he would initiate a correspondence with the incendiary Unitarian clergyman and active abolitionist Theodore Parker, would avidly collect all his writings, and would share them with Lincoln. The relationship was to last until Parker's death in 1860 and allowed the Boston minister unobtrusive access to the future president, as well as the opportunity to wield political and religious influence, since Herndon records that he and his partner held long discussions about what they read. Of the antislavery activists Herndon considered Parker "grander than all the others," so it was inevitable that Parker's views on what Herndon terms the great issue of slavery would not only be brought to Lincoln's attention but also benefit from his partner's enthusiastic support.[28] And it would not be unexpected in that case for Lincoln to absorb Parker's ideas and apply them in his own writings. The reader would nevertheless be justified in asking, Why, if Parker's importance to Lincoln extended to more than the Gettysburg Phrase, has it not previously received more attention?

One reason that Theodore Parker's influential role has so long been overlooked is that for many years it was actually carefully concealed. Lincoln's political career could have suffered serious damage in the years preceding the American Civil War if he had been linked to a person of Parker's antislavery convictions, so the letters exchanged between Parker and Herndon during this period often stress the necessity for secrecy, secrecy that turned out to have long-term effects. Nor was Lincoln himself averse to such secrecy. Publicly, of course, he held abolitionists at arms length and did all he could to maintain a politic distance from their more radical positions. Privately, however, the situation could be quite different, as Parker was allowed to understand.

On April 8, 1857, for instance, Herndon writes the minister of some backroom politics involving a move by a few key border newspapers to support each other in *"accidentally"* shifting toward Republicanism in 1860, a maneuver with the potential of greatly benefiting the young party as well as one of its early members, Abraham Lincoln:

> I had a very—most entertaining, conversation on yesterday with one of the leading emancipationists of M[iss]o[uri]—, and one of the leading Republicans of this state. Do not ask who they are—will tell you all about it ere long. . . . These two men are *more than ordinary men*—the conversation was in my office, and suppose was

> confidential;—therefore I keep dark and request you to do so on the M[iss]o[uri] man's account—don't care for the Ill[inois] man. You know the Ill[inois] man.

According to Joseph Fort Newton, the two men were most likely Frank Blair of Missouri and Abraham Lincoln (the Illinois man about whom Parker would certainly not need to worry and whose identity he could easily surmise), "who were at that time trying, with the aid of their friend George D. Prentice of the Louisville *Journal*, to make such a move."[29] Herndon's request of Parker, clearly based on his understanding of his partner's wish, is thus designed to prevent the political gambit by the press (as well as Lincoln's contact with the Missouri emancipationist) from reaching the public eye.

Less than a year later Lincoln also was capable of slipping useful information and even a word of warning to one of the most prominent of the Illinois abolitionists, Owen Lovejoy, described by Herndon as "a radical, fiery, brave, fanatical man" who was "full of the virus of Abolitionism."[30] Not long before Lincoln was to deliver his House Divided speech on June 16, 1858, and in the same year during which his famous debates with Stephen Douglas would take place, the soon-to-be senatorial candidate sent a rather revealing letter to Lovejoy. Had the letter fallen into the hands of Douglas or one of his associates, it would unquestionably have provided Senator Douglas with ammunition for his repeated charge in the debates that Lincoln was a closet abolitionist, in league with prominent antislavery activists such as Joshua R. Giddings, Frederick Douglass, and Lovejoy himself. In his letter to Lovejoy, concerning and in support of the congressman's efforts to retain his seat in the U.S. House of Representatives, Lincoln displays unclouded awareness of the awkward situation in which he could find himself were the letter to become public, yet he dares to take the risk.

> Hon: O. Lovejoy. Springfield
> Dear Sir March 8, 1858.
>
> I have just returned from court in one of the counties of your District, where I had an inside view that few will have who correspond with you, and I feel it rather a duty to say a word to you about it.
>
> Your danger *has been* that democracy would wheedle some republican to run against you without a nomination, relying mainly on democratic votes. I have seen the strong men who could make

> the most trouble in that way, and find that they view the thing in the proper light and will not consent to be so used. But they have been urgently tempted by the enemy; and I think it is still the point for you to guard most vigilantly. I think it is not expected that you can be beaten for a nomination; but do not let what I say, as to that, lull you.
>
> Now, let this be strictly confidential; not that there is anything wrong in it; but that I have some highly valued friends who would not like me any the better for writing it.
>
> Yours very truly
> A. Lincoln
>
> P.S. Be glad to hear from you.[31]

It is evident from this letter that Lincoln harbored no illusions about what would happen if what he had just penned to Lovejoy were to come to light: he could be seen as adopting a position that might weaken his connections with a number of "highly valued" and most probably highly influential "friends," possibly casting a shadow over his own ambitions for higher office. The suggestion that Lovejoy keep the message "strictly confidential" thus illustrates to what extent Lincoln felt he could trust the committed abolitionist, and the high regard in which he obviously held him.

That this regard was reciprocated can be seen in the speech Lovejoy delivered on June 30, 1858, accepting his party's nomination, an address coming fewer than two weeks after Lincoln's House Divided speech. Lovejoy responded positively, if cautiously, to the question of whether he was "for Lincoln" in the upcoming Senate race, explaining to his listeners that he had decided to back Lincoln "because he is a true hearted man, and that, come what will, unterrified by power, unseduced by ambition, he will remain true to the great principles upon which the Republican party is organized."[32]

Lincoln's friendship with and respect for the Illinois congressman would prove enduring, and its closeness is manifested in a letter he sent John H. Bryant upon the death of Lovejoy in May 1864:

> My personal acquaintance with him commenced only about ten years ago, since when it has been quite intimate; and every step in it has been one of increasing respect and esteem, ending, with his life, in no less than affection on my part. It can be truly said of him

> that while he was personally ambitious, he bravely endured the obscurity which the unpopularity of his principles imposed, and never accepted official honors, until those honors were ready to admit his principles with him. Throughout my heavy, and perplexing responsibilities here, to the day of his death, it would scarcely wrong any other to say, he was my most generous friend.[33]

The date and content of this letter combine to reveal that the intimacy and trust Lincoln experienced with Lovejoy presumably had their beginnings in the same crucible year of 1854 during which the Kansas-Nebraska bill began stirring strong sentiments with respect to the slavery issue. And there seems little doubt that, had Lincoln believed at the time that causes he held dear might be jeopardized in any way by Lovejoy's electoral success, he would not have taken the trouble to promote the abolitionist's political welfare.

For Owen Lovejoy was not only a passionate abolitionist in his own right. He was also the brother of Elijah P. Lovejoy, the dedicated abolitionist newspaper editor whose printing presses had been thrown into the Mississippi River and who on November 7, 1837, because of his radical views, was murdered by a mob in Alton, Illinois. The repercussions of this outrage were felt throughout the United States, leading among other things to a public protest meeting as far away as Boston at the venerable Faneuil Hall. It was at this meeting and in defense of Elijah Lovejoy that Wendell Phillips, a man who would one day earn the respect of William Herndon and become one of Theodore Parker's strongest antislavery allies, first revealed to the Boston public the oratorical skills that were to serve the abolitionist cause so well.[34]

Back in Illinois Herndon, too, was shocked by Lovejoy's fate into adopting a more radical position. He relates that "This cruel and uncalled for murder had aroused the anti-slavery sentiment everywhere. . . . I, although acting nominally with the Whig party up to 1853, struck out for Abolitionism pure and simple."[35] What effect Herndon's commitment to that cause may have had on his law partner can only be surmised. But a speech Lincoln made not long after the Alton lynching reveals much about the thinking of the man who would later pen the secretive but supportive letter to Owen Lovejoy in 1854, and who would still later write the House Divided speech and the Gettysburg Address. Since many of the ideas expressed in that early speech were to surface often throughout Lincoln's career, they deserve a moment of our attention at this point.

❧ In his "Address Before the Young Men's Lyceum of Springfield, Illinois," on January 27, 1838, the youthful Lincoln sought to awaken his listeners to "the increasing disregard for law which pervades the country; the growing disposition to substitute the wild and furious passions, in lieu of the sober judgement of Courts; and the worse than savage mobs, for the executive ministers of justice."[36] As a case in point he took "the State of Mississippi" where "they first commenced by hanging the regular gamblers: a set of men, certainly not following for a livelihood, a very useful, or very honest occupation; but one which, so far from being forbidden by the laws, was actually licensed by an act of the Legislature, passed but a single year before" (109). As Lincoln described it, things did not stop there, however. The hangings had spread "from gamblers to negroes, from negroes to white citizens, and from these to strangers; till, dead men were seen literally dangling from the boughs of trees upon every road side; and in numbers almost sufficient to rival the native Spanish moss of the country, as a drapery of the forest" (110). Lincoln further recounts how in St. Louis, Missouri, "A mulatto man, by the name of McIntosh, was seized in the street, dragged to the suburbs of the city, chained to a tree, and actually burned to death; and all within a single hour from the time he had been a freeman, attending to his own business, and at peace with the world" (110).

By selecting examples from two of the lowest-ranking social groups Lincoln was evidently attempting to strengthen his argument through seeking justice for those with the weakest defenses against uncontrolled violence. "Abstractly considered," judged Lincoln, "the hanging of the gamblers at Vicksburg, was of but little consequence. They constitute a portion of population, that is worse than useless in a[ny community; and their death, if no perni]cious example is set by it, is never matter of reasonable regret with any one" (110). "Similar too," Lincoln continued, "is the correct reasoning, in regard to the burning of the negro at St. Louis," (110) since it was to be assumed that the man would have been executed in any event for the murder he had committed. Nevertheless, the Illinois lawyer felt that "the example in either case, was fearful" because violence of that nature can rarely be delimited, and during the confusion mobs "will be as likely to hang or burn some one, who is neither a gambler nor a murderer [as] one who is; and that, acting upon the [exam]ple they set, the mob of to-morrow, may, an[d] probably will, hang or burn some of them, [by th]e very same mistake" (110–11). The danger, therefore, was that the innocent along with the guilty could well fall victim to unbridled mob brutality. What was worse, however, was that immunity of mob members to punishment, and lack of protection for peaceful citizens and their property, could cause the "*attachment* of the People" to their government to be "broken down and destroyed" (111). Lincoln believed that, were such a thing allowed to happen, the result could carry tragic portent: "Whenever this effect shall be produced among us; whenever the vicious portion of the population shall be permitted to gather in bands of hundreds and thousands, and burn churches, ravage and rob provision stores, throw printing presses into rivers, shoot editors, and hang and burn obnoxious persons at pleasure, and with impunity; depend on it, this Government cannot last" (111). Such vigilante "justice" ultimately threatens the governmental fabric of the nation.

Here, then, was the significant and menacing context in which the shooting of Elijah Lovejoy and the destruction of the editor's printing presses inscribed itself. And the man who would one day guide the nation through the bloodiest war it had ever experienced did not hesitate to propose what he viewed as an effective response to the present turbulent situation: "Let every American, every lover of liberty, every well wisher to his posterity, swear by the blood of the Revolution never to violate in the least particular, the laws of the country; and never to tolerate their violation by others. As the patriots of seventy-six did to the support of the Declaration of Independence, so to the support of the Constitution and Laws, let every American pledge his life, his property, and his sacred honor" (112). This credo, Lincoln hoped, would become "the *political Religion* of the nation" (112).

With these words the lawyer had concluded the primary thrust of his argument, but he went on to explain his perception of what should be done about faults in the legal system: "let me not be understood as saying there are no bad laws, nor that grievances may not arise, for the redress of which, no legal provisions have been made. I mean to say no such thing. But I do mean to say, that, although bad laws, if they exist should be repealed as soon as possible, still while they continue in force, for the sake of example, they should be religiously observed" (112).

Religious respect for the Constitution and the law was thus the bulwark of the democratic experiment and represented a continuation of the great tradition, begun by the founders, of risking all in support of the Declaration of Independence. The law, it is clear, was a sacred entity for Lincoln, and this was the light in which he wished his audience to see his view of the antislavery movement, so important to Elijah Lovejoy: "In any case that arises, as for instance, the promulgation of abolitionism, one of two positions is necessarily true; that is, the thing is right within itself, and therefore deserves the protection of all law and all good citizens; or, it is wrong, and therefore proper to be prohibited by legal enactments; and in neither case, is the interposition of mob law, either necessary, justifiable, or excusable" (113).

At this point Lincoln ran into difficulty, however. For it was obvious that if the founding fathers had fully respected the laws under which they were living at the time no Declaration of Independence would ever have been proclaimed; no revolution would have freed them from England's grip. Abraham Lincoln, a man for whom the law had made possible a better life and who clearly admired reason, balance, and logic, was thus attempting to deal evenhandedly with passion, powerful forces, strong characters, and concepts of justice that could not abide the slow workings of legal systems. These difficulties would surface again during his career, and again in connection with abolition. His response at this juncture is therefore worth considering for the light it casts on the views of the man who in 1854 would step forcefully onto the political stage of the United States.

Lincoln accords the American revolutionaries of 1776 full honor, while nevertheless sensing that there is serious danger in continuing to nurture revolutionary passions. "Passion has helped us; but can do so no more" (115), he maintains. "It will in future be our enemy. Reason, cold, calculating, unimpassioned reason must furnish all the materials for our future support and defence" (115). Extremism in any form is anathema to this man of the law. Hence, the aggressively revolutionary goals of the abolitionists do not find favor with him; and whether the law is applied to gamblers or mulattoes it must be the same for all, guided by reason rather than emotion. Lincoln recognizes, however, that exceptional and powerful personalities with the fire of revolution in their veins will always threaten to bend laws and countries to their own will, something he believes cannot but be destructive since such persons find no gratification "in supporting and maintaining an edifice that has been erected by others" (114). Lincoln holds that "Many great good men sufficiently qualified for any task they should undertake, may ever be found whose ambition would aspire to nothing beyond a seat in Congress, a gubernatorial or a presidential chair; *but such belong not to the family of the lion, or the tribe of the eagle*" (114). And returning to the extremism to be found on both sides of the slavery issue, Lincoln warns that the ambition of "an Alexander, a Caesar, or a Napoleon" ever "*scorns* to tread in the footsteps of *any* predecessor, however illustrious. It thirsts and burns for distinction; and, if possible, it will have it, whether at the expense of emancipating slaves, or enslaving freemen" (114).[37]

The crime committed by a pro-slavery mob against Elijah Lovejoy, involving murder as well as the stifling of free speech, thus represented one extreme to be avoided. But Lincoln did not feel this was all there was to the question, since Lovejoy himself had occupied another extreme by virtue of the views he held on abolition. What James Hurt sees in Lincoln's lines as "a rather startling reference to emancipation" thus loses its surprise factor and reveals itself to be sharply focused when seen in relation to the "distinction" Lovejoy had achieved for himself through his emancipationist inflexibility—and when considered within the context of Lincoln's balanced, reasoned refusal to allow his respect for the law to waver in the face of abolitionist ardor.[38] For Lincoln considers that, in the interest of the law, the extremes of both the emancipator and the enslaver are to be prudently avoided. His emphasis on treating the emotional topic of abolition in a cool, logical manner separated him sharply from the passion of Elijah Lovejoy and diverged just as sharply from that of the enslavers.

Nor was this the first time Lincoln had adopted a well-defined position on the subject. Almost a year earlier, on March 3, 1837, in the Illinois Legislature, he and Daniel Stone had co-signed a protest against resolutions drafted by a joint select committee of both houses and presented to the House on January 12 of that year. The opening argument of the protest read: "We believe that the institution of slavery is founded on both injustice and bad policy; but that the promulgation of abolition doctrines tends rather to increase than to abate its evils." This position, adopted many months prior to the murder of Elijah Lovejoy, placed Lincoln and Stone clearly at odds with the select committee's original proposal where it was "*Resolved by the General Assembly of the State of Illinois,* That we highly disapprove of the formation of abolition societies, and of the doctrines promulgated by them."[39]

The distinction that Lincoln and Stone undertook to draw might have seemed to outsiders like splitting hairs, but a critical feature of their protest was the use of the terms "injustice" and "evils," which raised the always awkward issue of the morality of slavery. This aspect of the question had not been addressed by the select committee, which simply ignored it and attempted to place full blame for any unrest involving the slavery issue at the feet of "abolition societies." Lincoln and Stone, refusing to countenance such a one-sided view, insisted on placing a balance-weight on the scales. And for Lincoln, the morality issue would remain central to his thinking throughout his career, tightly linked to the "bad policy" with which he felt it was hopelessly entangled. As a practical matter, however, this would not prevent him on at least two occasions from taking law cases involving slaves: in 1841 defending the interests of the slave, and in 1847 the interests of the owner. But as David Donald submits, this should not "be taken as an indication of Lincoln's views on slavery; his *business* was law, not morality" (emphasis added).[40] Nor should Lincoln and Stone's joint 1837 effort be seen as a passing whim. Lincoln's sense of slavery's inseparable connection with morality would lead him (during his term in the U.S. House of Representatives, for example) to vote, as he claimed, "over 40 times" for the Wilmot Proviso, which aimed at preventing slavery from being allowed into territory acquired by the United States in the Mexican War.[41]

When, in spite of the votes of Lincoln and like-minded colleagues, the Wilmot Proviso regularly succeeded in the House only to fail in the Senate, many antislavery congressmen in Washington, further frustrated and irked by the unsettling and distasteful experience of having to watch the slave system in action on a daily basis while attempting to concentrate on other matters of state, undertook to see it abolished within the District of Columbia. Lincoln, despite his views on the immorality of the institution, nevertheless backed away from all efforts that did not require the consent of the citizens of Washington.[42] Twelve years before, in 1837, he and Stone had taken a clear position on this point by declaring in their Illinois protest that "the Congress of the United States has the power, under the constitution, to abolish slavery in the District of Columbia; but that that power ought not to be exercised unless at the request of the people of said District."[43] By the time 1849 rolled around, Lincoln evidently still felt that adhering to such a path remained the wisest policy and in January prepared to offer, with the support of antislavery men such as the Ohio abolitionist Joshua Giddings, "A bill for an act to abolish slavery in the District of Columbia, by the consent of the free white people of said District, and with compensation to owners."[44] According to Lincoln, support for the bill unfortunately evaporated before he had time to introduce it, and he "*dropped* the matter knowing it was useless to prosecute the business at that time."[45]

While giving ground in the face of what he judged to be probable political defeat, however, Lincoln demonstrated that his 1837 view on the matter had not swayed in the intervening years. It was still his intention to see "ultimate extinction" of the "peculiar institution," and his bill was to have been a qualified step in the direction of limited abolition. He was not to have the chance to achieve this goal until April 16, 1862, when he signed into law what is known as the D.C. Emancipation Act, liberating the thirty-one hundred slaves who lived in the District of Columbia.[46] But the president's words on that occasion are revelatory of his patient persistence on this point of abolition principle in the years since he had undertaken his first initiative: "I have never doubted the constitutional authority of congress to abolish slavery in this District; and I have ever desired to see the national capital freed from the institution in some satisfactory way. Hence there has never been, in my mind, any question upon the subject, except the one of expediency, arising in view of all the circumstances."[47]

Around 1849 Lincoln is also reported to have expressed his definitive position on slavery to the man who had given him his start as a lawyer back in 1837. In an interview Herndon recorded not long after Lincoln's death John Todd Stuart, Lincoln's former mentor and partner, claimed that somewhere between 1848 and 1850 he had ventured the opinion, in a conversation with the rising Whig politician, that "'the time would soon Come in which or when we must be Democrats or Abolitionists.' 'When that time comes my mind is made up.' The Slavery question Can't be Compromised Said Lincoln in an Emphatic tone."[48]

The fact that, in 1854, the future president could covertly come to the aid of Elijah Lovejoy's brother Owen thus hints at a silent but perceptible shift toward abolitionist positions with regard to the "injustice and bad policy" he had publicly denounced in 1837. This should not be construed as a claim that Lincoln had adopted abolitionist views concerning either a rapid or a violent solution to the slavery problem, but the events of 1854 were evidently disturbing him by tilting the balance, as he saw it, away from "gradual extinction" of the institution, and in favor of the position of pro-slavery forces.

In 1854 it could also have seemed to Lincoln that the crucial question was being posed again in terms he had discussed in his Lyceum speech of 1838. Was reason or passion to prevail? Were the slow workings of the law, which could permit gradual colonization in Africa, to prove effective or was the heat of the abolitionists to carry the day? The Illinois lawyer knew which he preferred, but he was also coming to realize that with the passage of the Kansas-Nebraska bill time was running short and the legal system was not responding to the problem in ways that either satisfied him or promised to work.

❧ It therefore seems possible that inattention to such suggestive indications as Lincoln's 1854 letter to Owen Lovejoy, together with acceptance of the Great Emancipator's public stance on gradual abolition, has led to a tendency to discount the possible strength of Lincoln's antislavery sympathies, and hence to a failure to sufficiently consider the conceivable influence on him of Theodore Parker. But why, one might ask, have the inquisitive natures of historians not been stimulated to examine the likelihood that forceful influence could have been exerted on Lincoln's thinking by the persuasive views of a major abolitionist? After all, it cannot be claimed that Lincoln's letter to Lovejoy has been inaccessible, and it is well known that when Lincoln was in Washington as a member of Congress one of the persons with whom he shared lodgings was the Ohio abolitionist Joshua Giddings.[49] Nor has it been a secret that Herndon corresponded with Parker.

As it turns out, it is in Herndon's direction that we must look for one of the primary reasons that Parker's role with regard to Lincoln has attracted so little notice. Unintentionally, Herndon contributed in an integral way to causing Parker's importance to Lincoln to go almost unremarked. This occurred because, in his biography of Lincoln, Herndon cites the Parker sermon "The Effect of Slavery on the American People" as the source for the words "government of the people, by the people, for the people."[50]

Succeeding writers have consistently accepted this claim at face value. Henry Steele Commager, for instance, almost half a century following the publication of the biography comes to the conclusion that "There is some controversy as to the origin of the famous phrase that Lincoln used in the Gettysburg address, but Herndon is authority for the statement that Lincoln took it from Parker, and this suggestion seems entirely reasonable."[51] While prudently confining himself to the specific sermon mentioned by Herndon, Commager clearly inclines toward trusting the lawyer's version of events. In 1995 David Donald similarly concludes that Lincoln's "closing promise of survival for 'government of the people, by the people, for the people' may have had its origin in Daniel Webster's 1830 speech calling the American government 'made for the people, made by the people, and answerable to the people,' but more probably Lincoln derived it from a sermon of Theodore Parker, to which Herndon had called his attention, defining democracy as 'a government of all the people, by all the people, for all the people.'"[52]

Herndon's presence in the law office he shared with Lincoln permitted intimate access to his partner's thinking and activities during the years the two men worked together and furnishes one reason that historians, as a rule, have placed strong trust in the reliability of Herndon's reports.[53] Adopting this seemingly secure approach comports a certain danger, however. There is a distinct tendency to avoid questioning Herndon's assertions and to curtail inquiry at the point where he ceases reporting. Since the lawyer's account of Parker's influence on the Gettysburg Address is restricted to the Gettysburg Phrase, it seems that historians have consequently dismissed the possibility that Parker could have had any further significant connection with the speech and have turned the page without pursuing the issue. This in itself is troublesome enough, but the problem is compounded by the fact that Herndon's report in this instance turns out to be flawed.

The first person to draw attention to Herndon's mistake was Joseph Fort Newton in his *Lincoln and Herndon,* a 1910 treatment of letters exchanged, not, as might be expected, between the two men mentioned in the title but between Herndon and Parker. Newton points out that the Parker sermon mentioned by Herndon as the source for the Gettysburg Phrase could not have served the role assigned it.[54] Yet no one until now has heeded Newton's hint, or followed up on his lead, or traced the conceivable origins of much more than the Gettysburg Phrase. Why not?

Paradoxically, one reason can be laid directly at the doorstep of Newton himself. This has not been noticed, however, apparently because scholars wishing to consult the letters exchanged during the 1850s between Parker and Herndon have turned as a rule to Newton's handy one-volume work rather than to the original correspondence. In so doing they have exposed themselves to the risk involved in placing complete trust in that work, a risk similar in nature to placing unbounded faith in Herndon's biography. Of the few researchers who have taken the trouble to consult the actual letters not one has pointed out any of the defects that do in fact exist in Newton's treatment.

A surprisingly simple reason for overlooking such defects could conceivably be that the rare scholar who has gone to the trouble of consulting the original letters has experienced difficulty in deciphering the handwriting of one or both correspondents and has thus been distracted from perceiving any less conspicuous problems. Herndon, for example, writes a classically fluent hand, but there are moments when the reader must resort to context and magnifying glass in order to make out what he is saying. Considerably worse difficulties arise with Parker's scrawl, once described by his colleague Convers Francis as "transcendental chirography."[55] Parker himself freely admitted to a fellow clergyman that all the letters in his words were "natural celibates, unfit for wedlock."[56] And James Russell Lowell, badgered by the minister for failing to send a promised article for the journal Parker was editing at the time, flippantly replied:

> Your note was so illegible that I was unable to make out that part of it in which you reproached me for my remissness. I shall choose rather to treasure it as containing I know not what commendations of my promptitude and punctuality. I will have it framed and glazed and exhibit it to editors inquiring my qualifications, as the enthusiastic testimony of the Rev. Theo. Parker, and fearlessly defy all detection.[57]

Confronted with such legibility problems it is understandable, if not completely excusable, that scholars should have preferred to trust to Newton's published transcriptions rather than to invest in the painstaking and time-consuming struggle required to surmount the obstacles involved in making out Parker's or Herndon's handwriting. Newton himself can also be forgiven for misreading a word or phrase now and again. Nor would any of this necessarily be of critical importance were there no shortcomings in Newton's edition of the Herndon-Parker correspondence extending to more than misread words or phrases. But there are.

A close comparison of Newton's transcriptions of the Herndon-Parker letters with their originals discloses serious gaps and omissions that are never mentioned, marked, or alluded to. This leaves readers of the "Herndon-Parker letters according to Newton" with the mistaken impression that they have received whole cloth, when in fact many significant pieces have been quietly trimmed away. Newton's approach to his material is cavalier: he often omits phrases or entire paragraphs, blends two or more letters into one without acknowledging the fact, or is careless about recording dates. Comparing Newton's abridged version with the original letters suggests that many of his alterations were undertaken not with the intention of obscuring meaning but with the goal of providing smoother textual flow. Yet certain elements of Herndon's letters are edited out with such regularity that Parker's role tends to be masked, thus creating a misleading picture of how much the minister's opinions and ideas meant to Herndon—and, indirectly but more important, to Lincoln.

One component of the letters that Newton often deletes is Herndon's frequent expression of gratitude and indebtedness to Parker. In the absence of those portions of the letters where Herndon openly expresses such feelings, it is easy for the reader to miss the importance Parker and his writings had for Herndon and his law partner. To gain a clearer understanding of the significance of these omissions it will consequently prove helpful to briefly survey some of the material Newton silently excised from the letters.

Herndon informs Parker on June 29, 1857, "I did as you requested—gave Mr. Lincoln your best wishes: he returns them. I send you this day one of Mr. Lincoln's speeches." On July 4, however, Herndon cautions the minister to keep the earlier letter "*whol[l]y private—my name*—no use in saying this I know." This request is omitted by Newton. In Herndon's letter of August 4, 1857, conflated by Newton with a letter of July 29 of the same year and left undated, we find the lines "P.S. The reason why I wrote to you and said 'private' not long since was on Mr. Lincoln's account not my own. Base politicians would charge him with sending you matter. That was the reason and that alone that made me say 'private.'" In this instance, the words "*Whol[l]y private*—the world would not understand" go unmentioned. From a letter of December 19, 1857, Newton also leaves out "Can you not write to me a few lines and say what you are doing by way of writing—speech making etc. etc.—? Can you not give me your opinion of political moves—." In addition, Newton jettisons "no further—not public." And with Herndon's letter of February 20, 1858, following the words "Excuse the length of this," the rest of the sentence, "—could not cut it off," is simply suppressed. The omitted words were apparently without value for Newton. Yet they are vital to understanding Herndon's inability to restrain his ebullient nature, a quality that more than once in his life would cause him serious problems—not the least of these with Parker himself, as subsequently shall be demonstrated.

From Herndon's letter of June 1, 1858, Newton expunges, along with a quantity of other material, "Your predictions—all through your speeches—are soon to be verified, and then I will put you down, as I have Douglas, a prophet, and only in that particular will I liken you to Douglas. The saw-drawn parallel you would not like, would you?" Relegated to oblivion as well is the following passage: "By the by, I see that [Charles Lennox] Remond says you are not a good anti-slavery man—*glad he said that.* I will explain sometime—cannot now—. Are you going to speak, or have you so done, before the anti-slavery society New England? If you do, and you publish your speech send it me, and I will be much obliged." A parenthetical request inserted at the beginning of a Herndon letter dated September 25, 1858, is also deemed unimportant and excluded from Newton's work: "I said *Confidential*—still say so; yet you may give your friends *a hint*—not telling your informant or showing the letters."

The foregoing instances demonstrate that much of the material systematically deleted by Newton pertains to the confidential nature of Herndon's information, and the degree of trust he was placing in Parker's discretion. Secrecy was an essential element of the exchange; and it was important to both men, since, as Herndon made clear to the minister on August 4, 1857, his reason for requesting Parker's circumspection "was on Mr. Lincoln's account." From another perspective, as Newton observes, "No doubt Lincoln, knowing that Douglas was eager to link him with the

Abolitionists, and thus fasten the odium of that name upon him, had warned Herndon about urging Mr. Parker to attack Douglas for his local tricks."[58]

An additional area where omissions consistently occur is in connection with the importance Parker's sermons and speeches held for Herndon. In the following extract from Herndon's letter to Parker of February 1857, for instance, Newton discards the final sentence: "I have an idea that there are no laws in nature as usually understood and supposed. I infer this much from your three most excellent sermons on 'Providence.' I had this opinion sometime since; but re-read your sermons to fortify or disprove my positions." Newton also eliminates from many transcriptions Herndon's specific requests for the preacher's sermons, a regular feature of the lawyer's letters, beginning with his initial correspondence with Parker in 1854.

As a result of such frequent deletions, the reader receives the impression that Herndon's reliance on Parker's religious and political writings was much less extensive than the original letters prove it to be. And if William Herndon had not been the partner and closest associate of Abraham Lincoln during the years preceding Lincoln's presidency, the story of the Herndon-Parker correspondence could probably stop here without any great loss. But Herndon *was* Lincoln's law partner, all the while maintaining an active exchange of letters with, and regularly receiving the published writings of, the acknowledged abolitionist Theodore Parker during the critical period leading up to the American Civil War.

CHAPTER TWO

Concealing Lincoln's Abolitionism

❧ Because Herndon served as the bridge connecting Lincoln to Parker, Newton's omissions from the letters exchanged between Herndon and Parker take on potentially profound significance for anyone wishing to understand what the minister's writings can have meant to the man who was to be elected president of the United States in November 1860. A return to the unedited Herndon-Parker correspondence is therefore imperative in order to comprehend how Parker's letters and published works could exert influence, through Herndon, on Lincoln. The pivotal position in this transmission process was occupied of course by Herndon, and he was not unconscious of his role. In the following passage from his biography of Lincoln, he addresses the question of slavery, emphasizing how important he considered his own personal input to having Parker's influence bear Lincolnian fruit:

> Every time a good speech on the great issue was made I sent for it. Hence you could find on my table the latest utterances of Giddings, Phillips, Sumner, Seward, and one whom I considered grander than all the others—Theodore Parker. Lincoln and I took such papers as the *Chicago Tribune, New York Tribune, Anti-Slavery Standard, Emancipator,* and *National Era.* On the other side of the question we took the *Charleston Mercury* and the *Richmond Enquirer*. . . . In addition I purchased all the leading histories of the slavery movement, and other works which treated on that subject. Lincoln himself never bought many books, but he and I both read those I have named. After reading them we would discuss the questions they touched upon and the ideas they suggested, from our different points of view. . . . I remember once, after having read one of Theodore Parker's sermons on slavery, saying to Mr. Lincoln substantially this: "I have always noticed that ill-gotten wealth does no man any good. This is as true of nations as individuals. I believe that all the ill-gotten gain wrenched

> by us from the Negro through his enslavement will eventually be taken from us, and we will be set back where we began." Lincoln thought my prophecy rather direful. He doubted seriously if either of us would live to see the righting of so great a wrong; but years after when writing his second Inaugural address, he endorsed the idea. Clothing it in the most beautiful language, he says: "Yet if God wills that it [the war] continue till all the wealth piled by the bondsman's two hundred and fifty years of unrequited toil shall be sunk, and until every drop of blood drawn by the lash shall be paid by another drawn by the sword, as was said three thousand years ago, so still it must be said, 'The judgments of the Lord are true and righteous altogether.'"[1]

What Herndon unabashedly underscores here is a sense of the key role he felt he had played in events where he was both actor and observer. The Illinois lawyer pictures himself as the indispensable factor in Lincoln's use of a concept gleaned from Parker. And although Herndon accords Parker credit for having been a possible source for some of Lincoln's greatness, he has no trouble whatsoever remembering—even after the passage of many years—that it was actually he himself who was the vital catalyst in the process.

Herndon's assumption of self-importance is not unusual, as can be seen in connection with a prophecy he claims to have made concerning Lincoln's House Divided speech. Admitting that he initially questioned the wisdom of using the famous metaphor "a house divided against itself," Herndon recalls that when Lincoln later asked "a dozen or so of his friends" to comment on the speech before it was to be delivered, "Some condemned and not one endorsed it." By then, however, the lawyer affirms that he had reversed his original position: "I was the last to respond. Although the doctrine announced was rather rank, yet it suited my views, and I said, 'Lincoln, deliver that speech as read and it will make you President.' At the time I hardly realized the force of my prophecy."[2] A few years prior to this (but still long after Lincoln was president), Herndon had told Jesse Weik that when Lincoln first read the speech to him in their joint office he said to his partner: "The speech is a good one—written with great power and will bring you permanently before the American public. It is in advance of the age, but deliver it just as you have written it," and that Lincoln "subsequently consulted some friends about it—some had one view of it and some an other [*sic*]. Some wanted this sentence struck out and some that etc. and then in the presence of the crowd he asked my opinion again and I emphatically said to him—Lincoln deliver and publish your speech just as you have written it: it will make you President of the United States."[3]

What would appear to be exaggerated self-promotion by Herndon describes, in Donald's view, "one of those incidents which seem almost too good to be true," but, he hastens to add, "there are three witnesses—Herndon, William Jayne and John Armstrong—who confirm the essential story."[4] However, upon closer examination of the story, clear problems emerge. As far as is known Lincoln was focusing at that moment on becoming the senator from Illinois, not the president. As David Zarefsky points out, "from the perspective of 1858, the 1860 presidential election appeared to be in the distant future."[5] This suggests that Herndon's prediction, written long after Lincoln's death, may have been inspired by—and added later in the light of—intervening events. Another difficulty arises when we note that the earliest testimony to the truth of the tale, that of Armstrong, was recorded twelve years after the fact, and by Herndon himself.[6]

It is not inconsequential that Armstrong's report, though belated, predates Herndon's by fifteen years and Jayne's by thirty.[7] Given such lengthy time spans, and the fact that almost verbatim repetition of much of the same material occurs in all three accounts, the possibility cannot be dismissed that interaction between the three men resulted in some textual contamination. It should also be noted that Jayne's *Abraham Lincoln: Personal Reminiscences of the Martyred President* includes many stories and anecdotes concerning events that he had not personally witnessed. In recounting the "House Divided" story he neither claims to have been present on the occasion described by Herndon nor mentions any Herndon prophecy with regard to the 1860 presidential race.[8]

A more cautious and less grandly prophetic reaction by Herndon than that described in his and Armstrong's much later accounts may nevertheless be discovered in the contemporary reports Herndon was sending his friend Theodore Parker during the summer of 1858. Two days following the presentation of Lincoln's House Divided speech on June 16, Herndon forwarded a copy of the speech to Parker, along with the following note:

> Enclosed is the Speech of Mr Lincoln's Speech [*sic*] at our recent Republican Convention. The speech is very good—read it. We have had the best & largest convention ever held in our state—more talent and more virtue.
>
> Send me your late speech in pamphlet form when out.[9]

On July 8, 1858, after receiving the minister's July 1 letter containing a copy of the requested sermon, an expression of thanks for Lincoln's *"admirable"* speech, and an articulation of the view that Stephen Douglas had erred in not switching to the Republican party, Herndon shares with his friend a more extended evaluation of the situation:

> I thank you for yours of July 1st, and agree with you that Douglas has blundered. We feel that he has committed great faults, and cannot ever recover therefrom. He is dead. Had we a fair apportionment in this State we Republicans could beat him 20 on joint ballot: but as it is, the apportionment having been made when we were very young & wild—not so densely populated as now—*he may* defeat us. . . . Our State ticket will be elected without much trouble; but as to Lincoln there may be some doubts. These doubts will energize us, fire us, move us.
>
> Mr Lincoln's speech is quite compact—nervous—eloquent: it is the best Executive Expression of the ideas of political-Republicanism, as at present organized, that I have seen. Stump orators will take higher and more lofty grounds. Prudence is written all over the political world, and we cannot help it—Do not blame us for not jumping higher just now. Remember *your* great law of the historic continuity of the development of ideas, and then you will say—*"all is right."*

Herndon alludes again to Lincoln's House Divided speech on July 24, 1858, explaining to Parker that the candidate has been obliged to improve on the tactics he employed on June 16: "Mr. Lincoln takes broader & deeper grounds *now* than he did in his Springfield Speech. I told you the speakers would do so, and even Lincoln had to follow."[10]

In none of these messages, sent at the time to a man Herndon held in the highest regard, is there evidence that the presidency was under conscious consideration by either of the Springfield law partners. Immediate problems with apportionment, Douglas, and strategy hold their attention, with no time or space consecrated to weighing the possible results of a future political race even less certain of success than the present one promises to be. While Herndon is clearly satisfied with Lincoln's speech, it is equally obvious that he considers it less ambitious and "lofty" than Parker might have wished. Nor does any of the drama found in Herndon's story about predicting the presidency for Lincoln appear in his contemporary letters to the minister.

Herndon's only prediction to Parker concerning Lincoln's political future does not occur until August 31 when he somewhat tentatively offers "as my opinion, and the opinion of good honest Republicans that we will crush out Douglas—anti-slaveryism. I give it *now* as my *present* opinion that Lincoln will be the next U.S. Senator for Ill[inois]," adding, *"Private except to special friends."* Although the two men, at Parker's August 28 initiative, soon begin to consider possible presidential candidates (Parker's view, not fully shared by Herndon, is that "the Republican party will nominate *Seward* for the Presidency, and elect him in 1860"), neither ever mentions Abraham Lincoln in connection with the nation's highest office. Moreover, following Lincoln's defeat for the Senate, and despite Parker's reassuring assessment on November 13, 1858, that Douglas will fail in his bid to become a presidential candidate in 1860, Herndon shares with Parker on November 23, his deep-seated fear that Douglas may yet take the ultimate prize: "there is a kind of victory fatality—a manifest destiny—hanging 'round loose' about Douglas, and this idea makes me dread the future as a child does the dark."[11] The possibility cannot be totally excluded, of course, that throughout this hectic period Herndon was maintaining strategic silence regarding his hope for and the prospect of a run for the presidency by Lincoln. But considering the enthusiasm for the House Divided speech, which Herndon claimed in later years to have felt and expressed just before the speech was delivered, it would seem that at least a gentle hint of such a hope might have seeped into the letters in which he shared so much sensitive political information with his abolitionist friend Theodore Parker.

Whatever the amount of accuracy that may be attributed to Herndon's subsequent accounts of the encouragement he claims to have given Lincoln regarding the House Divided speech, the candidate's effort did not lead in the end to victory in the senatorial election. In fact, a number of Lincoln's friends were of the opinion that the speech lost him the race. In Herndon's hindsight this detail gets swiftly passed over, in favor of praise for his own judgment and loyalty:

> Lincoln did deliver it just as he had written it and read it to my [*sic*] in our office. Soon after the election was over and Lincoln was defeated hundreds of friends flocked into the office and said to Lincoln—"I told you that that speech would kill you." This mystified Lincoln: he would say to them, "You don't fully comprehend its importance; but I suppose you all have or will desert me for that speech. There is one man who will stick to me to the end: he understands it and its importance and that man is Billy Herndon my good old and long tried friend."[12]

According to his own reports, then, William Herndon acted as midwife at the birth of two of Lincoln's most highly esteemed utterances: the Second Inaugural Address and the House Divided speech. With the latter, moreover, he dons a cloak of clairvoyance and assumes the honor of predicting the presidency for his partner, at a time when that office could only have been a dim blur (if that) on Lincoln's horizon, given the attention he was then dedicating to gaining a seat in the U.S. Senate. We find again, with Lincoln's First Inaugural Address, that Herndon recalls having provided the president with the wherewithal:

> Mr. Lincoln sometime in Jany or Feby 1861 asked me to loan him Henry Clay's great, his best speech in 1850, and likewise told me to get him President Jackson's Proclamation against Nullification in 1832–33, I think and the Constitution. I did loan him Clay's speech of '50—Gen Jackson's proclamation, and the Constitution of the U. States. Lincoln was perfectly familiar with Webster's reply to Calhoun and Haynes [*sic*] in 1833, I think. . . . Lincoln, as soon as I got him what he wanted, went over to Smith's store on the south side of the public [square?], went upstairs above Smith's—his brother-in-law, and got his room and then and there wrote his first Inaugural. . . . It is my opinion that these books and speeches were all the things that he used in the writing of his first Inaugural.[13]

In connection with three major Lincoln speeches, therefore, Herndon lays claim to having made an active personal contribution. Not a bad role at all for a man whom some might consider only a minor player. It should come as no surprise, therefore, to find him associating himself closely with what would become Lincoln's most famous speech, the Gettysburg Address.

❧ When Lincoln referred to "government of the people, by the people, for the people," he used a triple formulation that, as Garry Wills points out, is "the point on which most historians grant Parker's influence on Lincoln."[14] And the president's use of what would become known as the Gettysburg Phrase is the specific connection between him and Parker that has seen the most lively traffic in the years since Herndon and Weik first published their biography. In that work Herndon apparently had little difficulty recalling—almost forty years later—his return from a visit he had made to the eastern United States in March and early April 1858:

> I brought with me additional sermons and lectures by Theodore Parker, who was warm in his commendation of Lincoln. One of these was a lecture on "The Effect of Slavery on the American People," which was delivered in the Music Hall in Boston, and which I gave to Lincoln, who read it and returned it. He liked especially the following expression, which he marked with a pencil, and which he in substance afterwards used in his Gettysburg address: "Democracy is direct self-government, over all the people, for all the people, by all the people."[15]

Newton adds the following commentary to Herndon's claim:

> the phrase, in one form or another had been a favorite with Parker for years, often taking the exact form in which Lincoln used it. In a speech delivered in 1859 we find it embedded in a passage of great power, while his first use of it was in a letter to Samuel J. May, in 1846, where it is simply "a government of all, by all, for all." But the testimony of Herndon is sufficient as it relates to Lincoln, even if in his biography he is mistaken in the title of the address which he gave to his partner. . . . The address he mentions, "The Effect of Slavery," was delivered on the 4th of July following.[16]

Newton is correct as to the title of the address, but he is mistaken as to "the exact form." For although Parker often varied his phrasing, never did he employ the precise formula used by Lincoln: "of the people, by the people, for the people." Many writers over the years, apparently unaware of Newton's observation, have therefore drawn unquestioningly on Herndon's account of the importance of "The Effect of Slavery on the American People" to the Gettysburg Address. This has allowed the lawyer's assertion concerning the Gettysburg Phrase to become one of the most often repeated and widely accepted errors in American historical writing. For the facts show that Parker's speech was not delivered "in the Music Hall in Boston" until July 4, 1858, as Newton accurately points out, and was not printed until after that date. Thus, despite Herndon's affirmation to the contrary, it could not have been in his luggage in April 1858.

One reason Parker's effort could not have been available to Herndon in pamphlet form prior to April is because it was the minister's custom to publish sermons and speeches only after they had been delivered. Parker biographer John Weiss reports, for example, that "A sermon 'Of Slavery' was preached January 31, 1841, repeated by request January 4, 1843, and then published."[17] The grounds for such a delay seem to have been financial. When Parker was still paying for the publication of his works himself, he waited until the demand made itself felt before risking his capital, as occurred with his sermon "The Excellence of Goodness," delivered on January 26, 1845, at James Freeman Clarke's church. Such was also the case with "The Transient and Permanent in Christianity"; with "The Pharisees" and "Primitive Christianity," which were printed in *The Dial* after having been delivered at Parker's West Roxbury church; and with all his other published sermons of the period. Some even included the words "and now published by request" on their covers.

That this was still his practice in 1858 may be deduced from the fact that on April 4 of that year (the day before Herndon arrived back in Springfield from his trip east), Parker preached the first of two sermons on "A False and True Revival of Religion." The sermon was immediately published as having been "Phonographically Reported by James M. W. Yerrinton," and contained on page 2 the following "Note from the publisher. Mr. Parker stated previous to his discourse that the subject under consideration would be treated in two sermons. The first (the present) on A False Revival, and the second on A True Revival. The second discourse, which is immediately connected with the present, will be published on Tuesday, April 13th," or, in other words, as soon as possible following its expected delivery on Sunday, April 11.[18] Shortly afterward

Parker could write Senator John Hale: "I am glad you like my revival sermons. They sold 10,000 in ten days, and the demand still continues. They were stereotyped in forty-eight hours after they were preached; but they struck off 5000 copies before they stopped the press to stereotype the matter."[19] This was taking place, it should be noted, at precisely the moment Herndon professes in the Lincoln biography to have already been in possession of Parker's Fourth of July speech, and handing it to his partner.

Herndon was therefore in error regarding particulars related to the Gettysburg Phrase, but the Herndon-Weik Collection in the Library of Congress does, indeed, contain a copy of Parker's "The Effect of Slavery on the American People," the speech Herndon mentions in the Lincoln biography. This copy is endowed with a vertical, slightly curved line in the margin next to a triple formulation corresponding to the one Herndon quotes: "Democracy is Direct Self-government, over all the people, for all the people, by all the people."[20] Nowhere on the pamphlet, however, is there any actual handwriting to provide unequivocal proof that Lincoln either read that particular copy or made that particular sign. In the absence of such corroborating evidence, one is left to draw one's own conclusions concerning the origin of the mark, and Herndon, knowing his partner's habits and manner of marking what he read, may have felt fully warranted in making his seemingly arbitrary assumption in regard to the parenthesis-shaped line, even many years after the date in question. Yet it is equally possible that someone other than Lincoln—and that must include Herndon himself—could have made the mark. If we consider the date of delivery of Parker's sermon, and his modus operandi with respect to the publication of his sermons and speeches, it would seem difficult to accept Herndon's account of the manner in which Lincoln adopted the Gettysburg Phrase from the Boston preacher. There are nonetheless grounds for not rejecting out of hand Herndon's assertion that Lincoln read this particular speech and marked this phrase.

The exact formulation of the phrase Herndon mentions appears on page 5 of the pamphlet, beside which may be found the penciled symbol referred to above. In addition, a mark of exactly the same nature occurs on page 4 next to the sentence "The political and ecclesiastical functionary is the servant, the people master, now." There is a clear logical correlation between the two marked sentences, both of which stress the fundamental role of the people in controlling their own destiny. And if Herndon actually had this particular copy of the pamphlet before him as he wrote (as is almost certain, since it is the only one of that title to be found in the Herndon-Weik Collection used in writing the Lincoln biography), his discovery of pencil marks on the two facing pages could have seemed to him sufficient proof that his memory was correct, and that here without doubt was the source of Lincoln's inspiration. Herndon would have had no need to read further, since the apparently incontrovertible evidence would have appeared perfectly adequate to document the point.

It is still difficult, however, not to suspect that it might have been Herndon himself who added those seemingly innocent marks on facing pages, in order to provide credibility for a story that promised to redound to his own glory. Such a supposition could find support in his mistaken claim that it was this specific sermon he had brought back with him from Boston in April. Yet the pamphlet itself appears to absolve the lawyer of any intentional deception.

Fortuitously, this particular Parker sermon is exceptional in containing not one but two formulations of the Gettysburg Phrase, the second of which reads: "Slavery is in flagrant violation of the institutions of America—Direct Government,—over all the people, by all the people, for all the people."[21] Since this second formulation occurs near the end of the pamphlet, nine pages later than the first, it conceivably went unnoticed once Herndon had come across the first one. Such an explanation is bolstered by the fact that the second rendering of the phrase is embellished with a pencil mark similar in all respects to the others in the pamphlet. Had Herndon been aware of the pencil-marked second occurrence at the time he was writing (as he surely would have been had he recently made the marks himself), it would have been only logical to mention it in connection with the first, in order to make his case more convincing for Lincoln's having made the marks and appropriated Parker's concept. The fact that Herndon neglected to draw attention to this significant piece of evidence could therefore indicate that he failed to carefully peruse the entire pamphlet prior to writing his account. This in turn would imply that, if the markings were indeed his, they had been done far enough in the past for him to have forgotten about the second occurrence. This is, of course, within the realm of possibility. It would seem far more likely, however, that Herndon's failure to note the second appearance of the phrase points to his having been inattentive, perhaps hasty, but innocent of any intent to deceive. Then, too, the likelihood that he had a copy of the sermon, in all probability this particular copy, in front of him as he wrote is enhanced by his ability to recall its exact title and the precise location of its delivery, despite the impossibility of his having been in possession of the document as early as he claims, or to have been present at its delivery on July 4, so many years before.

Herndon's account of the origin of the Gettysburg Phrase is further complicated by yet another detail. Had the phrase been used only once by Parker, and in the sermon cited by Herndon, reasons might yet be found that could lend strength to the lawyer's story. But, as several writers have pointed out, a careful reading of Parker's antislavery sermons of the 1850s reveals that variations of the Gettysburg Phrase, which Parker often referred to as the "idea" of democracy, appear in almost every one.[22] Parker's first use of such a phrase, as Newton correctly notes, seems to have occurred in a private letter to Samuel J. May of November 13, 1846, where the minister affirmed: "Let the world have peace for 500 years, the aristocracy of blood will have gone, the aristocracy of gold has come and gone, that of talent will have also come and gone, and the aristocracy of goodness, which is the democracy of man, the government *of* all, *for* all, *by* all, will be the power that is."[23] Parker's earliest *public* use took place on December 22, 1847, in "Letter to the People of the United States Touching the Matter of Slavery," where, in speaking of the principles upon which the United States was founded, he explained to his audience: "The priesthood, nobility, royalty, did not share these ideas—nor the sentiments which led to them. These ideas were of the people; they must form a democracy, the government of all, for all, and by all—a commonwealth with no privileged class—a state without nobles or kings, a church without prelate or priest."[24]

Since we know from Herndon's earliest letters to Parker that he took special pride in possessing all of the minister's writings it can be assumed that Lincoln, in reading and discussing with his partner the works of the highly regarded son of Massachusetts, encountered the phrase more than the single time mentioned by Herndon. It is also probable that, having run into the phrase on several occasions, Lincoln remembered it and, as Herndon attests, marked it in the pamphlet in question, subsequently employing a slightly edited version of it at Gettysburg. In light of this, it would now seem reasonable to ask, Might not Parker's writings also have been at the origin of other formulations or ideas used by Lincoln in his famous address? Indeed, if one reflects on the prominence attained by Lincoln's speeches over the years, and if one takes into consideration Herndon's esteem for Parker, it seems little short of astounding that the possibility Parker might have influenced additional aspects of those speeches has gone so long unnoticed.

One of the reasons for this neglect could be Herndon's faulty account in his Lincoln biography of the source of the Gettysburg Phrase, which has blinded historians to the importance of Theodore Parker by directing their attention uniquely toward the sermon on "The Effect of Slavery on the American People." As this sermon contains little beyond the Gettysburg Phrase for which Lincoln might seem tributary to Parker, it is not surprising that Herndon's account has been taken at face value, and that Lincoln's debt to Parker has been regarded as minimal. In addition, an awareness of Newton's mistreatment of the Herndon-Parker correspondence would suggest that historians might have had their curiosity piqued much sooner had Newton pared less from the letters and been more particular about presenting accurate transcriptions of them. The fact remains, however, that while Herndon's explanation of specific details concerning the *manner* in which one of the most famous phrases in American history found its way into the Gettysburg Address may have been inaccurate, there is little doubt, as shall later be demonstrated more fully, that Theodore Parker served as the source for that phrase.

❧ Curiously, Herndon's comments concerning the critical nature of his own contribution to the Gettysburg Address and the House Divided speech occur within two pages of each other in his biography of Lincoln, although the speeches themselves were delivered over five years apart. Some justification for this can be advanced on the grounds that Herndon's trip east and the delivery of the House Divided speech both occurred in 1858, within a few months of each other. But the lawyer's error with respect to the date of the Parker speech he considered to be the source of the Gettysburg Phrase would at least hint at his inclining toward self-aggrandizement at the time he was composing his biography several decades afterward.

Herndon was not insensitive to the fact that such a charge might be leveled at him, and and attempted to head off the possibility almost twenty years prior to publishing the above account. In February 1870 he interviewed John Armstrong, who was present on the occasion when Lincoln appealed to his friends for their views on the House Divided speech before delivering it publicly. The interview, as recorded by Herndon, is matched by his own later narrative of events (including his prediction of a Lincoln candidacy for president in 1860) on all significant points, and often in specific phrasing.[25] A copy of the interview was also sent to Ward Hill Lamon on February 19, 1870.[26] A follow-up letter of February 25 confirms: "I sent you some days since more at the request of Jno Armstrong than of myself a short account of what I had to say on Lincoln's house divided against itself speech—should not have sent it for the same reason that I have refused—failed to say more—write more to you—namely I do not wish to be considered a blow—boast—or fool who wishes to be noticed &c. &c."[27] In spite of such protestations, and although fully warranted in doing so, Herndon nonetheless hesitated only a few days before forwarding the interview to Lamon. His self-proclaimed modesty is further undercut by the fact that, in the Lincoln biography, he quotes extensively from the Armstrong interview without crediting Armstrong in any way.[28]

Although it is apparent Herndon did not shy away from the limelight, there is no question but that it was often well earned. Our historical knowledge concerning Lincoln would be far poorer without the labors he expended in collecting eyewitness accounts of events in the former president's life for the biography he coauthored with Weik; and the history of the United States would be much the poorer had Herndon not brought to the law office he shared with Lincoln an extensive range of written material that contained thoughts and perceptions on which the future president might draw. Many of those writings were from the pen of Theodore Parker, and not only did the minister not begrudge them, there is evidence they were sent gratis.

Herndon's first letters to Parker reveal the significance he attached to being kept fully informed of the preacher's ideas, as well as those of other Massachusetts writers and thinkers of a similar mindset. When Herndon asked to be sent speeches and sermons, Parker showed himself more than willing to comply. He tells his friend on July 1, 1858: "I send my speech in pamphlet form. Please never think of paying me for what I send, and oblige Yours truly Theodore Parker."[29] On August 23, Herndon also expresses his appreciation for four sermons he has recently received, and for the minister's largesse in not wishing to accept remuneration for them:

> The first 2 are excellent,—the 3d is eloquent, scientific, and grand—You have almost, in this, excelled yourself; and the fourth is graceful, loving and hopeful. I wish this *resume,* these last four sermons of yours, was in the hands of every American citizen, so that he might see what *the* religion is. I thank you very kindly for these sermons—am much obliged to you. I have no way of paying for them—you will not take my money, but to read, and when having done so, to teach the ideas to others. I say I thank you for them.

Immediately afterward the lawyer switches to an important current event, the first of the Lincoln-Douglas debates:

> Now for politics in Ill[inois]. Mr Lincoln spoke at Ottawa on Saturday. Mr. Douglas also spoke there: this was their first place of meeting. We have not heard from them, but we Republicans know how the debate ended, if Lincoln was well. Lincoln will deliver a speech there that will do himself credit. He is too much of a Kentucky gentleman to debate with Douglas; i.e., he will not condescend to lie: he will not bend to expediency: he will not hug shams, and so he labors under a disadvantage in this State; yet he will take hold of Douglas and prove the conspiracy to enslave America on him. He has got the documents and will shoot the charge home.

This exchange provides evidence that Parker knew where his speeches were going, understood in what manner they might prove influential, and realized the importance of keeping this line of communication open. The intrusion of minor financial considerations was simply not to be tolerated. In addition, the minister was careful to assure Herndon on September 23, 1858, of his discretion in regard to the information with which he was regularly being entrusted: "Your last letter—just come to hand, is quite important. I shall keep it confidential but consider the intelligence and 'govern myself accordingly.'"[30]

Herndon, on the other hand, never one to be satisfied with only what Parker chose to send, could not resist trying to put spurs to his friend. On February 20, 1858, for instance, we find him making the following request of the now seriously ailing preacher: "I want you to make a sermon—speech on or about the 4th day of July, taking this subject, in substance—"The Sweep of Liberty"—the path along which Freedom has traveled since its birth, giving its history etc. When delivered publish—."[31] Herndon's pleasure and appreciation at the result of his enjoinder is expressed on July 24 of the same year: "I this day received from you your Fourth-of-July Oration. I thank you most sincerely. I have read it carefully, and say it is most Excellent—quite eloquent. Again I thank you for it."[32]

The "Oration" for which Herndon thanked Parker so profusely does indeed deal with human liberty, albeit from the point of view of slavery. In examining the effects of the slave system on America, Parker refers to Ionian Homer, Arminius, Alexander Von Humboldt, the history of the Hebrew people, and other historical figures, periods, and events before he makes the claim that "the poor negro has no history to look back upon; no science, no arts, no literature, not even a great war, no single famous name!" Nevertheless, declares Parker, "Nothing can save slavery. It is destined to ruin. Once I thought it might end peacefully: now I think it must fall as so many another wickedness, in violence and blood." This, because "Slavery is in flagrant violation of the institutions of America—direct government, over all the people, by all the people, for all the people."[33]

It thus turns out that the speech that in February Herndon had urged Parker to write for presentation "on or about the 4th day of July," and for which he expressed his appreciation on July 24 (clearly revealing he had just read it for the first time), was "The Effect of Slavery on the American People." This is the same speech that Herndon claimed in the Lincoln biography to have brought back with him in April from his visit to Boston, the speech he affirmed was the source for the Gettysburg Phrase. In view of Herndon's personal involvement with the conception and creation of this particular work, it is little wonder that in later years it should have held a special place in his memory. Nor is it surprising that he felt able to be so positive so many years after the fact that it was precisely here that the germ of Lincoln's famous phrase could be found. There is nevertheless clear irony in the realization that Herndon himself—in this letter of July 24, thanking Parker for a sermon not delivered until July 4, but which the lawyer would later claim to have already had in his possession back in April—should be the one to furnish final, irrefutable proof of the inaccuracy of his account of the origin of the Gettysburg Phrase.

❧ Meanwhile, it was not only in the area of politics that Theodore Parker's notions were acting upon the future president. Herndon recalled several years after Lincoln's death, in connection with his religion, "I used to loan him Theodore Parker's works."[34] And Herndon's views of Parker's religious writings are divulged in a letter to the minister of December 27, 1856, in which he acknowledges that whenever he met a young lawyer "who had an ideal of the perfection of purposes—who was really religious in the good sense of actual religion, I gave him a list of books and made him buy them. You know probably what I recommended and whose books."[35]

In the Lincoln biography, Herndon also quotes from a letter from Jesse W. Fell, dated September 22, 1870, relating that after Fell presented Lincoln with a copy of William Ellery Channing's works:

> Subsequently the contents of these volumes, together with the writings of Theodore Parker, furnished him, as he informed me, by his friend and law partner, William H. Herndon, became naturally the topics of conversation with us; and, though far from believing there was an entire harmony of view on his part with either of those authors, yet they were generally much admired and approved by him.
>
> No religious views with him seemed to find any favor except of the practical and rationalistic order; and if, from my recollections on this subject, I was called upon to designate an author whose views most nearly represented Mr. Lincoln's on this subject, I would say that author was Theodore Parker.[36]

Fell forwarded a copy of the letter to Herndon, accompanied by a cover letter containing the following postscript: "Of course I did not Know Mr. L. half as well as you, but have written from my Stand-point. Am I not correct in my Statement as to his views being pretty well represented by Parker?—I so understood him in *substance* tho' not in *terms*—or words.—"[37] The question received its affirmative reply when Herndon elected to include the account in his Lincoln biography.

Buttressing Fell's testimony is a letter Herndon sent Weik on December 29, 1885, in which he states:

> I kept many of my books in my office—especially the new ones and read them. Mr Lincoln had access to all such books as I had and frequently read parts of the volumes—such as struck his fancy. I used to read to him passages in the books that struck me as eloquent, grand, poetical, philisophic [*sic*] and the like. I would talk in my own peculiar vein to Lincoln about what I read and thought: he would like or dislike what I read and thought—would discuss the subject with me, sometimes animatedly. Sometimes we would get into a philosophic discussion—sometimes on religious questions and sometimes on this question or that.

Herndon goes on to specify "the kind of books which Lincoln had access to and sometimes peeped into. I had all the following books, i.e., the writers of the works, their names, and the books, etc., they wrote. If I did not have all I had the most of them."[38] Third on a list of twenty authors, following (Ralph Waldo) Emerson and (Thomas) Carlyle, appears the name Parker.

Finding Emerson's name so prominently positioned on this list is quite understandable when we recall that Herndon informed Parker in his second letter to the minister that "I do you and Emmerson [*sic*], or rather *truth,* some good here. I have made presents of your sermons and some of Emmerson's rather than not have them read."[39] Emerson, like Parker, was an ordained Unitarian minister who approached the Christian religion from a rationalist point of view. And Lincoln's respect for Emerson's thinking caused him to make the effort not only to hear the "Sage of Boston" lecture in 1843 but to receive him at the White House after becoming president.[40] Herndon's listing of Emerson and Parker in close conjunction thus points to the value he placed on the thinking of these two men, and just what potential their ideas possessed to influence Lincoln's own. It was to the religious notions of Parker, however, that Herndon—and through Herndon, possibly Lincoln—seems to have been most forcefully drawn.

Key to this attraction was apparently the fact that Parker was a renegade Unitarian who sought to understand Christianity by means of his own logical reasoning and intuitive natural instincts. In 1841, for example, he had preached his revolutionary sermon entitled "A Discourse on the Transient and Permanent in

Christianity," asserting that Christianity was not dependent on Jesus being the son of God, on "the infallible inspiration of the Bible," or on miracles. The minister held that "the great truths of morality and religion, the deep sentiment of love to man and love to God, are perceived intuitively, and by instance, as it were, though our theology be imperfect and miserable." With regard to the Bible Parker asked, "Did Christ ever demand that men should assent to the doctrines of the Old Testament, credit its stories, and take its poems for histories, and believe equally two accounts that contradict one another?" He further declared that "It is hard to see why the great truths of Christianity rest on the personal authority of Jesus, more than the axioms of geometry rest on the personal authority of Euclid or Archimedes. The authority of Jesus, as of all teachers, one would naturally think, must rest on the truth of his words, and not their truth on his authority."[41]

For Lincoln, an admirer of logic and of Euclid and a skeptic as to the divine origin of the Scriptures, this reasoned treatment of what Parker qualified as "natural religion" could indeed have seemed appealing, even reassuring, with regard to the lawyer's own reflections on the subject.[42] For Parker explained that "it is not so much by the Christ who lived so blameless and beautiful eighteen centuries ago that we are saved directly, but by the Christ we form in our hearts and live out in our daily life, that we save ourselves, God working with us both to will and to do." In the minister's conception, "Christianity is a simple thing, very simple. It is absolute, pure morality; absolute, pure religion; the love of man; the love of God acting without let or hindrance." From Parker's perspective, "we never are *Christians* as he was the *Christ,* until we worship, as Jesus did, with no mediator, with nothing between us and the Father of all."[43] As a careful reader of the Bible, conscientiously alert to questions of humane justice and morality, and averse to committing himself to any particular faith or denomination, Abraham Lincoln probably found little to quarrel with in such views.

It is also well known that Lincoln was hard to pin down with respect to his personal religious beliefs, and Theodore Parker never got the chance to discuss his own with the Illinois lawyer.[44] But Herndon's connection to Lincoln—together with Parker's reasoned perception of a personalized, private, and self-determined form of morality-based Christianity, independent of miracles and mysticism—opens a portal to speculation concerning Lincoln's possible absorption and application of some of the Boston minister's concepts. A hint of the support Parker might possibly offer may be seen in Lincoln's curt comment to a delegation of Christian ministers visiting the president at the White House in 1862: "These are not, however, the days of miracles, and I suppose it will be granted that I am not to expect a direct revelation."[45] In later chapters we shall observe, moreover, that Parker and Lincoln harbored a shared conception of the Declaration of Independence as treating equality and human rights as "both natural and divine," possessing "their authority from God and nature."[46] Hence, the possible importance of Lincoln's awareness of Parker's religious convictions—as interwoven with the minister's political views, thus justifying the interaction of religion and politics—should not be underestimated. We shall see that as these strands twined together, they permitted the creation of a powerful and productive bond.

❧ The Herndon-Parker letters in their unadulterated form, together with the Herndon-Weik biography of Lincoln and Herndon's letters to Weik, offer a relatively clear, if not unfailingly objective, picture of the exchange of views that took place with Herndon as intermediary between Parker and Lincoln. In the years leading up to his presidency, Lincoln was inclining, ever so slowly, toward seeing slavery abolished by one means or another, yet for political reasons he could not allow himself to be considered in the abolitionist camp nor specifically connected in any way with abolitionist thinking. Under such conditions Herndon served admirably as a silent conduit, allowing Lincoln to gain recognition among Massachusetts abolitionists such as Parker, William Lloyd Garrison, and Wendell Phillips, and to profit from and better comprehend their ideas and concerns regarding the major problems of the period. In such a manner Theodore Parker chanced to acquire influential, if secondhand, access to the man who would shortly become, in the eyes of many, the most important American of his era.

But wherein lay the magnetism that *pulled* Herndon so strongly to Parker and, despite personal tensions and complications, held the two men together over the difficult years from 1854 to 1860? In seeking an answer to this question it should be realized that a remarkable feature of the tie between the Illinois lawyer and the Boston minister was that principle won out over passion in keeping their friendship alive. By all rights the relationship should not have survived at all, since on the two occasions when the pair met face-to-face the result was nothing short of disastrous. Their first encounter took place in the fall of 1856 when Parker, at Herndon's request, lectured in Springfield only to have a number of things go wrong. The crowd was small. As Donald explains, "It was the very worst time of the year, immediately prior to a presidential election, and Springfield people, tired out by constant campaign addresses, neglected to attend."[47] According to Newton, the lecture had not "been properly advertised, but advertising would have done little good in Springfield where Parker was held to be a dangerous man both politically and theologically."[48]

There was also some confusion about payment. Remorsefully Herndon wrote Parker on November 12, by way of excusing himself:

> Enclosed is a letter from Mr. Post: he made the arrangements with Mr. Wells in reference to your lecture. You will see what he says; and then you can throw the blame where it justly belongs. Had you spoken to me the night I left you at the tavern; and told me how this matter stood, I should have felt much better than I did after you went away. I regret all this proceeding very much; yet I do not know where I am to blame. I hope you will have the goodness to separate me from the "mass." You have been shamefully wronged by some one. By the by did not H. Ward Beecher have a difficulty with Mr. Wells? What say you—Will you place me right in your estimation, if you can?

The note from Herbert Post included with Herndon's letter confirms that "I was the person who made arrangements with Mr. E. T. Wells to have you lecture here. There was nothing said about the price—no am[oun]t. was agreed to or suggested."[49] And while both Herndon's letter and Post's note clearly point to a problem with financial arrangements, Parker's November 17 response downplays that difficulty. On the face of things Parker would seem to wish to resolve the issue amicably, but he carefully refrains from explicitly absolving Herndon of blame: "Don't think I had any hard thoughts about the lecture at S[pringfield]. I was more concerned at the smallness of the audience than aught besides. I felt a little delicacy about naming the matter to you—and should not have thought any more of it had not you written for an explanation of my *looks*. There *was* a misunderstanding between Mr. Beecher and Mr. Ward [*sic*]; but I shall have none, with anybody."[50]

To a casual observer Parker's unemotional explanation would appear to put an end to the matter, but there is evidence to suggest this did not occur—at least not at once. Although scholars have paid the fact no attention, Parker's original letter bears a large and surprising doubled "X," crossing out the entire passage cited above. One X is drawn in brown ink, like that used in the letter itself, but somewhat thicker and of a deeper hue, while the other is in thick lead pencil. The surprise stems from the fact that no other letter in the collection displays such marks. And since the paragraph in question opens the letter, it is unlikely that Parker would have sent a message of such a sensitive nature in this condition. It is also improbable that he would have continued writing on the same sheet of paper after crossing out the first thirteen lines with both a pen and a pencil—or have changed from pen to pencil and back to pen in mid-missive—particularly when it is realized that those lines fill almost the entire page. Nor is it likely that one or both Xs were added by Parker after the letter had been completed, since neither mark serves to prevent the reader from understanding the words and sense of the passage. It should also be noted that whereas both Herndon and Parker regularly employed brown ink, only Herndon frequently underlined words or ideas with a wavy line similar to the one used in the large ink-drawn "X."[51]

A more plausible explanation for the marks, therefore, is that when Herndon did not receive the open-armed absolution requested of Parker on November 12, he reacted strongly to what he construed as an all too measured and not fully frank response by the minister, scrawling the doubled X himself, possibly on two separate readings of the letter, with a different writing instrument at hand on each occasion. External evidence favoring this assumption may be found in Herndon's next letter to Parker, penned on December 27. The obviously dispirited lawyer finally feels obliged to grapple with the irksome task of providing clarification for his discontent with the situation and with Parker himself at the time of the minister's visit:

> I had hoped to have a long chat with you on the evening you were here, and to state to you things as they exist West and which you will scarcely get unvarnished for *a long time to come;* but an unexpected misunderstanding came over us, and *cut me through;* thus depriving me of the pleasure. This may however be to your

> advantage—to your gain. I could not sit still in your presence—nor in any other person's, and be fretted like an annoyed child without knowing whence the trouble. I always escape from so unpleasant a situation. I was at that time worn down, having spoken I think nearly a hundred times—was not well—had neglected my person—my clothes—my home—office all—all and suppose I did not cut a very handsome figure before you. I regret but could not do otherwise. Friend; pardon all—forget and forgive—remember only the good—the motives and intentions.[52]

This letter posted two days after Christmas, almost two months following the preacher's Springfield lecture, makes apparent how distressed Herndon had felt about the situation, in addition to disclosing that the lawyer was still smarting under what he perceived as a rebuke from the preacher. It is also evident that it took Herndon quite some time after receiving Parker's letter to work himself up to expressing the belief that, notwithstanding his friend's soothing words, there had indeed been a misunderstanding, and that the minister had failed to be candid with him. When these belated revelations of Herndon's true feelings are taken into account, it becomes simpler to grasp why he believed he had just cause for anger at Parker's muted response to his request for forgiveness—and why, in addition, he might well feel like striking out the letter's offending passage, not once but twice, with a large X.

Yet, less than two years following this episode in a turn of events that would have been difficult to foresee, time had already healed hurt feelings enough for Herndon to repay Parker's visit to Springfield with a sojourn in Boston on his trip east. According to Herndon the journey was undertaken when he "inferred" that it might prove politically helpful to Lincoln's 1858 Senate race against Stephen Douglas. Lincoln had purportedly expressed the wish that "someone could put a flea in Greeley's ear—see Trumbull—Sumner, Wilson—Seward—Parker—Garrison—Phillips and others, and try and turn the currents in the right directions."[53] Herndon consequently made stops in Washington, D.C., New York, and Boston.

In Washington Herndon saw all the congressmen Lincoln had mentioned, with the exception of Sumner. He even spoke with Douglas, who though ill at the time met with the visitor from Illinois and assured him that his own course did not put him in "opposition to Mr. Lincoln or his party."[54] Then it was on to New York where Herndon carefully placed the "flea" in Greeley's ear concerning Lincoln's worry that the influential editor of the *New York Tribune* was pulling him "down in order to elevate Douglas." Lincoln's worry was not without foundation: Horace Greeley was under the impression that Douglas had shifted to the antislavery ranks, and he was therefore pressing the case for returning the Little Giant to the Senate. Since Greeley was encouraging Illinois Republicans to back the Democratic senator rather than the Springfield lawyer in the upcoming race, it would appear from Herndon's report that a somewhat nervous Lincoln felt that placing "a flea" was certainly in order, and that his partner was the man to do it.[55]

Herndon dutifully undertook the task, but without much success. He was obliged to inform Lincoln that Greeley "evidently wants Douglas sustained and sent back to the Senate. He did not say so in so many words, yet his *feelings* are with Douglas. I know it from the spirit and drift of his conversation."[56] Having nevertheless done what he could, the lawyer then continued on "to Boston—saw Gov Banks—Theo Parker—Garrison—Phillips—and put them all right, if they were not right before, which is more than likely. I was gone about one month." Herndon "did not then think that the trip was necessary at all, but to assure Lincoln, to pacify him, to make him feel better, I went, and did all that I could for friend Lincoln."[57]

The journey took place in the spring of 1858, and Herndon explains to Parker in a letter dated May 29, written several weeks following his return home, that during his trip to Massachusetts he had hoped "to see the places of Revolutionary Memory, and those living *institutions* of Boston—Garrison, Parker and Philips [*sic*]." Once again, however, the meeting between the lawyer and the minister turned sour, and the result was no happier than before. In his letter of May 29, he illuminates one of the reasons for his disappointment:

> Yours of 13th April is before me and in answer to which let me say—I would have been much and highly pleased to have met at your house a few friends, but as it was I did not. . . . Could I have had the pleasure of having sat down and talked to you—3 of you [the other two being William Lloyd Garrison and Wendell Phillips]—I should have liked it much, but as it so happened I did not: it was not my fault: I was in Boston ten whole days, and no living man came to see me.

Why this occurred is not clear, but Herndon seeks to downplay the importance of the incident, for himself as well as for his relationship to Parker: "This is all right: I do not complain, though I must say what I once said to you—I was somewhat disappointed—*disappointed* is all: and now suppose I was disappointed—do you suppose that this will make me dislike you—alter my respect for you? God forbid! You know me to little purpose if you think I am so small and malicious as that."[58]

Nonetheless, Herndon subsequently reveals that Parker was not as forthcoming as he might have been, and that the reason for this reticence may have been Herndon's own bubbly Western garrulity, which he is the first to acknowledge. Yet once again he attempts to keep it from causing a break in relations between him and the Boston preacher: "I very much wanted to know the social and political condition Northwards—do [*sic*] Southwards, as that is my native home. We of the South now in the west have the *'let go'*—the *gasseous gush*—why did you not say—. We are too social—too talkative, and *that* is our fault. I *demonstrated* this at your house—whol[l]y forgot myself—*You* chained me—blame yourself—. Now, Mr. Parker, let this matter drop from your fingers and sink with the ocean forever."[59]

From all appearances Parker did let the matter drop; but he was apparently not the only person Herndon met during his stay in Boston who had not openly embraced the visitor from Illinois. On April 7, 1858, two days after his arrival back in Springfield, Herndon wrote to Parker: "I watched you all closely, and am not deceived. I say this: Your men are generally cold—probably not more selfish than other men, but they are *cold*—Understand me—I do not say this indiscriminately of all—: Your women are warm—matronly—spontaneously good—." Nevertheless, Herndon frankly avowed that not all the difficulties could be blamed on his hosts: "I know my faults positive and negative. I was not reared in great cities or in costly halls and am not up to their civilities, or rather forms of civilities—. I blunder here and err, and all that I can say is—'Excuse'—'Forgive my trippings'—."[60]

On the other hand, one of the highlights of his trip had been listening to Parker preach a sermon which he found "deep—rich—broad and generous, giving all their due." He was also "gratified at the *immensity* of your audience—was surprised at the number of men and women who came to hear you—to hear and grow wiser through you." Boston had been only one of the stops on his journey, however, and all things considered, Herndon felt that "My whole trip was one of delight—amusement—pleasure and profit, bating a little for disappointments—. I am highly gratified with the results of my short travel, *in spite* of rebuffs—."[61]

Years afterward, when he described the trip to his friend Weik, Herndon would not recall those disappointments and rebuffs. He related only that "I had a good time of it—was treated well by all persons—saw the cities etc. etc." What Herndon would recall instead would be the import for Lincoln's future success of what he had managed to achieve: "I think now that things began more and more to work for Lincoln's success. I say I *think* so, but do not *know* the cause, unless it be my assurance that Lincoln, to the anti-slavery cause, was as true as steel—as firmly set as Garrison etc. etc."[62]

Meanwhile, however, Herndon's usual optimism seems to have blunted the edge of any negative memories of his treatment in Boston; and he indicates on June 1, 1858, that he has already gotten over his sense of having been slighted, truly wishing bygones to be bygones. He opens a letter to Parker with the words: "I want to talk politics to you a moment leaving all other things 'way behind.'"[63] The lawyer's wish was to be granted: although the two friends were never to meet again, their correspondence continued to flow as if nothing untoward had ever transpired.

❧ Hence, despite the contrast between the ebullient Westerner and the reserved Easterner, and the personal tensions and differences that could arise between them when they were together, both Parker and Herndon clearly desired to continue what was felt to be a mutually rewarding exchange. Both seemed to realize they were riding the crests of waves that were of critical consequence to the future of the country, and they could fathom the value of joining hands to work toward what they conceived to be constructive solutions to the problems of the day. It was in their letters that they found they could best meet, however; it was there that they could agree on goals to be achieved; and there, if not in their direct personal contact, that they were able to find sustenance in what each could offer the other.

That both Herndon and Parker shared eclectic reading habits, together with a convergence of views on other subjects, no doubt contributed considerably to enabling them to overcome their inability to achieve harmony in each other's company. But for Herndon there was something still deeper. In a letter to Parker dated March 30, 1857, he enclosed a note to the minister's wife, Lydia, in which he confessed that "The reason I write to him is this—He is about the only man living who can hold me steady. That is a decided compliment. I never told him this much, but an opportunity is now offered and I quickly seize the occasion." It took Herndon until April 17 of the following year to admit as much to Parker: "Your guidance holds me steady—calm. . . . There may be some *special* things that you and I may differ on, but that makes no difference."[64]

Herndon's letters to Parker witness to the fact that the "steadiness" referred to touched a wide variety of subjects, including religion, philosophy, nature, personalities, and politics. On August 31, 1858, the Illinois lawyer stresses to his friend that "I always tell you the truth—never dodge." He affirms in a letter of September 20, 1858, marked "Whol[l]y Confidential" that he goes as deeply into sensitive issues as possible, pointing out, with regard to Stephen Douglas: "I told you all I dared when in Boston." On October 4, Herndon also takes pains to make clear to Parker that he will go as far as is ethically appropriate in sharing any important information that comes his way, and for whose accuracy he can vouch:

> I wrote to you about a certain *U[nited States] sen[ator],* and you say that hint—that man, chagrins you. I am sorry for this, but I cannot help it. However, I promise you that ere long you shall have the man's name, if it is not too great a breach of confidence. I will think about it—ask my good friends too what to do. I hope you do not doubt my word, as I have always been true to you, and all others on all occasions [this sentence is omitted by Newton]. I state nothing but facts that I *know.*

A few weeks after this, on November 23, 1858, Herndon confirms to Parker that "I landed at home from Washington and East generally, and told our people what I told you. What I told you by word and by writing I *know* to be true. I have no *private* opinion on politics that I do not tell you."[65]

What Herndon endeavors to underline is the reliability of his information and of himself. In his effort to be true to Parker, he is also straightforward about acknowledging indebtedness—which could extend even to the actual phrasing of perceptions. In a letter of January 24, 1857, for instance, he allows: "The forest trees stand out boldly against the infinite blue—look shrivelled in their 'cold and naked anatomy'—St[at]ed[?] this from you I think." As early in their correspondence as April 23, 1855, Herndon also frankly concedes that he may owe the minister in thought and word more than even he himself fully realizes, requesting that he be excused if he has incurred such a debt: "Mr. Parker if you see any expressions in those pieces which are yours in essence remember, you impressed the hard steel upon a softer plate." (It will be well to recall such expressions of indebtedness at later stages of this work when Lincoln's own debt to Parker is considered.)[66]

Central to the Herndon-Parker correspondence was always the lawyer's wish to receive the older man's views and approbation. His letters frequently contain such questions as "Can you not write to me a few lines—give your ideas," or, "What can we do? that is *the* question. Anything which you may suggest to me I will try and profit by."[67] Reflecting on speeches by Senator William Seward, Herndon asks: "By the by, those speeches are brave bold manly inexorably earth-true speeches, but is it—was it, prudent, wise-sagacious *in Seward* to alter them? What say you? What think you?" The following day he explains his reason for so often seeking Parker's opinions and approval: "There are some men in the world whose keen approbative judgements we always desire—court, to respond yes or no to acts done by us. You are at once liberal—candid and philosophic, and therefore you are amongst that class of minds courted, by others whose judgements are looked up to. . . . Our course or Greel[e]y's I want you to approve. If our course was wrong, say so—If Greel[e]y's, say so."[68]

Parker for his part was also beholden to Herndon. On September 20, 1858, for instance, the lawyer confides to Parker that, back in October of 1857, Greeley, Douglas, Thurlow Weed, and Seward had met "by accident or otherwise" in Chicago and made a secret deal to get Douglas elected senator and Seward president.[69] Knowledge of this maneuver aids Parker in understanding the background of the current political situation, and he indicates as much in a letter to his friend dated September 23, 1858: "That 'accidental' meeting in Chicago is quite remarkable, and explains many things which seemed queer before!" The preacher also solemnly promises to keep Herndon's information confidential. And on November 13, 1858, in what would turn out to be his final substantive letter to Herndon, Parker again expresses appreciation for shared intelligence: "I am your debtor for three letters—very instructive ones too." Despite Parker's interest in the information Herndon is furnishing, he nevertheless feels compelled to reveal: "I should not have allowed the account to run on so, had I not been sick, a surgical operation laid me on my bed for nearly three weeks—and of course I wrote only with another's hand and but little even in that wise."[70]

As it turned out, the minister's illness and weak physical condition were far more serious than either he or Herndon realized. As late as January 15 of the following year, however, Herndon was still urging his friend on as if he were in robust health:

> I hope you will let your four lectures on Washington, Adams, Jefferson, and Franklin come out soon. Can you not do this without infringing too much on your calculations? By the by, *no man has yet let out a philosophic idea* of *the causes* of the American Revolution, or the principles which lay thereunder—no, not one. *Can you not do this* in some of your lectures? Again, I never have seen or read or heard of a good lecture on the sweep of human liberty—say commencing at India and ending in America—Think of this—.[71]

Whatever Parker may have thought of Herndon's suggestions, his dwindling strength was not to allow him to bring them to fruition. Nor was the ailing preacher destined to reach his fiftieth birthday. On May 13, 1860, less than a year prior to Abraham Lincoln's inauguration as president of the United States, Parker's body would be placed in a modest grave in Florence, Italy.

❧ It is evident that Herndon valued Parker's thinking and found inspiration in his words. Apparent as well is his wish to have Parker's approval of his and Lincoln's course of action, in spite of the necessity for keeping the abolitionist minister's name from ever being openly linked in any manner with that of the future president. Parker in turn was exceedingly sensitive to the need to prevent his reputation as a radical from throwing Lincoln's middle-of-the-road balancing act out of kilter in Illinois; and if he wished to praise Lincoln, he did it via Herndon. We find an instance of this strategy revealed on June 29, 1857, when Herndon writes Parker, "Thank you for yours of the 24th inst. I did as you requested—gave Mr. Lincoln your best wishes: he returns them. I send you this day one of Mr. Lincoln's speeches in the State Journal." Although on July 29 Herndon tells the preacher that he is again sending speeches ("one by Sen Douglas;—one by Sen Trumbull, and one by Mr. Lincoln. Mr. Lincoln has gone to N.Y. or he would have sent to you himself"), this seems to be the closest Lincoln and Parker ever come to direct contact. And, whether for the reason given or from diplomatic reticence on Lincoln's part, it is Herndon, not Lincoln, who ultimately carries out the task.[72]

The following year, upon receiving from Herndon a copy of Lincoln's House Divided speech, Parker predicts victory for the aspiring politician in the fall senatorial election but intimates to his friend that he will stay out of the spotlight to keep from besmirching the new senator's reputation with his own abolitionist views. After extending "Many thanks for your letter and for *the admirable speech of Mr. Lincoln,*" Parker proceeds to forecast victory for Lincoln in the fall election, telling Herndon, "I think I shall congratulate *you* on *his* Senatorial dignity next winter" (emphases added).[73] Theodore Parker's praise will not and can not travel directly or in writing to the man he hopes will become the next senator from Illinois; it will obligatorily stop first at the desk of William Herndon, from there to be transmitted orally. No revealing paper trail can be allowed to exist. The close link between Parker and Herndon, as well as Herndon's reports on how he and Lincoln shared their reading matter, make it nonetheless more than likely that Parker's quiet, indirect word of praise will not fail to reach its intended recipient.

❧ Theodore Parker's ability to be circumspect about sharing too much of what he knew can also be deduced from what was to be Herndon's final letter to him. On December 15, 1859, Herndon informs the minister, who had traveled to Europe for health reasons, that "John Brown's raid in Virginia has somewhat awoke us to the 'irrepressible conflict'—has roused us to the greatness and grandeur of America's coming events; his death has sent a thrill of horror through the American world. His deeds are sweeping from the great tall heads to the mass of our people. You have no idea of the influence of John Brown's acts."[74] Herndon's words in this instance betray something he plainly did not know and had not divined: his friend Parker possessed only too clear an idea of the situation involving the fiery abolitionist Brown.

One reason the preacher's absence from the country was judicious at this moment—in addition to its importance to his failing health—was that he was an active member of the Secret Six, a group of Boston luminaries who had aided Brown morally and financially prior to his ill-fated attack on the arms depot at Harpers Ferry, Virginia. The well-intentioned but amateur circle had not been sufficiently circumspect in its use of the mails, however; and because Brown had recorded names and activities of friends and associates in his private notebooks, Parker risked being legally implicated in the affair. Brown had written Parker on February 2, 1858, for example:

> I am again out of Kansas, and am at this time concealing my whereabouts, but for very different reasons, however, than those I had for doing so at Boston last spring. I have nearly perfected arrangements for carrying out an important measure, in which the world has a deep interest, as well as Kansas, and only lack from 500 to 800 dollars to enable me to do so. The same object for which I asked for secret-service money last fall. It is my only errand here, and I have written some of our mutual friends in regard to it, but none of them understand my views so well as you do, and I cannot explain without them first committing themselves more than I know of their doing. . . . Cannot you, either by direct or indirect action, do something to further me. Do you not know of some parties whom you could induce to give their abolition theories a thorough practical shape? . . . Do you think any of my Garrisonian friends either at Boston, Worcester or in any other place, can be induced to supply a little "straw" if I will absolutely make "bricks"?

In a letter to Thomas Wentworth Higginson, Franklin B. Sanborn indicated that the "straw" had been forthcoming: "Stearns has given $100 and promises $200 more . . . Mr. Parker has raised $100 and will do something more," and by the time Brown returned to Kansas he was close to $1,500 better off. Brown's private notebook was particularly incriminating, containing a number of entries such as: "March 7th 1858 wrote Theo Parker asking him to write me (enclosing to Stephen Smith, Lombard St. Philadelphia) saying what he would do about tracts."[75] Thus, had Parker been in the United States at the time, he almost certainly would have been called before a congressional committee to testify concerning, and perhaps be indicted for, conspiracy.[76] Herndon's letter of

December 15 establishes that Parker had never shared any such information with him nor divulged Parker's damning connections with Brown.

It was no doubt better that way. Brown's raid in October 1859 preceded the selection of candidates for the presidential election of 1860 and inclined political parties to prefer conservatives who condoned neither violent measures nor the active abolition of slavery. Lincoln's clearly enunciated opposition to violent pro- or anti-abolitionist activity had been public since 1838 and was well suited to the requirements of the Republican party. A hint of even an indirect link to Brown could have scuttled his chances for the nomination. Parker's tie to Herndon and Lincoln was therefore much more effective for being unseen and, considering the minister's connection with Brown, for being unknown. This allowed Lincoln, the future Republican candidate, to defend his party to "the Southern people" with an unsullied conscience: "You charge that we stir up insurrections among your slaves. We deny it; and what is your proof? Harper's Ferry! John Brown!! John Brown was no Republican; and you have failed to implicate a single Republican in his Harper's Ferry enterprise."[77]

CHAPTER THREE

Parker and Politicians

❧ Although Abraham Lincoln could claim in good conscience not to be connected to John Brown, and perhaps with a somewhat less clear conscience not to be linked to abolitionism, this was not the case with Theodore Parker, as Brown was well aware. On February 2, 1858, only a few months before Lincoln was to deliver his House Divided speech, Brown wrote from Rochester, New York, to Thomas Wentworth Higginson, an abolitionist Unitarian minister and Parker confederate:

> I am here *concealing my whereabouts* for good reasons (as I think) not however from any anxiety about my personal safety. I have been told that you are both a true *man:* and a true *abolitionist;* "and I partly believe," the whole story. Last fall I undertook to raise from $500 to $1000, for *secret service,* and succeeded in getting $500. I now want to get for the *perfecting* of BY FAR the most *important* undertaking of my whole life; from $500 to $800 within the next sixty days. I have written Rev. Theodore Parker, George L. Stearns and F. B. Sanborn Esqrs. on the subject; but do not know as either Mr. Stearns or Mr. Sanborn are abolitionists. I suppose they are.[1]

This passage makes plain that Brown harbored no doubts about Parker's commitment to abolitionism. He was clearly convinced that, cognizant of his background and intentions, the minister would not hesitate to oppose the U.S. government on the slavery issue by contributing to *"secret service."* It is also important to realize that although Brown has often been characterized as a fanatic, this was not the light in which he was viewed by his Massachusetts supporters. Higginson, for instance, described him as

> a man whose mere appearance and bearing refuted in advance some of the strange perversions which have found their way into many books, and which have often wholly missed the type to which he be-

> longed. In his thin, worn, resolute face there were the signs of a fire which might wear him out, and practically did so, but nothing of pettiness or baseness; and his talk was calm, persuasive, and coherent.

Nor did the plan presented by Brown to his Boston benefactors arouse any significant worries, since it was

> simply to penetrate Virginia with a few comrades, to keep utterly clear of all attempt to create slave insurrection, but to get together bands and families of fugitive slaves, and then be guided by events. If he could establish them permanently in those fastnesses, like the Maroons of Jamaica and Surinam, so much the better; if not, he would make a break from time to time, and take parties to Canada, by paths already familiar to him. All this he explained to me and others, plainly and calmly, and there was nothing in it that we considered either objectionable or impracticable; so that his friends in Boston—Theodore Parker, [Samuel Gridley] Howe, Stearns Sanborn, and myself—were ready to coöperate in his plan as thus limited.

It was this plan, as conceived by Brown and presented to his patrons, that received acceptance and financial backing, whereas Higginson assures us that "Of the wider organization and membership afterwards formed by him in Canada we of course knew nothing, nor could we foresee the imprudence which finally perverted the attack into a defeat."

The close, quiet involvement of Theodore Parker with John Brown, the man many consider to have provided the spark that ignited the American Civil War, exposes the deep immersion of the minister in the political reality of his time. Parker's active participation also demonstrates his intention to influence that reality through exploiting whatever avenues might lead toward the final abolition of slavery. By no means the least important of these involved cultivating and maintaining a steady correspondence with a wide variety of contemporary leaders, as well as with their friends and associates. And because of William Herndon's direct contact with Lincoln, Parker's Illinois friend turns out to have provided one of the most significant ties to the future president. Lincoln was not, however, the only important contemporary of Parker's to come within range of the minister's energetic aura. The broad network of links that Parker nurtured with men at the heart of the nation's power structure plus the wide-ranging effort he dedicated to abolishing slavery can perhaps best be understood through a consideration of the extent to which he corresponded during the 1850s with U.S. senators from the Northeast.

Parker was quick to comprehend that some gentle influence in the right places could potentially prove of critical importance to the nation, and he accordingly initiated first an exchange of letters and subsequently an exchange of views with Senators Charles Sumner, Henry Wilson, John Hale, and William Seward. The minister had also been a friend of Horace Mann for many years prior to the educator's election to Congress, and their correspondence continued unabated after Mann took on his new post. Through such contacts Parker doubtless hoped to obtain an even wider audience for ideas concerning the burning issues of his era, and from the letters exchanged between the Massachusetts parson and these Northeastern politicians it appears that the stratagem bore its desired fruit. Almost every letter from one of these men to Parker—particularly those sent between 1852 and 1858—acknowledges receipt of one or more of the clergyman's most recent speeches or sermons. Even more important, there is often a word of appreciation for information or ideas already employed in congressional debates.

William Seward, who after an unsuccessful bid to gain the Republican nomination for president was to serve as Abraham Lincoln's secretary of state, was one of those who had Parker to thank for help in carrying on the battle to free the slaves. Seward wrote Parker in 1852, "The Country as Mankind will come to know that they owe you a great debt. I, for one, am willing to acknowledge it now." The sort of debt Seward wished to acknowledge is clearly revealed in the senator's last-ditch attempt to halt the ominous Kansas-Nebraska bill during debate in the Senate in May 1854. It was to a letter from Parker that he turned for some of the insights and intelligence he shared with the nation on that occasion, and he later candidly apologized: "Your letter of the 19th of May 1854 met me on my return to this city [Washington] the day before the passage of the Nebraska Bill in the Senate. I took the liberty of borrowing some of your own ideas and some of your own borrowed Latin for use in my hurried speech on that occasion and I now humbly beg your pardon for it." Considering Parker's strong feelings regarding the principles Seward was championing, and the exhaustive efforts the minister regularly expended in obtaining a hearing for his ideas, it is not likely that he reflected long before granting the senator's requested absolution.[2]

It was, after all, Seward's conviction that he in politics and Parker in religion were doing approximately the same work, although in widely different fields. Because the senator viewed these fields as interdependent, he considered Parker's contribution indispensable to accomplishing anything concrete in either of the two areas. As a politician Seward could therefore applaud the minister on August 10, 1852, for having perceived "two things which anti-slavery men are too slow in learning . . . that the work of propagandism is moral as well as political and the moral part being the basis of the other, must precede. They too often look to Washington for both when it is apparent that only the latter can be done, and that that can only be done to the extent that the Country is prepared to sustain them who do it." For approval of his own course of action in the antislavery struggle, Seward, as his letters make evident, looked beyond Washington, D.C., to Boston and to Parker. This may be seen, for example, in a letter he wrote the preacher in March 1858, in which he confides: "I am glad that you are satisfied with my speech, I should not be content with it myself if you were not satisfied." And Seward once praised Parker as "just such a person as I think can only fight the battle against slavery in Boston successfully." In requesting a copy of the minister's latest speech in June 1858, Seward frankly announced that he would "have use for it often hereafter," remarking that "You do not know I am sure how great a work you have done."[3]

Seward, on the other hand, felt that *he* knew quite well wherein lay Parker's greatness. He explained to the minister, "You have discovered clearly that the negative anti-slavery policy of the time is soon to cease because it has practically effected all that it can and that a positive action directed towards the removal of slavery from the country is to be adopted. And you have indicated, I think justly, the ground on which reformers can maintain themselves constitutionally in adopting this policy."[4] Seward's realization that this man of peace did not shy away from the possible necessity for armed opposition to the slave system acquires additional significance when we note that his letter was written almost three years prior to the outbreak of the Civil War, the "positive action" to which he clearly refers. This was a full two years before the senator realized the precise direction in which Parker's thought was tending.

That Seward was correct in assuming it was civil war the unconventional minister had in mind is made plain in the following excerpt from a letter Parker wrote Senator John Hale on October 21, 1856: "If Buchanan is President I think the Union does not hold out his four years—it must end in civil war, which I have been preparing for these six months past. I buy no books except for pressing need. Last year I bought $1,500 worth—this year I shall not order $200 worth. I may want the money for cannons."[5] It was Parker's considered belief that the 1856 presidential election would produce what could prove the most important crisis in the national history of the United States, and he was fully expecting James Buchanan to be elected. During the months preceding the writing of this letter, he had consequently been plying Hale with requests for books published by the "Army or Navy Department" on "the Strength of Cannon," and had requested "an inventory of all the Military Stores of the United States."[6]

Stirring Parker's fears of open conflict was the violent physical attack on Senator Charles Sumner of Massachusetts that had occurred that spring. In many ways, Sumner could be considered a protégé of Parker. The preacher had taken it upon himself to congratulate the future senator in 1845 on the occasion of Sumner's Fourth of July speech entitled "The True Grandeur of Nations," and thereafter the relationship between the two men ripened rapidly. They stood together on the platform before the Boston public in condemning the Mexican War in 1846, and Sumner's election to Daniel Webster's Senate seat in 1851 was largely a result of the stand he took alongside Parker and the abolitionists against the rendition into the hands of Southern slaveholders of the runaway slave Thomas Sims.[7]

Upon Sumner's election, Parker expressed to the new senator his hopes that he would be in "morals not politics," and that he would become known as "the Senator with a conscience."[8] But when Sumner still had not spoken out against slavery after nine months in office, Parker began to worry that the senator was not going to prove as effective an antislavery pillar as originally hoped, and, knowing that Samuel Gridley Howe was Sumner's closest friend, shared with Howe his concern that if Sumner "does not speak, then he is *dead—dead—dead.*" Long aware of Parker's worry, Howe, only a few weeks before, had apprised his friend of Parker's misgivings, saying, "A wise man likes to know how the wind blows, though he may have determined not to vary his course, even for a tempest. I wrote to Parker saying that he was lacking *faith.*"[9] To his private journal Parker confided, "Sumner has disappointed me by his nine months of silence. His election was a triumph—but a few more such triumphs will ruin us."[10] Parker did not conceal from Sumner his unhappiness with the senator's course of action, and Sumner complained to Howe that "Parker is too impatient. If by chance or ignorance of the currents here I have got into the rapids, my friends should not abandon me."[11]

Sumner's sensitivity to the minister's impatience is understandable, but Parker was certainly not abandoning him. It seems, rather, that the spirited preacher was merely attempting to encourage the fledgling senator to take wing and strive to reach the heights of which he was capable. Not long after this when Sumner finally did speak (possibly goaded to it by the reaction of Parker and others to his silence), the preacher was predictably among the first to offer warm felicitations on a job well done: "You have made a grand speech," he wrote. "It was worthwhile to go to congress to make such a speech in the Senate. . . . You have now done what I all along have said you would do, tho' I lamented that you did not do it long ago."[12]

Thereafter, Parker would often have occasion to commend Sumner for speeches against the "Slave-Power" and was ever in the vanguard of those sending thanks for the job Sumner was doing. Parker's friendship for the senator, and his personal interest in the work Sumner had undertaken, did not, however, keep him from appraising objectively Sumner's capabilities. At the death of Robert Rantoul, the former U.S. senator from Massachusetts, Parker noted: "he was a man of more effective power than Sumner. . . . Sumner he led by his argument or example; Sumner he *drove* by force of Christianity; Sumner he pulled by the beard or the hair."[13] What is of particular significance here is the preacher's realization that Sumner was susceptible to being pulled and pushed. Parker obviously hoped that with the right push the senator could be induced to use his enormous powers for the cause dear to the abolitionists; and, as ever, the minister was by no means hesitant about lending his own shoulder to the effort if need be. The direction in which Parker was pushing Sumner was not without danger, however.

In a letter Sumner sent Parker in June 1854, just two weeks after the Kansas-Nebraska bill had cleared its final hurdle (and only one day after Herndon's second letter to the minister), the senator described how menacing the situation in Washington had become: "The threats to put a bullet through my head—and hang me—and mob me—have been frequent. I have always said; 'Let them come: they will find me at my post.'" The following day he informed Parker: "Here in Washington I am attacked as chief firebrand, associate, and even leader of Phillips and Parker."[14] But despite the senator's antislavery efforts and his connections to such abolitionists, it would take almost two years more before the passions of his enemies would lead to physical action.

Sumner was at his post in the Senate on May 22, 1856, when Congressman Preston S. Brooks of South Carolina attacked him with a gold-headed, gutta-percha cane. The reason for Brooks's attack was Sumner's explosive "Crime against Kansas" speech delivered on May 19 and 20. Just two days before presenting that speech Sumner had informed Parker it would be coming:

> I have read and admired your speech in the *Post.* It is a whole sheaf of spears against slavery. Alas! alas! the Tyranny over us is complete. Will the people submit? When you read this I shall be saying—in the Senate—they will not! Would that I had your strength. But I shall pronounce the most thorough Philippic ever uttered in a legislative body.

In the fierce Kansas-Nebraska debates two years prior to this, Sumner had been praised for defending Massachusetts in broadsides leveled at Senators Stephen Douglas, James Mason, and Andrew Butler (Brooks's aging cousin); and the "Crime against Kansas" speech reveals that Sumner had not forgotten the earlier acrimony. Irritated in the present instance by what he felt were bullying tactics employed by Douglas, Sumner again attacked him unsparingly, while at the same time colorfully branding Butler the Don Quixote of slavery. Parker was quick to praise the effort. On May 21, 1856, he wrote, "My Dear Sumner,—God bless you for the brave words you spoke the other day, and have always spoken, of which I hear report in the papers."[15] Brooks, on the other hand, incensed at what he considered insufferable insults to the South as well as to the senators Sumner had denounced, undertook to defend the honor of his cousin, his state, and his region in the classic manner of a superior to an inferior: with a whipping. The beating he administered to Sumner—much of it as the Massachusetts senator sat trapped behind his immovable senate desk—was brief but effective, and Sumner's head was a bloody mass as his friends carried him from the Senate chamber that day.[16]

Sumner was never to fully recover from the cudgeling he endured, but this did not prevent him from being overwhelmingly reelected to his senate seat the following January.[17] Notwithstanding his fragile physical condition, this was cause for celebration within the ranks of his friends and supporters. And on January 24, 1857, sensitive to the long-range importance of Sumner's success, Herndon dashed off an enthusiastic congratulatory letter to Parker:

> We have just heard that Hon Chas Sumner has been re-elected to the United States Senate by the Legislature of Old Mass. God bless her. Let me congratulate you: and Humanity through you, upon the great event in *the History of the moves of Liberty.* Humanity can be reached only through the individual—I use *you.* May Sumner live—may you live,—he senatorially and you ministerially, to strike the last link, & *shiver it too,* from the last slave that breathes the free air of heaven.

It would take some years yet before Sumner could actually resume effective work in the Senate, and he was to suffer for the rest of his life from excruciating pain that no doctor in the United States or Europe was capable of assuaging.[18] But in spite of the torment his infirmity caused him, the senator ultimately became an element of consequence in the abolitionists' offensive. Following the 1860 presidential election, for instance, he lost no opportunity of making his antislavery views known to Abraham Lincoln.[19] Even after Parker's death, therefore, the minister's spirit—via Sumner—would continue to whisper its insistent message in the president's ear.[20]

❧ The attack upon Charles Sumner caused serious anxiety among other Northern senators, and Senator Henry Wilson wrote Theodore Parker three days after the beating that additional "threatened assaults upon several northern men creates much feeling and excites deep interest for the coming week." The following day he called upon the minister for aid: "Do you think that we could get in Boston $1,000 or $1,500 for purposes of defence here? I shall be at home next week, and I want to have a plain talk with you. I can say nothing more now than to hint that we mean to protect ourselves and punish the assailants of the past if we have the power."[21] Although Parker promised to forward Wilson the requested funds, the amount needed finally came to only $200, thanks to generous contributions from unidentified persons that Wilson, a former cobbler, described only as "my Shoe and Leather Dealing friends." Throughout this three-month period, however, Wilson did not hesitate to offer Parker such counsel as: "Be very careful in regard to this matter as it is one of great delicacy."[22]

Wilson, like Sumner, was a beneficiary of Parker's steady backing. The minister had written him a long letter upon his election to the Senate, admonishing him to stand firm for freedom and warning of the reefs upon which he could run aground if not prudent in his actions. Later that year, when Wilson finally found time to respond, he assured Parker that the letter had not been simply filed away with other messages of congratulation: "I sometimes read over the letter you were so kind as to send to me when I first took my seat in the Senate. You dealt frankly with me in that letter, and I thank you for it, and I hope to be better and wiser for it. . . . If I can so labor as to advance the cause of universal and impartial liberty in the country, I shall be content, whether my action meets the approbation of the politicians or not."[23] That Parker should have been the man in Boston to whom Wilson turned when the real battle began thus illustrates more concretely than flowery phrases of commendation how influential a position the minister occupied in relation to several of the most important men in the United States during the 1850s and indicates one of the reasons that his friendship was so vital to William Herndon. Parker's reaction to Wilson's request for "defence" money is noteworthy as still another example of just how great a distance separated this Unitarian preacher from the nonresistance or pacifism of abolitionists such as William Lloyd Garrison.

Parker was consistently vigilant in trying to ensure that antislavery action by any one of his allies would never fail to receive both recognition and appreciation. Each time one of his friends in Congress took a stand on a critical issue, a note of praise arrived from the Boston preacher. "I do not know how to thank you enough," he wrote Wilson on July 7, 1855. "You do nobly at all places, all times. If the rest of your senatorial term be like this part, we shall see times such as we only wished for but dared not hope as yet. There is a North, a real North, quite visible now."[24] Braced by such unshakable moral backing, it is not surprising that Sumner, Wilson, Seward, Hale, and Mann stood at the forefront of the Northern men in Congress battling the South's "Black Power" and felt themselves secure on their northern flank.

Parker comprehended only too clearly, however, that inducing politicians to take up and promote the antislavery ideas expounded in the sermons and letters with which he regularly plied them was most likely to be an effort of years. Although he was personally willing to expend that effort and endure the opprobrium to which it often gave rise, he was nonetheless conscious of the difficulties that confronted his friends in Washington when they dared to stake out unpopular positions. His unclouded understanding of these obstacles was expressed publicly as early as 1856 in an address entitled "The Present Aspect of the Anti-Slavery Enterprise":

> It is easy for Mr. Garrison and Mr. Phillips or me to say all of our thought. I am responsible to nobody, and nobody to me. But it is not easy for Mr. Sumner, Mr. Seward, and Mr. Chase to say all of their thought; because they have a position to maintain and they must keep in that position. . . . The anti-slavery non-political reformer is to excite the sentiment, and give the idea; he may tell his whole scheme all at once, and if he will. But the political reformer, who, for immediate action, is to organize the sentiment and idea he finds ready for him, cannot do or propose all things at once; he must do one thing at a time, tell one thing at a time.[25]

In order to "excite the sentiment, and give the idea," Parker was therefore careful to have copies of each of his latest sermons or speeches—as soon as possible after they had been delivered and printed—on the desks of his favorite congressmen. In this way there was always a chance that he could influence the direction taken by one or more of these politicians if or when they found themselves inclined to venture a cautious step toward resolving the slavery question.

Parker's dedication in this regard illustrates the value he placed on such efforts, as well as the intensity and depth of his own commitment. Active on many fronts in the struggle against slavery, he was not a person to fail to explore the potential of any path that might lead to a beneficial contribution to the cause. At the beginning of his career he wrote a friend: "I fear lest I have missed it capitally in becoming a minister, that as a lawyer, or in other departments of thought and action I might have been more useful, and at the same time free from a certain restrain-bond (invisible, but strong as fate) which convention has tied up every minister withal."[26]

Stretching those "restrain-bonds" on "thought and action" to the breaking point was something Parker never hesitated to do, however; and there is consequently no mystery why, in spite of personal differences with the Illinois lawyer William Herndon, he maintained regular correspondence with this man he knew to be at the center of Western politics. Nor is it surprising that, as a minister with invisible limits imposed upon him, Parker could sympathize with politicians such as Lincoln who felt the need to be exceedingly careful in gauging the length of the strides that could be taken toward changing the views of their constituents. Parker knew only too well that the "political reformer" could do merely "one thing at a time, tell one thing at a time," and he was patient yet unrelenting in his drive to force the issue of slavery to a climax. It would also appear that, although the question of "influence" is generally shrouded in mist difficult to dissipate, Parker—through his connection to, and with the blessing of, Herndon—was in as favorable a position to influence the thought of the rising Western politician Abraham Lincoln as any writer of the period; and from the evidence thus far presented was not averse to doing so. It will therefore prove useful at this stage of the discussion to consider some of the qualities in the preacher that might have appealed to Lincoln and conceivably spoken to him in a manner similar to that experienced by his partner.

❧ Theodore Parker had graduated from Harvard and drew his sustenance from Unitarianism, as well as the long-settled East, whereas Abraham Lincoln was a man of the West who admitted to religious skepticism and had learned law by the seat of his pants. Despite such differing backgrounds, a number of fundamental similarities chanced to exist between the two men. These may best be grasped, perhaps, through a comparison of the perceptions found in two revealing essays, Jacques Barzun's "Lincoln the Writer" and Thomas Wentworth Higginson's "Theodore Parker."[27]

Almost a century after Lincoln's death Barzun made the following observation:

> Lincoln's detachment was what produced his mastery over men. Had he not, as president, towered in mind and will over his cabinet, they would have crushed or used him without remorse. Chase, Seward, Stanton, the Blairs, McClellan had among them enough

> egotism and ability to wreck several administrations. . . . It was not until he was removed from their midst that any of them conceived of him as an apparition greater than themselves. . . . John Hay, who saw the long struggle, confirms Herndon's judgments: "It is absurd to call him a modest man. No great man was ever modest. It was his intellectual arrogance and unconscious assumption of superiority that men like Chase and Sumner could never forgive." (64–65)

Higginson, writing in 1899, remembered that his friend and contemporary "Theodore Parker was so strong and self-sufficing upon his own ground, he needed so little from any other person, while giving so freely to all, that one would hardly venture to add anything to the autobiographies he has left" (34–35). What is more, Higginson wrote, "He made his great qualities seem so natural and inevitable, we forgot that all did not share them. We forgot the scholar's proverbial reproach of timidity and selfishness, in watching him. While he lived, it seemed a matter of course that the greatest acquirements and the heartiest self-devotion should go together" (59). Lincoln and Parker are pictured in the above descriptions as strongly independent, distant, and not unconscious of the abilities and gifts with which they were endowed. In connection with Higginson's comments regarding Parker, we may also recall Herndon's strong feeling of having been rebuffed and held at a distance by the minister's cool reserve both times that the two men met.

An additional, somewhat unexpected, parallel between Parker and Lincoln can be discerned in how some of their contemporaries perceived their writing styles. In Barzun's view:

> Lincoln has indeed had praise as a writer, but nearly all of it has been conventional and absentminded. . . . Thus, in the Hay and Nicolay edition of Lincoln's works, a famous editor of the nineties writes: "Of style, in the ordinary use of the word, Lincoln may be said to have had little. There was nothing ambitiously elaborate or self-consciously simple in Lincoln's way of writing. He had not the scholar's range of words. He was not always grammatically accurate. He would doubtless have been very much surprised if anyone had told him that he 'had' a style at all."
>
> Here one feels like asking: Then why discuss "Lincoln as a writer"? The answer is unconvincing: "And yet, because he was determined to be understood, because he was honest, because he had a

> warm and true heart, because he had read good books eagerly and not coldly, and because there was in him a native good taste, as well as a strain of imagination, he achieved a singularly clear and forcible style, which took color from his own noble character and became a thing individual and distinguished. . . . "
>
> So the man who had no style had a style after all—one that was clear, forcible, individual and distinguished. (59–60)

To those who have read some of Parker's sermons, it may come as no surprise to learn that Higginson felt Parker, too, failed to achieve "the finest literary execution":

> A delicate literary ear he might have had, perhaps, but he very seldom stopped to cultivate or even indulge it. . . . Theodore Parker's most scholarly performances were still stump speeches. Vigorous, rich, brilliant, copious, they yet seldom afford a sentence which falls in perfect cadence upon the ear; under a show of regular method, they are loose and diffuse, and often have the qualities which he himself attributed to the style of John Quincy Adams,—"disorderly, ill compacted, and homely to a fault." (51)

With respect to Lincoln's writing, Barzun explains that, "In his own day, Lincoln's prose was found flat, dull, lacking in taste. It differed radically in form and tone from the accepted models—Webster's or Channing's for speeches, Bryant's or Greeley's for journalism. Once or twice, Lincoln did imitate their genteel circumlocutions or resonant abstractions. But these were exercises he never repeated." Barzun considers that Lincoln's "style, well in hand by his thirtieth year and richly developed by his fiftieth, has the eloquence which comes of the contrast between transparency of medium and density of thought" (66).

Of Parker's style, Higginson allows that while the minister's prose was in some ways effective, it certainly could not have been said to sparkle:

> The deeds make the man, but it is the style which makes or dooms the writer. History, which always sends great men in groups, gave us Emerson by whom to test the intellectual qualities of Parker. They coöperated in their work from the beginning, but not in the same mutual relation as now; in looking back over the rich volumes of the "Dial," the reader now passes by the contributions of Parker

> to glean every sentence of Emerson's, but we have the latter's authority for the fact that it was the former's articles which originally sold the numbers. (54–55)

Higginson is nevertheless careful to provide balance for his judgment by recounting that

> I have always remembered a certain lecture of his on the Anglo-Saxons as the most wonderful instance that ever came within my knowledge of the adaptation of solid learning to the popular intellect. Nearly two hours of almost unadorned fact,—for there was far less than usual of relief and illustration,—and yet the lyceum audience listened to it as if an angel sang to them. So perfect was his sense of purpose and of power, so clear and lucid was his delivery, with such wonderful composure did he lay out section by section, his historical chart, that he grasped his hearers as absolutely as he grasped his subject,—one was compelled to believe that he might read the people the Sanskrit Lexicon, and they would listen with ever fresh delight. Without actual grace or beauty or melody, his mere elocution was sufficient to produce effects for which melody and grace and beauty might have sighed in vain. I always felt that he well described his own eloquence while describing Luther's in one of the most admirably moulded sentences he ever achieved,—"The homely force of Luther, who, in the language of the farm, the shop, the boat, the street, or the nursery, told the high truths that reason or religion taught, and took possession of his audience by a storm of speech, then poured upon them all the riches of his brave plebeian soul, baptizing every head anew,—a man who with the people seemed more mob than they, and with kings the most imperial man." (47–48)

In spite of himself then (and in a manner reminiscent of the critic of Lincoln's style quoted by Barzun), Higginson witnesses to the force of at least a certain kind of style possessed by the Boston minister and finds himself recognizing Parker's "eloquence." Although in Higginson's view Parker does not measure up to Emerson's literary skills, his "sense of purpose and power" is "perfect," his "delivery" is "clear and lucid," and we are told, somewhat paradoxically, that, "Without actual grace or beauty or melody, his mere elocution was sufficient to produce effects for which melody and grace and beauty might have sighed in vain." Hence, the man who in

Higginson's judgment could seldom produce "a sentence which falls in perfect cadence upon the ear" is also the person who produced the "admirably moulded" sentence on Luther. It would seem that Parker, like Lincoln, did after all possess his own sort of style.

In the sentence describing Luther's "homely force" in using "the language of the farm, the shop, the boat, the street, or the nursery" to tell "the high truths that reason or religion taught," a sentence seen by Higginson as describing Parker's personal eloquence, we find a clear parallel with Barzun's evaluation of Lincoln's language:

> As a lawyer Lincoln knew that the courtroom vocabulary would achieve this purpose [to avoid misunderstanding] if handled with a little care. But it would remain jargon, obscure to the common understanding. As an artist, therefore, he undertook to frame his ideas invariably in one idiom, that of daily life. He had to use, of course, the technical names of the actions and documents he dealt with. But all the rest was in the vernacular. His first achievement, then, was to translate the minute accuracy of the advocate and the judge into the words of common men. (68)

The importance to both Parker and Lincoln of the ability to use everyday language in making their ideas generally accessible is unquestionably a key element in the style of each. As Higginson says of Parker:

> it was in popularizing thought and knowledge that his great and wonderful power lay. Not an original thinker, in the same sense with Emerson, he yet translated for tens of thousands that which Emerson spoke to hundreds only. No matter who had been heard on any subject, the great mass of intelligent, "progressive" New England thinkers waited to hear the thing summed up by Theodore Parker. . . . No matter how well others seemed to have hit the target, his shot was the triumphant one, at last. Thinkers might find no new thought in the new discourse, leaders of action no new plan, yet, after all that had been said and done, his was the statement that told upon the community. (46–47)

Much in this description could apply just as well to Abraham Lincoln. And, tangentially, it would do well to keep in mind Higginson's final sentence when the extent of Parker's possible influence on Lincoln is subsequently considered.

A further feature of Parker's speeches and sermons that Higginson highlights as being of significance to those who came to listen to the minister's message was "his thorough Americanism of training and sympathy. Surcharged with European learning, he yet remained at heart the Lexington farmer's boy, and his whole harvest was indigenous, not exotic" (48). "Americanism"—unadorned—is also the element that Barzun considers fundamental to Lincoln's style:

> The four main qualities of Lincoln's literary art—precision, vernacular ease, rhythmical virtuosity, and elegance—may at a century's remove seem alien to our tastes. Yet it seems no less odd to question their use and interest to the present when one considers one continuing strain in our literature. Lincoln's example, plainly, helped to break the monopoly of the dealers in literary plush. After Lincoln comes Mark Twain, and out of Mark Twain come contemporaries of ours as diverse as Sherwood Anderson, H. L. Mencken, and Ernest Hemingway. Lincoln's use of his style for the intimate genre and for the sublime was his alone; but his workaday style is the American style par excellence. (73)

Parker's style may not have been the American style par excellence, but it was a style both acceptable and eminently understandable to the multitudes of Americans and visitors to America who made their way in droves to attend his sermons and lectures.[28] It was a style that, like Lincoln's, avoided "literary plush" in order to spend the time and clarity thus gained in penetrating to the heart of issues.

Another aspect common to the writing of Parker and Lincoln is their dependence on deliberate, logical tactics in treating the question at hand. Barzun affirms that, for Lincoln, "Demonstration was . . . the one proper goal of argument; he never seems to have considered it within his power to convince by disturbing the judgment through the emotions. In the few passages where he resorts to platform tricks, he uses only irony or satire, never the rain-barrel booming of the Fourth-of-July orator" (68). Higginson relates, of Parker, "he early learned, so he once told me, that the New England people dearly love two things,—a philosophical arrangement and plenty of statistics. To these, therefore, he treated them thoroughly" (47). Both Lincoln and Parker thus chose "demonstration" over soul-wringing, preferring to convince through reasoned argument rather than by Barzun's "disturbing the judgment through the emotions" (68). It may be observed as well that what Barzun describes as "The four main qualities of Lincoln's literary art—precision, vernacular ease, rhythmical virtuosity, and elegance"—are features evident also in Parker's writing. Although in none of these domains can it be averred that Parker reaches Lincoln's level of achievement, the minister's sermons and speeches often contain the less polished makings of the stuff that dreams are made of—"stuff" that, as Herndon informs us, was no secret to Lincoln.

In Barzun's analysis of Lincoln's writing, attention is drawn to "One superior gift he possessed from the start and developed to a supreme degree, the gift of rhythm" (68–69). For anyone who has read or listened to Lincoln's prose, this claim needs no further justification. Nor is it a secret that the rhythm detectable in Lincoln's later speeches is often owed to biblical cadences, rhetoric, or quotations. It may be suggested, also, that on the subject of rhythm Higginson fails to do justice to Parker. One need only recall the sentence describing Luther, or Higginson's realization that Parker "might read the people the Sanskrit Lexicon, and they would listen with ever fresh delight," to understand that something was going on that Higginson could not fully grasp or explain.

A careful reading of Parker's sermons and speeches makes clear that what Higginson describes but does not discern are the slow, tide-like rhythms of Parker's productions. The inevitability of the conclusions toward which he steadily, adamantly presses generates a quietly developing undercurrent, signaled primarily by gentle, rolling, rhythmical waves. The motions are those of the sea. In addition they are, at times, biblical. It is not incomprehensible, therefore, that Higginson, a minister himself, would clearly feel or sense them, without necessarily apprehending how their effect was achieved or that they might be the expression of a subtle skill, whether or not consciously perceived as such by Parker or his listeners. Nor is it difficult to understand why Lincoln, so conscious of biblical rhythms and balance himself, might easily respond to them.

The essays of Barzun and Higginson again prove revelatory with regard to a major difference existing between Lincoln and Parker: the manner in which they approached the act of writing. It is Barzun's conclusion that

> Lincoln wrote slowly—meaning, by writing, the physical act of forming letters on paper. This would augment the desirability of being brief. Lincoln wrote before the typewriter and the dictating ma-

> chine, and wanting to put all his meaning into one or two lucid sentences, he thought before he wrote. The great compression came after he had, lawyerlike, excluded alternatives and hit upon right order and emphasis.
>
> Obviously this style would make use of skips and connections unsuited to speechmaking. The member of the cabinet who received a terse memorandum had it before him to make out at leisure. But an audience requires a looser texture, just as it requires a more measured delivery. (70)

Such a method is at clear variance with Higginson's perception of the method employed by Parker. According to Higginson, the minister once

> said of Dr. Channing,—"Diffuseness is the old Adam of the pulpit. There are always two ways of hitting the mark,—one with a single bullet, the other with a shower of small shot: Dr. Channing chose the latter, as most of our pulpit orators have done." Theodore Parker chose it also. . . . In the perpetual rush and hurry of his life, he had no time to select, to discriminate, to omit anything, or to mature anything. He had the opportunities, the provocatives, and the drawbacks which make the work and mar the fame of the professional journalist. (51–52)

But Parker was nothing if not thorough, and Higginson, although betraying a certain New England reserve, bravely strives to clarify as well as credit the preacher's accomplishments:

> No matter what theme might be announced, the people got the whole latitude and longitude of Theodore Parker, and that was precisely what they wanted. He, more than any other man among us, broke down the traditional non-committalism of the lecture room, and oxygenated all the lyceums of the land. He thus multiplied his audience very greatly, while doubtless losing to some degree the power of close logic and of addressing a specific statement to a special point. Yet it seemed as if he could easily leave the lancet to others, grant him only the hammer and the forge. (54)

From Higginson's description it gradually becomes apparent that the measured approach to speech-making of Parker, a translator of thick German tomes, had the advantage of leaving little doubt in the listener's mind as to what views he held on a given subject. There was thus no risk that Herndon—and via Herndon, Lincoln—could mistake the tenor of the minister's message or miss its import. And once the steel had been heated in the forge and beaten by the hammer of Theodore Parker, it is just possible it was ready for Abraham Lincoln to fashion into a lancet. But what kind of steel, we might ask, was Parker making ready for that lancet? And in what manner would Lincoln's House Divided speech and Gettysburg Address ultimately benefit from the well-tempered quality of that metal?

CHAPTER FOUR

Lincoln's "House Divided" Revisited

❧ Of the writings of Theodore Parker from which Abraham Lincoln could draw sustenance as he struggled to find his place on the political stage of the mid-1850s, much of importance may be found in "A Sermon of the Dangers which Threaten the Rights of Man in America," delivered on July 2, 1854, two days before Independence Day celebrations. Although it might at first appear that the date of delivery should have allowed Lincoln to see the sermon prior to his Springfield or Peoria speeches the following October, it is quite conceivable that the amount of time required for Parker to have it published and subsequently sent to Herndon was insufficient to make this possible. This could go far toward explaining why no trace of the "Rights of Man" sermon can be discerned in either of Lincoln's October efforts, whereas a segment of Parker's earlier "New York speech" may well be reflected there (see Chapter 1). But whatever the circumstances and dates surrounding Herndon's acquisition of the sermon, its potential for influencing Lincoln's thinking in important ways mandates that we turn our attention at this point to the tribute Parker felt would be appropriate for the Fourth of July observance. And as we now know just how strongly Herndon felt *pulled* to the Boston minister, and how the interaction between Herndon, Parker, and Lincoln operated, there would seem to be reasonable grounds for examining the possible effect of Parker's sermon on Lincoln's House Divided speech, a speech that looked back to 1854 and the agitated situation stemming from Stephen Douglas's Kansas-Nebraska bill.

Yet once again, Herndon gets in the way, distracting scholars from giving Parker's work the consideration it might otherwise receive. For while it is Herndon who informs us that "Lincoln now from 1854 to 1861 was in his glory—had hopes—bright hopes, to fill his aspirations," it is also Herndon's account of the debt owed by the first sentence of Lincoln's House Divided speech to Daniel

Webster's Reply to Hayne that has served to divert attention from what succeeds that sentence.[1] Over thirty years after Lincoln wrote and presented the House Divided speech, Herndon told readers of his Lincoln biography that "If any student of oratorical history, after reading Lincoln's speech on this occasion will refer to Webster's reply to Hayne in the Senate, he will be struck with the similarity in figure and thought in the opening lines of both speeches. In fact it may not be amiss to note that, in this instance, Webster's effort was carefully read by Lincoln and served in part as his model."[2]

Lending credence to Herndon's accounts has consequently led historians to bestow the laurel wreath of "influence" on the man whom some at the time termed "the Godlike Daniel." Richard N. Current, for instance, echoes Herndon in affirming that "In preparing his House-Divided speech of 1858 [Lincoln] used the Reply to Hayne as a kind of model, and while working on his First Inaugural he again had before him that masterpiece of Webster's." Donald goes even further and specifically asserts that the first eighteen lines of the House Divided speech were created "In conscious imitation of the opening of Daniel Webster's celebrated reply to Robert Hayne."[3]

Such a convergence of views on the part of highly respected scholars would appear to settle the question once and for all, especially since, as Wills correctly points out, an examination of Webster's Reply to Hayne together with his speech "The Constitution Not a Compact" reveals that "every element" of Lincoln's argument in the First Inaugural "was taken from Webster." This does not, however, authorize the conclusion that the same holds true for the House Divided speech; and a comment made by Wills merits attention in this regard. Referring to Lincoln's well-documented ability to be diplomatically reserved on occasion, Wills notes that "Lincoln was accused during his lifetime of clever evasions and key silences."[4] This remark deserves to be weighed in conjunction with George M. Fredrickson's careful demonstration that Lincoln "quoted [Henry] Clay, paraphrased him, and at times virtually plagiarized from him, not merely for the practical political purpose of winning recalcitrant Whigs to the Republican cause but because he indeed thought of himself as taking up where Clay had left off." Nor, according to Arthur Lehman Goodhart, would direct appropriation of this nature have been considered improper by the lawyer, since it is a "legal trait" that

> can be found in Lincoln's frequent use of what he himself had said on a previous occasion, or in his borrowing whole sentences from other writers without referring to his sources. The best-known illustration of this is the famous phrase "government of the people, by the people, for the people" in the last line of the [Gettysburg] Address. This had, almost certainly, been taken from an address delivered by Theodore Parker. . . . Such borrowing is intentionally used by most lawyers because their whole training is directed to reliance on precedents; for them a legal statement has added force if it can be shown that it is not a novel one. The highest compliment that can be paid to a lawyer is to say that he is a sound thinker; it is less flattering to suggest that he is an original one.[5]

These observations raise the distinct possibility that there was influence on Lincoln's speeches of which Herndon was unaware and that Lincoln did not openly acknowledge. It is this possibility that I shall consider, by way of establishing that whether or not Lincoln ever realized it (or, as is far more likely, was strategically silent on the subject), Theodore Parker's "Rights of Man" sermon was considerably more of an influence on Lincoln's House Divided speech than was Webster's Reply to Hayne. Before examining this influence, however, it is important to pay heed to the claim made on behalf of Daniel Webster, and to consider Webster's contribution to Lincoln's effort.

❧ It was on January 26, 1830, that Webster rose from his seat in the U.S. Senate to rebut Robert Y. Hayne's defense of the notion that a state possessed the right to reject federal legislation it deemed injurious to its rights or sovereignty. Considering this doctrine of John C. Calhoun's a threat to the Constitution and to the Union, the "Great Daniel" began his Reply in the following manner:

> Mr. President,—When the mariner has been tossed for many days in thick weather, and on an unknown sea, he naturally avails himself of the first pause in the storm, the earliest glance of the sun, to take his latitude, and ascertain how far the elements have driven him from his true course. Let us imitate this prudence, and before we float further on the waves of this debate, refer to the point from which we departed, that we may at least be able to conjecture where we now are. (Reply, 271)

DANIEL WEBSTER

(Courtesy of the Massachusetts Historical Society)

In comparison, the first sentence of Lincoln's House Divided speech carries the same fundamental message, with far fewer words and decidedly less drift:

> If we could first know *where* we are, and *whither* we are tending, we could better judge *what* to do, and *how* to do it.[6]

Placed alongside the opening lines of Webster's answer to Hayne, the similarity "in figure and thought" of Lincoln's lines is undeniable. Both men propose that an effort be made to take bearings before attempting to define a course in which movement might acquire some promise of progress. It is nonetheless important to recall that Herndon specifies only "the opening lines of both speeches" and claims that Webster's speech "served in part" as Lincoln's "model." The "part," therefore, was conceivably more limited than many readers have heretofore assumed. Although the measure of Herndon's precise meaning will probably never be known, a comparison of the two speeches, together with selections from other Webster utterances, reveals that Lincoln was unquestionably indebted to the senator from Massachusetts.

Webster in his Reply to Hayne took the position that "The domestic slavery of the Southern States I leave where I find it,—in the hands of their own governments. It is their affair, not mine" (281). This was a position Lincoln himself supported for many years, and that this was still the case in 1858 can be seen in the first of the Lincoln-Douglas debates where Lincoln stated: "I have no purpose directly or indirectly to interfere with the institution of slavery in the States where it exists. I believe I have no lawful right to do so, and I have no inclination to do so."[7]

The heart of Webster's speech, however, was his assertion that "The Union itself is too full of benefit to be hazarded in propositions for changing its original basis." He declared: "I go for the Constitution as it is, and for the Union as it is" (Reply, 281). He stressed this point in closing his speech with resounding rhetoric on behalf of the Union:

> I have not allowed myself, Sir, to look beyond the Union, to see what might lie hidden in the dark recess behind. I have not coolly weighed the chances of preserving liberty when the bonds that unite us together shall be broken asunder. . . . God grant that in my day, at least, that curtain may not rise! God grant that on my vision never

> may be opened what lies behind! When my eyes shall be turned to behold for the last time the sun in heaven, may I not see him shining on the broken and dishonored fragments of a once glorious Union; on States dissevered, discordant, belligerent; on a land rent with civil feuds, or drenched, it may be, in fraternal blood! Let their last feeble and lingering glance rather behold the gorgeous ensign of the republic, now known and honored throughout the earth, still full high advanced, its arms and trophies streaming in their original lustre, not a stripe erased or polluted, nor a single star obscured, bearing for its motto no such miserable interrogatory as "What is all this worth?" nor those other words of delusion and folly, "Liberty first and Union afterwards"; but everywhere, spread all over in characters of living light, blazing on all its ample folds, as they float over the sea and over the land, and in every wind under the whole heavens, that other sentiment, dear to every true American heart,—Liberty *and* Union, now and for ever, one and inseparable! (342)

Webster's commitment to the concept of the Union admits no impediment. He clearly spurns the kind of independence that would permit states' rights advocates to justify secession or civil strife on behalf of the "liberty" of individual states. He and Lincoln thus agree that the kind of revolution permitted in 1776 is no longer an option, a point Lincoln made in his Lyceum speech of 1838, that paralleled the view Webster had presented in 1830 and also went counter to Thomas Jefferson's concept of the primacy of states' rights.

In support of Herndon's assertion concerning the importance of Webster's influence on Lincoln's House Divided speech, we should also note that, toward the close of the speech, Lincoln declares:

> Two years ago the Republicans of the nation mustered over thirteen hundred thousand strong.
>
> We did this under the single impulse of resistance to a common danger, with every external circumstance against us.
>
> Of *Strange, discordant,* and even, *hostile* elements, we gathered from the four winds, and *formed* and fought the battle through, under the constant hot fire of a disciplined, proud, and pampered enemy. (House Divided, 380)

Lincoln then asks: "Did we brave all *then,* to *falter* now?—*now*— when that same enemy is *wavering,* dissevered and belligerent?"

(380). Considering that in Lincoln's day the sentence from the closing paragraph of Webster's speech beginning with "When my eyes" and ending with "fraternal blood" was perhaps the most widely known utterance of the Massachusetts senator, and that, according to Herndon, "Lincoln thought that Webster's great speech in reply to Haynes [*sic*] was the very best speech that was ever delivered,"[8] Lincoln's "*wavering,* dissevered and belligerent" must be seen as indebted to Webster's "dissevered, discordant, belligerent."[9] Even Webster's "discordant," although not included in Lincoln's three-word series, appears a few lines earlier in the House Divided speech and is italicized. An essential point, however, is that Lincoln uses Webster's words in an entirely different context and for a different purpose than Webster. He borrows the senator's vocabulary and some of his rhetorical flourishes but not his logic. This can be demonstrated through a closer look at the substance of Webster's speech.

The central focus of the debate with Hayne was the doctrine of nullification that had recently been adopted by the legislature of South Carolina. In essence this doctrine claimed that a state had the constitutional right to refuse to be bound by federal laws it deemed inimical to its rights or sovereignty. Webster saw the doctrine as a major threat to the union of the states, arguing:

> The great question is, Whose prerogative is it to decide on the constitutionality or unconstitutionality of the laws? On that, the main debate hinges. The proposition, that, in case of a supposed violation of the Constitution by Congress, the States have a constitutional right to interfere and annul the law of Congress, is the proposition of the gentleman. I do not admit it. If the gentleman had intended no more than to assert the right of revolution for justifiable cause, he would have said only what all agree to. But I cannot conceive that there can be a middle course, between submission to the laws, when regularly pronounced constitutional, on the one hand, and open resistance, which is revolution or rebellion, on the other. (Reply, 320–21)

For Webster it followed that nullification was equivalent to allowing a willful child to have its own way to the detriment of the family. Such foolish and risky permissiveness was therefore to be rejected except, of course, in the case of the kind of oppression that had led the original thirteen states to unite in revolution against a common tyranny. Webster's position was firm: "I say, the right of a State to annul a law of Congress cannot be maintained, but on the ground of the inalienable right of man to resist oppression; that is to say, upon the ground of revolution. I admit that there is an ultimate violent remedy, above the Constitution and in defiance of the Constitution, which may be resorted to when a revolution is to be justified" (321).

But to permit a minirevolution by one or more states within the Union, upon each occasion of unhappiness with a federal government decision, did not serve the common good, and Webster could "not admit, that, under the Constitution and in conformity with it, there is any mode in which a State government, as a member of the Union, can interfere and stop the progress of the general government, by force of her own laws, under any circumstances whatever" (Reply, 321). He reasoned that "The people . . . erected this government. They gave it a Constitution, and in that Constitution they have enumerated the powers which they bestow on it. They have made it a limited government. They have defined its authority" (334). The senator further realized that the nullification doctrine could ultimately lead to open conflict between states supporting the laws laid down by the federal government and those choosing to decide for themselves which of the federal statutes suited them: "Direct collision . . . between force and force, is the unavoidable result of that remedy for the revision of unconstitutional laws which the gentleman contends for. It must happen in the very first case to which it is applied" (334), and Webster directed his listeners' attention to the fact that "To resist by force the execution of a law, generally, is treason. Can the courts of the United States take notice of the indulgence of a State to commit treason?" (339). Then, seeking to lighten the mood while driving home his point, Webster resorted to a half-serious joke about hanging, the usual punishment for treasonable acts: "it is rather an awkward business, this dying without touching the ground! After all, that is a sort of hemp tax worse than any part of the tariff" (338).

In the end, however, neither treason nor nullification was necessary if one accepted Webster's view that the ultimate power of decision lay not with the representative governments of the states but with the individuals who peopled each of the separate states of the nation:

> If any thing be found in the national Constitution, either by original provision or subsequent interpretation, which ought not to be in it, the people know how to get rid of it. If any construction, unacceptable to them, be established, so as to become practically a part of the Constitution, they will amend it, at their own sovereign pleasure. But while the people choose to maintain it as it is, while they are satisfied with it, and refuse to change it, who has given, or who can give, to the State legislatures a right to alter it, either by interference, construction, or otherwise? (Reply, 340)

This powerful defence of the Union, and its constitutional foundation in the will of the people rather than in the will of state legislatures, soon came to be considered classic and, as Herndon indicates, was probably not far from Lincoln's consciousness as he undertook to prepare a speech on a major threat to the Union, a threat even greater in his day than it had been in Webster's. Lincoln, like Webster, was challenging the views of a man he saw as posing a major danger to the Union if left unopposed: for Webster it was Hayne; for Lincoln, Stephen Douglas. And Lincoln's opening words to his House Divided speech do, indeed, condense the flowing prose of the opening paragraph of Webster's effort into that single, poetically balanced, alliterative sentence: "If we could first know *where* we are, and *whither* we are tending, we could better judge *what* to do, and *how* to do it" (House Divided, 372). In addition, unmistakable echoes of Webster's speech can be distinguished in the stressed and balanced use of "where," "whither," "what," "how," since with Webster's Reply to Hayne we find the Massachusetts senator at one stage offering to "tell the gentleman *when,* and *how,* and *why* New England has supported measures favorable to the West" (Reply, 293) and then, following a thorough exegesis, closing with "I hope that by this time, Sir, the honorable gentleman is satisfied; if not, I do not know *when,* or *how,* or *why* he ever will be" (294).

A related echo of these words can also be detected in a speech Webster delivered in Buffalo, New York, on May 22, 1851. On this occasion he tells his audience:

> Gentlemen, believe me, I know where I am. I know to whom I am speaking. I know for whom I am speaking. I know that I am here in this singularly prosperous and powerful section of the United States, Western New York, and I know the character of the men

> who inhabit Western New York. I know they are sons of liberty, one and all; that they sucked in liberty with their mothers' milk; inherited it with their blood; that it is the subject of their daily contemplation and watchful thought. . . . I hope these observations will satisfy you that I know where I am, under what responsibility I speak, and before whom I appear.[10]

Herndon makes no mention of the Buffalo speech in connection with Lincoln's House Divided effort, but it is quite probable, considering Lincoln's admiration for Webster and the fact that they had once served together in Congress, that this more recent endeavor by the great orator was also in the future candidate's mind as he began the work of preparing the opening salvo in his bid for the U.S. Senate seat from Illinois.

Enhancing the possibility that Lincoln knew this oration at the time he was writing his own is the fact that, in the same speech, we find Webster asking the major question of the day:

> Can we preserve the union of the States, not by coercion, not by military power, not by angry controversies; but [also] can we of this generation, you and I, your friends and my friends,—can we so preserve the union of these States, by such administration of the powers of the Constitution as shall give content and satisfaction to all who live under it, and draw us together, not by military power, but by the silken cords of mutual, fraternal, patriotic affection? That is the question, and no other.

And the senator left no doubt as to what answer he would give to that question:

> Gentlemen, I believe in party distinctions. I am a party man. There are questions belonging to party in which I take an interest, and there are opinions entertained by other parties which I repudiate; but what of all that? If a house be divided against itself, it will fall, and crush every body in it. We must see that we maintain the government which is over us. We must see that we uphold the constitution, and we must do so without regard to party.[11]

The biblical quotation "a house divided against itself" is known to have been employed by Lincoln as early as March 4, 1843, in a campaign circular; it was thus a passage by no means foreign to him.[12] It is possible that Webster's use of it in his Buffalo speech could have recalled it to Lincoln's consciousness, although there was plainly no need for that. Nor does the basic content of the House Divided speech lean more than lightly either on Webster's Reply to Hayne or on the Buffalo speech. Some historians nonetheless cite Lincoln's first fifteen or twenty lines and (following Herndon's lead) attribute to Lincoln a copycat approach to Webster's well-known reply.[13]

Close examination of the efforts of both Lincoln and Webster reveals this assumption to have little basis in fact. And it would appear that, by drawing attention to Webster's influence on the first sentence of the House Divided speech, Herndon has inadvertently deflected scholars from discovering a more plausible source for the speech's opening philosophical section. While it seems beyond doubt that the initial sentence of the House Divided speech is owed to Webster's Reply to Hayne, and that to create this opening line Lincoln polished and skillfully honed Webster's first two sentences, thereafter the logic of the senatorial candidate's argument breaks away sharply from that of the Massachusetts leader. Webster follows up the taking of bearings manifest in his opening lines with a request for a reading of the resolution on public lands (the subject originally under discussion), after which he continues: "We have thus heard, Sir, what the resolution is which is actually before us for consideration; and it will readily occur to every one, that it is almost the only subject about which something has not been said in the speech, running through two days, by which the Senate has been entertained by the gentleman from South Carolina" (Reply, 271). Webster subsequently launches on a loquacious defence of himself, aspects of the debate itself, and New England before turning to questions concerning slavery, nullification, and the Union.

After adopting Webster's strategy in his opening sentence Lincoln, on the other hand, could not have diverged more radically from the arguments of the Massachusetts senator. This becomes apparent from the crucial opening section of Lincoln's speech:

> If we could first know *where* we are, and *whither* we are tending, we could better judge *what* to do, and *how* to do it.
>
> We are now far into the *fifth* year, since a policy was initiated, with the *avowed* object, and *confident* promise, of putting an end to slavery agitation.

> Under the operation of that policy, that agitation has not only, *not ceased,* but has *constantly augmented.*
>
> In my opinion, it *will* not cease, until a *crisis* shall have been reached, and passed—
>
> "A house divided against itself cannot stand."
>
> I believe this government cannot endure, permanently half *slave* and half *free.*
>
> I do not expect the Union to be *dissolved*—I do not expect the house to *fall*—but I *do* expect it will cease to be divided.
>
> It will become *all* one thing, or *all* the other.
>
> Either the *opponents* of slavery, will arrest the further spread of it, and place it where the public mind shall rest in the belief that it is in course of ultimate extinction; or its *advocates* will push it forward, till it shall become alike lawful in *all* the States, *old* as well as *new—North* as well as *South.*
>
> Have we no *tendency* to the latter condition? (House Divided, 372-73)

Both Lincoln and Webster have at heart the maintaining of the Union, as is obvious from the words that bring Webster's speech to its ringing close and from Lincoln's concern regarding the continued existence of a house divided against itself. But Lincoln is dealing with the immediate threat to the Union posed in his day and is analyzing the theoretical, long-range implications as well as the practical expression of that threat.

Following his opening philosophical exposition of the fundamental problem facing the nation, Lincoln proceeds to describe in the remainder of his speech "that now almost complete legal combination—piece of *machinery* so to speak—compounded of the Nebraska doctrine, and the Dred Scott decision" (House Divided, 373). He asks anyone who doubts its existence to "consider not only *what work* the machinery is adapted to do, and *how well* adapted; but also, let him study the history of its construction, and trace, if he can, or rather *fail,* if he can, to trace the evidences of design, and concert of action, among its chief bosses, from the beginning" (373). The quiet conspiracy he perceives has as its goal to further the spread of slavery rather than aim at its gradual eradication. And, in Lincoln's view, it runs counter to the wishes of the founding fathers, who understood only too well the evil involved in enslaving another human being, and who (as Lincoln maintains in his final debate with Douglas on October 15, 1858) in their far-seeing wisdom even carefully omitted the word *slavery* from the Constitution in order that the document, at some future date after slavery had finally been abolished from American soil, would not require revision.[14] Thus, it is treachery to what Lincoln considers the ideals of the founders that arouses his wrath. And it is Stephen Douglas, the man who in 1854 instigated the repeal of the Missouri Compromise, who receives the majority of his thunderbolts.

An interesting sidelight here is that one of the most important of the founders, Thomas Jefferson, expressed near the end of his life his support for "a general emancipation and *expatriation*" of America's slave population, although simultaneously opposing the Missouri Compromise. In Jefferson's opinion: "A geographical line, coinciding with a marked principle, moral and political, once conceived and held up to the angry passions of men, will never be obliterated; and every new irritation will mark it deeper and deeper."[15] But Lincoln in this instance was siding with Henry Clay in believing that only such a line stood a chance of providing the delimiting basis requisite to ultimate extirpation of the blight of slavery from American soil.

Lincoln's argumentation owes little to Webster's Reply to Hayne, however. Webster had set forth his conception of principles concerning the constitutionality of secession, and although this question was certainly not far from Lincoln's consciousness, it is not the issue at stake here. Rather than the constitutionality of secession the immediate problem is the constitutional right of a territory to exclude slavery, together with what Lincoln perceives to be a conspiracy to betray the ideals of the Revolution; and his approach is of necessity quite different from Webster's. The era is a new one, and Lincoln must confront the new problems this era brings with it.

Thus, although it cannot be gainsaid that Lincoln borrowed some superficial features as well as some rhythms and phrasing from Webster for use in the House Divided speech, the most prominent of which is probably to be found in the opening sentence, Herndon's claim that Webster's Reply to Hayne "served in part" as Lincoln's "model" has led historians to exaggerate both the "part" and the "model." Of far more consequence is the fact that Lincoln found in the work of the Massachusetts senator a spirit of unwavering support for the Union, as well as for a unity of purpose between the states and an indivisible destiny for the country as a whole. All of these lent support to his own beliefs and instincts. It was this spirit and this mantle that the older man bequeathed to the unknown from Illinois; and Abraham Lincoln would do his utmost to avoid dishonoring Daniel Webster's gift.

❧ Much occurred on the national stage between Webster's demise in 1852 and Lincoln's 1858 delivery of the House Divided speech, a speech that would have been poor indeed had it merely imitated Webster's Reply to Hayne and failed to address what had transpired in the intervening years. Fortunately it did neither. Nor was its purpose to simply emulate in form and content Webster's celebrated achievement. Lincoln was speaking to the men who had just nominated him as the Republican party's "first and only choice" for the U.S. Senate seat from Illinois. He was making them aware of his political perceptions, position, and prowess. To do this he needed to outline the framework within which he intended to wage his struggle for the office, and to define the goals he would strive to reach if elected. Accordingly, he opened with a statement of his philosophical stance on the major issue of the day: "slavery agitation."

For Lincoln, the future of the United States allowed only two alternatives with regard to slavery: the country would find itself either with or without it in *"all* the States, *old* as well as *new—North* as well as *South"* (House Divided, 373). The threat that slavery would prevail came, in Lincoln's view, from a multipronged offensive by the forces of the South's "black power." The first two of the prongs included "the Nebraska doctrine" and "the Dred Scott decision," which made up an "almost complete legal combination," a "piece of *machinery* so to speak." The "Nebraska doctrine" referred, of course, to Stephen Douglas's 1854 Kansas-Nebraska Act, which had repealed the "Congressional prohibition" against allowing slavery into nonslave territories. Lincoln had vehemently opposed that act in the fall of 1854, deeming it a powerful attack on the founding fathers' ultimate goal of seeing slavery gradually but completely eradicated from American soil. In the House Divided speech, Lincoln again speaks of placing it "in the course of ultimate extinction" (373). He realized, however, that a critical feature of the debate on the bill had been the fact that, while its opponents were unwilling to agree to a clause that would have permitted the *inclusion* of slavery in a territory, its supporters had refused to countenance an amendment that would allow slavery to be *excluded* from one. Lincoln therefore adopted the position that the failure to approve an exclusion clause meant a very dangerous loophole had intentionally been left open, betraying sinister long-range plans to extend slavery's tentacles into all the territories. More immediately menacing, from Lincoln's point of view, was the fact that Douglas (whom he identifies at this early stage of his speech simply as "the leading advocate of the Nebraska bill") was requested on the floor of the Senate "to state *his opinion* whether the people of a territory can constitutionally exclude slavery from their limits" (374) but refused to take a stand. Douglas allowed only that "That is a question for the Supreme Court" (374). Once the court had taken a decision on the Dred Scott case, however, Douglas began claiming that it was *not* for the court to decide. For Lincoln, it therefore appeared that the senator's inconsistent position did not bode well.

Lincoln explains in his speech that the Dred Scott case began in 1854, at the same time as the "Nebraska bill was passing through congress" (House Divided, 374) with decisions on both occurring in May of that year. The final Supreme Court decision, "involving the question of a negro's freedom, by reason of his owner having voluntarily taken him first into a free state and then a territory covered by the congressional prohibition, and held him as a slave for a long time in each" (374) was, as Lincoln tactfully phrased it, "deferred" until after the election of President James Buchanan, a man who could be trusted to continue the pro-slavery policies of his predecessor, Franklin Pierce. The suspicious link between the delay and the election was reinforced in Buchanan's inaugural address, when he personally urged the American people to abide by whatever decision might come, only to have that decision handed down just two days following the inauguration, hard on the heels of his message.

In essence, the Dred Scott decision denied the right of citizenship to American blacks and took the position that residence in a free state or territory did not constitute grounds on which freedom could be granted. Chief Justice Roger Taney further held that, since the founding fathers had not mentioned blacks in the Declaration of Independence and the Constitution, there were no legal grounds for respecting any rights to which these noncitizens might lay claim. The decision was issued on March 6, 1857, and June 26 of that year found Lincoln speaking out forcefully at Springfield against the opinion of the Court as well as against Stephen Douglas's backing of the Court's position. With spirited respect for the law, Lincoln declared: "We think [the Court's] decisions on Constitutional questions, when fully settled, should control, not only the particular cases decided, but the general policy of the country, subject to be disturbed only by amendments of the Constitution as provided in that instrument itself. More than this would be revolution." Revolution was the last thing the law-abiding attorney wanted, however, and although believing that "the Dred Scott decision is erroneous," he made clear that he would limit himself strictly to legal means in opposing it: "We know the court that made it, has often over-ruled its own decisions, and we shall do what we can to have it over-rule this. We offer no *resistance* to it."[16]

In doing what he could to have the decision overruled, Lincoln nevertheless embraced the view that the authors of the Declaration of Independence "intended to include *all* men, but they did not intend to declare all men equal *in all respects*. They did not mean to say all were equal in color, size, intellect, moral developments, or social capacity. They defined with tolerable distinctness, in what respects they did consider all men created equal—equal in 'certain inalienable rights, among which are life, liberty, and the pursuit of happiness.' This they said, and this meant."[17] Lincoln's interpretation of the Declaration to mean that equality between all human beings extended in a well-delimited fashion only to "certain inalienable rights" was apparently designed to cover his back with those who might otherwise find his attitude too liberal or even extreme. But he was also challenging Douglas's June 12 claim that the signers of the Declaration of Independence "referred to the white race alone, and not to the African, when they declared men to have been created free and equal—that they were speaking of British subjects on the continent being equal to British subjects born and residing in great Britain" and that "The declaration was adopted for the purpose of justifying the colonists in the eyes of the civilized world in withdrawing their allegiance from the British crown, and dissolving their connection with the British country."[18] Lincoln rejected this view out of hand, countering that "The assertion that 'all men are created equal' was of no practical use in effecting our separation from Great Britain; and it was placed in the Declaration, not for that, but for future use. Its authors meant it to be, thank God, it is now proving itself, a stumbling block to those who in after times might seek to turn a free people back into the hateful paths of despotism."[19]

Lincoln's opposition to the Dred Scott decision was based on his conviction that "obvious violence" had been done by the highest judicial power in the land to the sacred spirit of the Declaration of Independence.[20] In his House Divided speech, Lincoln wishes to underscore Douglas's support for and association with that violence. He accordingly reminds his listeners that shortly after the Supreme Court decision was announced, Douglas (to whom he now refers as the "reputed author of the Nebraska bill") acted in the interest of pro-slavery forces by finding "an early occasion to make a speech at this capitol indorsing the Dred Scott Decision, and vehemently denouncing all opposition to it" (House Divided, 374–75). In his own Springfield speech of 1857, Lincoln had attacked Taney and Douglas jointly, and although a year has passed since the speech was delivered he still sees these two men as instrumental in shaping a state of affairs that has only worsened since then. He therefore encourages his audience to see both the men and the situation in the same light and makes plain that the Kansas-Nebraska Act and the Dred Scott decision are inseparably connected by the devious actions of one key individual, as yet unnamed.

By avoiding mention of Douglas's name until late in the speech Lincoln subtly prompts his listeners to perceive for themselves the identity of the major villain connected with both the Kansas-Nebraska Act and the Dred Scott decision. This tactic not only allows Lincoln to repeatedly link the senator with what he regards as infamous deeds but renders more dramatic the moment when he will actually utter Douglas's name. Lincoln exploits an analogous strategy when addressing Douglas's recent apparent about-face on the slavery issue. The Democratic senator had openly diverged from the view of President Buchanan and his own party in opposing the Lecompton constitution, which promised to allow Kansas into the union as a slave state. But in speaking of this difference of opinion Lincoln carefully selects a word that is dismissive of its possible importance. By labeling the difference a "squabble" Lincoln downplays the significance of what he treats as a disingenuous stratagem.

He then quotes to deadly effect Douglas's claim in his speech on the Lecompton controversy not to *care* whether the slavery clause is voted down or up, so long as the vote is a fair one. Lincoln, it should be noted, was taking more advantage of Douglas's "don't care" phrase than was strictly justified, since Douglas had been explaining only that he opposed the Lecompton constitution on *any* grounds, and not only because of its slavery clause.[21] The phrase proved too tempting, however, and Abraham Lincoln, the seasoned politician, took full advantage of it in characterizing Douglas's position as amorphous, and equivalent to creating a moral vacuum that invited slavery to do as it liked while the senator calmly looked the other way.[22] Interpreting the situation to his listeners, Lincoln also lightly hints at the possibility of an avalanche effect developing in conjunction with the phrase: "The several points of the Dred Scott decision, in connection with Senator Douglas' 'care not' policy, constitute the piece of machinery, in its *present* state of advancement" (House Divided, 375).

By this point in his speech, Lincoln's audience has been vouchsafed the view that Douglas is a principal mover in promoting the present pro-slavery policy in the United States. The senator, Lincoln submits, has shown his colors with the Kansas-Nebraska Act, the exclusion amendment, the Dred Scott decision, and with his "care not" policy, designed to *"educate* and *mould* public opinion, at least *Northern* public opinion, to not *care* whether slavery is voted *down* or voted *up"* (House Divided, 376). Then, having methodically painted Douglas into a pro-slavery corner, Lincoln begins to pepper the senator—and those he regards as flying the same colors—with questions concerning slavery-associated actions from 1854 onward. His targets, besides Douglas, are Pierce, Buchanan, and the Supreme Court; and he intimates that each major development to date has taken place through what he terms "preconcert." Although lacking cold proof of an actual plot, Lincoln does not hesitate to affirm:

> We can not absolutely *know* that all these exact adaptations are the result of preconcert. But when we see a lot of framed timbers, different portions of which we know have been gotten out at different times and places and by different workmen—Stephen, Franklin, Roger and James, for instance [Stephen Douglas, Franklin Pierce, Roger Taney, James Buchanan]—and when we see these timbers joined together, and see they exactly make the frame of a house or a mill, all the tenons and mortices exactly fitting, and the lengths and proportions of the different pieces exactly adapted to their respective places, and not a piece too many or too few . . . in *such* a case, we find it impossible to not *believe* that Stephen and Franklin

> and Roger and James all understood one another from the beginning, and all worked upon a common *plan* or *draft* drawn up before the first lick was struck. (House Divided, 377)

Lincoln's charge, as Harry V. Jaffa argues, "was never intended to impute guilty purposes in the legal sense." Rather, "he is attempting to convince the people that they cannot entrust their liberties to the Democratic Party of Taney, Pierce, Buchanan, and Douglas." Jaffa further maintains, "it is important to keep in mind that the evidence Lincoln assembles in the speech is not so much evidence of a plot as it is evidence of a *tendency* toward a condition in which slavery shall be lawful everywhere in the United States."[23]

Lincoln's logic is carefully developed and reveals just how closely he has studied the different—and, with Justices McLean and Curtis, differing—opinions of the members of the Supreme Court on the Dred Scott decision. He predicts, moreover, that slavery will soon be legalized by an appropriate decision on the part of the Court, "declaring that the Constitution of the United States does not permit a state to exclude slavery from its limits" (House Divided, 378). Lincoln is convinced that such a decision is inevitable if Douglas's "doctrine of 'care not whether slavery be voted *down* or *up*,' shall gain upon the public mind sufficiently to give promise that such a decision can be maintained when made" (378–79). The "niche," Lincoln argues, has already been prepared, and "Welcome or unwelcome, such a decision *is* probably coming, and will soon be upon us, unless the power of the present political dynasty shall be met and overthrown" (379). Unless it *is* overthrown, declares Lincoln, that "dynasty" will wreak havoc even in the non-slave North: "We shall *lie down* pleasantly dreaming that the people of *Missouri* are on the verge of making their State *free;* and we shall *awake* to the *reality,* instead, that the *Supreme* Court has made *Illinois* a *slave* State." Therefore, "To meet and overthrow the power of that dynasty, is the work now before all those who would prevent that consummation" (379). This is the project to be undertaken; this the enemy to be confronted.

Douglas's renegade position on the Lecompton constitution is a fly in Lincoln's ointment, however. The Illinois railsplitter is well aware that the Republican party's membership rolls contain many defectors from the Democratic ranks who might easily be tempted to return to the fold and support Douglas, if it could be shown that the senator has truly reversed his position on the slavery question. As Don E. Fehrenbacher notes: "If any sizable number of Illinois Republicans were captivated by the Little Giant's new antislavery image, his re-election to the Senate would be ensured."[24] This possibility is one Lincoln must clearly head off before it has a chance to take hold and is unquestionably one reason for his unceasing, all-angles attack on Douglas in this speech. We therefore see Lincoln at this point striving both to decimate Douglas and to indicate that he himself is the man who can take the place of the "Little Giant" in the U.S. Senate. Somewhat tentatively, but thoughtfully and persistently, Lincoln calls into question Douglas's qualifications for meriting Republican support:

> There are those who denounce us *openly* to their *own* friends, and yet whisper *us softly,* that *Senator Douglas* is the *aptest* instrument there is, with which to effect that object. *They* do *not* tell us, nor has *he* told us, that he *wishes* any such object to be effected. . . . [but] How can he oppose the advances of slavery? He don't *care* anything about it. His avowed *mission is impressing* the "public heart" to *care* nothing about it. . . . He has done all in his power to reduce the whole question of slavery to one of a mere *right of property;* and as such, how can *he* oppose the foreign slave trade—how can he refuse that trade in that "property" shall be "perfectly free"—unless he does it as a *protection* to the home production? (House Divided, 379–80)

Hence, despite Douglas's *seeming* change of direction, despite the fact that "Senator Douglas holds, we know, that a man may rightfully be *wiser to-day* than he was *yesterday*—that he may rightfully *change* when he finds himself wrong" (380), Lincoln cautions his audience against placing blind faith in appearances: "can we for that reason, run ahead, and *infer* that he *will* make any particular change, of which he, himself, has given no intimation? Can we *safely* base *our* action upon any such *vague* inference?" For Lincoln, only one answer can be given to such questions concerning the senator, since "clearly, he is not *now* with us—he does not *pretend* to be—he does not *promise* to *ever* be." And now, having effectively disposed of Douglas, Lincoln can safely move on to subtly and unassumingly directing attention toward his own candidacy, and the need for the party to stand united in support of it: "Our cause, then, must be intrusted to, and conducted by its own undoubted friends—those whose hands are free, whose hearts are in the work—who *do care* for the result." Lincoln continues by recalling for his listeners that the still young Republican party is made up of members from a broad range of political backgrounds and persuasions, "*strange, discordant,* and even, *hostile* elements" that were "gathered from the four winds." The lawyer nevertheless reminds his audience that, in spite of incorporating such diverse "elements," the freshly founded, somewhat makeshift party managed to do well in the 1856 elections, "under the constant hot fire of a disciplined, proud, and pampered enemy." This is two years later, however, and Republican forces are clearly less ragtag. It is to these now seasoned troops that he appeals for support, rallying them with a rousing call to arms:

> Did we brave all *then* to *falter* now?—now—when that same enemy is *wavering,* dissevered and belligerent?
>
> The result is not doubtful. We shall not fail—if we stand firm, we shall not fail.
>
> *Wise councils* may *accelerate* or *mistakes delay* it, but sooner or later the victory is *sure* to come. (380–81)

These encouraging words conclude the speech Lincoln wrote in spring 1858 for delivery at the June 16 Illinois Republican State Convention, where he was to be selected as the party's candidate for the U.S. Senate. However, as Fehrenbacher discerns:

> The search for the origins of the House Divided speech leads back to the year of the Kansas-Nebraska Act and even beyond. Before 1854, according to Lincoln's own testimony, he had been opposed to slavery but had believed that it was in the course of ultimate extinction. . . . The Kansas-Nebraska Act, from his point of view, amounted to a revolution. It impaired the hope for ultimate extinction, opened the way for slavery's unlimited expansion, and made this corrosive issue paramount in American politics.[25]

In the House Divided speech, it is therefore logical for Lincoln to refer several times to the crucible year of 1854, beginning with a reference to Stephen Douglas's January 1854 bill that was to lead to the repeal of the Missouri Compromise. Following a brief but sharply chiseled exposition of his philosophical understanding of the instability inherent in a "house divided," Lincoln submits his appraisal of the current dilemma, offers a prediction for the future, and begins to elaborate on the direction in which he believes the country is moving.

❧ The opening philosophical concept that Lincoln developed in his speech did not originate with him, however. In 1854 Theodore Parker had preceded him in "A Sermon of the Dangers which Threaten the Rights of Man in America." The minister crystallized the problem in the following way: "There can be no national welfare without national unity of action. That cannot take place unless there is national unity of idea in fundamentals. Without this a nation is a 'house divided against itself;' of course it cannot stand. It is what mechanics call a figure without equilibrium; the different parts thereof do not balance" (Rights of Man, 362). As with Webster, Lincoln before him, and Lincoln again after him, Parker employs the "house divided" metaphor in this speech (its only occurrence in his writings, it seems) and predicts that slavery agitation will not come to an end before, as Lincoln was to put it, "a *crisis* shall have been reached, and passed—" (House Divided, 372). "Crisis" was a favorite word with Parker, one he used often in connection with America and the slavery problem, even titling one of his major sermons on the subject "The Present Crisis in American Affairs."[26] Although he does not use the word or a similar phrase in his "Rights of Man" sermon, he clearly refers to the notion. As usual, Parker was more prolix and less poetic than Lincoln would be, but the message he crafted was precisely the one Lincoln would later promote, albeit supplemented by a prediction that the crisis might well terminate in violence. Parker's analysis ran thus:

> These two ideas [slavery and freedom] are now fairly on foot. They are hostile; they are both mutually invasive and destructive. They are in exact opposition to each other, and the nation which embodies these two is not a figure of equilibrium. As both are active forces in the minds of men, and as each idea tends to become a fact—a universal and exclusive fact—as men with these ideas organize into parties as a means to make their idea into a fact, it follows that there must not only be strife amongst philosophical men about

> these antagonistic principles and ideas, but a strife of practical men about corresponding facts and measures. So the quarrel, if not otherwise ended, will pass from words to what seems more serious; and one will overcome the other. (Rights of Man, 366–67)

For Parker there was no possibility that the two ideas could ever peacefully coexist. He believed that the nation, in Lincoln's words, could not "endure, permanently half *slave* and half *free*" (House Divided, 372), and was convinced that "so long as these two antagonistic ideas remain, each seeking to organize itself and get exclusive power, there is no peace; there can be none" (Rights of Man, 367). For Parker in 1854 (as for Lincoln in 1858), "It is plain America cannot long hold these two contradictions in the national consciousness. Equilibrium must come" (368). Given this prospect, the minister felt that the only "question before the nation today is, Which shall prevail—the idea and fact of freedom, or the idea and fact of slavery; freedom, exclusive and universal, or slavery, exclusive and universal?" (367). And to Parker (as to Lincoln after him), it appeared that the nation was leaning toward the latter (375).

Even without the divisive force of the slavery question, Parker did not believe it was "possible for the Anglo-Saxons of America to remain as one nation for a great many years. . . . I, therefore, do not look on the union of the States as a thing that is likely to last a great length of time, under any circumstances. I doubt if any part of the nation will desire it a hundred years hence" (Rights of Man, 370). It was his opinion that

> a dissolution of the great Anglo-Saxon State seems likely to take place, when the territory is spread so wide that there is a practical inconvenience in balancing the nation on a single governmental point; when the numbers are so great that we require many centers of legislative and administrative action in order to secure individual freedom of the parts, as well as national unity of the whole; or when the Federal Government shall become so corrupt that the trunk will not sustain the limbs. Then the branches which make up this great American banyan-tree will separate from the rotten primeval trunk, draw their support from their own local roots, and spread into great and independent trees. All this may take place without fighting. Massachusetts and Maine were once a single State; now friendly sisters. (370–71)

But Parker did "not think this 'dissolution of the Union'" would "take place immediately, or very soon" (371). Believing that closely linked financial interests of the North and the South would succeed in holding the Union together for the moment, he concluded: "The instinct of American trade just now is hostile to American freedom. The money power and the slave power go hand in hand," and "for the present I think the Union will hold together" (374). Parker was nonetheless certain about what lay on the horizon and listed for his audience "three possible ways of settling the quarrel between these two ideas":

> This is the first: The discord may rend the nation asunder and the two elements separate and become distinct nations—a despotism with the idea of slavery, a democracy with the idea of freedom. Then each will be an equilibrious figure. . . .
>
> Or, second: The idea of freedom may destroy slavery with all its accidents—attendant and consequent. . . .
>
> Here is the third: The idea of slavery may destroy freedom, with all its accidents—attendant and consequent. (368)

Since the minister considered that the Union was not in danger of dissolution (at least not for the present), that effectively eliminated the first possibility and left, as was also the case with Lincoln, only two real options. Parker summarized those options in 1856, in his sermon "The Present Crisis in American Affairs," where he asked, "Shall slavery spread over all the United States, and root out freedom from the land? or shall freedom spread wide her blessed boughs till the whole continent is fed by her fruit, and lodged beneath her arms—her very leaves for the healing of the nations? That is the *ultimate* question."[27] Or, as Lincoln would phrase it in 1858, the nation would perforce "become *all* one thing, or *all* the other" (House Divided, 372).

Since Parker was assuming that the Union would hold together for the immediate future, he proceeded to "The next hypothesis": that "freedom may triumph over slavery" (Rights of Man, 375). And, as with Lincoln after him, the minister turns to the founding fathers for confirmation of their original intentions in that regard: "That was the expectation once, at the time of the Declaration of Independence; nay, at the formation of the Constitution" (375). But despite fundamental historical support for this position, the Boston preacher does not discount the final alternative:

"Shall slavery destroy freedom?" he asks. Unflinchingly, he stares the demon in the eye and feels himself obliged to admit, "It looks very much like it" (375). For Parker in 1854 (as with Lincoln in 1858), the "tendency" is unmistakable. Nor does the minister have any doubt about the outcome if slavery is allowed to obtain the upper hand:

> nothing is so remorseless as an idea, and no logic is so strong as the historical development of a national idea by millions of men. A measure is nothing without its principle. The idea which allows slavery in South Carolina will establish it also in New England. The bondage of a black man in Alexandria imperils every white woman's daughter in Boston. You cannot escape the consequences of a first principle more than you can "take the leap of Niagara and stop half way down." The principle which recognises slavery in the Constitution of the United States would make all America a despotism; while the principle which made John Quincy Adams a free man would extirpate slavery from Louisiana and Texas. (367–68)

How closely Lincoln paralleled Parker's pattern of logic may be observed by comparing the above lines with the following sentence from the House Divided speech: "Either the *opponents* of slavery will arrest the further spread of it, and place it where the public mind shall rest in the belief that it is in course of ultimate extinction; or its *advocates* will push it forward, till it shall become alike lawful in *all* the States, *old* as well as *new—North* as well as *South*" (372–73). Neither Parker nor Lincoln wore blinders as to what should be expected; nothing, in the view of either man, could be done by halves. The nation could not "endure, permanently half *slave* and half *free*" (372).

❧ At no point in the brief but explicit philosophical opening section of the House Divided speech does Lincoln digress in any major way from Parker's philosophy on the same subject, as expounded in the "Rights of Man" sermon. Nor, it should be noted, does the argument have its roots in Webster's Reply to Hayne. It is also worth considering here a judgment on the pivotal opening section of Lincoln's speech, offered by Lincoln's friend Leonard Swett in a letter to Herndon dated January 17, 1866:

> You will remember, in his campaign against Douglas in 1858, the first ten lines of the first speech he made defeated him. The sentiment of the "house divided against itself" seemed wholly inappropriate. It was a speech made at the commencement of a campaign, and apparently made for the campaign. Viewing it in this light alone, nothing could have been more unfortunate or inappropriate. It was saying just the wrong thing; yet he saw it was an abstract truth, and standing by the speech would ultimately find him in the right place. I was inclined at the time to believe these words were hastily and inconsiderately uttered, but subsequent facts have convinced me they were deliberate and had been matured.[28]

Swett recalls, in addition, being present at a dinner in 1859 with Lincoln and a group of intimate friends, where the speech was discussed: "We all insisted it was a great mistake, but he [Lincoln] justified himself, and finally said, "Well, gentlemen, you may think that speech was a mistake, but I never have believed it was, and you will see the day when you will consider it was the wisest thing I ever said."[29] Had Theodore Parker happened to have been present at the dinner where this exchange took place, he would undoubtedly have found grounds for agreeing with the future president.

Lincoln, meanwhile, having opened his House Divided speech with philosophical ideas closely evoking Parker's, next turned his attention to the more pressing question as to whether there was "no *tendency*" that the advocates of slavery would try to make it "lawful in *all* the States, *old* as well as *new—North* as well as *South*" (House Divided, 373). His thinking on this subject was in no way ambivalent:

> Let any one who doubts, carefully contemplate that now almost complete legal combination—piece of *machinery* so to speak—compounded of the Nebraska doctrine, and the Dred Scott decision. Let him consider not only *what work* the machinery is adapted to do, and *how well* adapted; but also, let him study the *history* of its construction, and trace, if he can, or rather *fail,* if he can, to trace the evidences of design, and concert of action, among its chief bosses, from the beginning. (373)

A key word here is "history," since Lincoln indicates that the history of the "piece of *machinery*" had begun, as he mentions in the second sentence of his speech, well over four years before—

and only four days after "The new year of 1854 found slavery excluded from more than half the States by State Constitutions, and from most of the national territory by Congressional prohibition" (373). The initiative of Stephen Douglas to repeal the Missouri Compromise is what Lincoln sees as the first step taken in the "construction" of the "piece of *machinery*" with "the evidences of design, and concert of action, among its chief bosses, from the beginning."

Although Lincoln's "own charge that there was a 'conspiracy' of the slave interests has been dismissed, even by many of Lincoln's admirers, as exaggerated if not deceptive," Wills points out that Theodore Parker

> often vilified Douglas as an agent of the Slave Power, and his description of the legal machinery and strategy of that Power *precedes Lincoln's and corresponds with it in every part.* The Slave Power, according to Parker, controlled the Supreme Court under Justice Taney, the presidency under Pierce and Buchanan, and the legislature through Douglas. These are the four men Lincoln attacked in his famous House Divided Speech of 1858.[30] (Emphasis added)

Wills also draws attention to the fact that "Recent historians have been less ready to charge Lincoln with exaggeration or special pleading when he talked of conspiracy. For one thing, it is now known that President Buchanan was secretly communicating with the Supreme Court and timing his own acts and words in expectation of the decision that was handed down on Dred Scott—a key contention in Lincoln's House Divided Speech."[31] Furthermore, as Jaffa explains:

> What is indubitable is that the proslavery political combination that placed Buchanan in the White House knew that a majority of the Supreme Court shared its political passion and would use its authority to place the interests of slavery beyond the control of electoral majorities. Lincoln's charge in the House Divided speech of a conspiracy to make slavery national was certainly well founded.[32]

In connection with Lincoln's conspiracy claims, it is important to realize that—after listing in his "Rights of Man" sermon eleven public measures that had been taken in support of slavery—Parker asked, "Are these the worst?" ominously answering his question with the words "Very far from it! Yet more dangerous things have been done in secret" (Rights of Man, 376). The minister neither elaborated on this assertion nor offered proof of its validity, but he did not shy away from making it. Thus, commencing with the critical period traversed by the nation in 1854, during which Lincoln also began, via Herndon, to be exposed to Parker's writings, the concept of an unholy alliance in the upper echelons of the U.S. government was continually being suggested to the future president.[33]

By 1856 Parker was referring openly to the Kansas-Nebraska Act in unmitigatedly blunt terms: "It is rather difficult to find all the facts concerning this Kansas business; lies have been woven over the whole matter, and I know of no transaction in human history which has been covered up with such abundant lying, from the death of Ananias and Sapphira down to the first nomination of Governor Gardner." Without fear of contradiction the minister could also affirm that "the President [Buchanan]—I have it on good authority—tried to bribe him [Andrew H. Reeder, appointed governor of the Kansas Territory by Buchanan's predecessor, Franklin Pierce, in June 1854, after passage of the Kansas-Nebraska bill], offering him the highest office then vacant—the ministry to China. Governor Reeder refused the bribe, and then was discharged from his office on the pretense of some pecuniary unfaithfulness." Abraham Lincoln interpreted Reeder's fate in a similar fashion in a letter to his friend Joshua Speed: "Poor Reeder is the only public man who has been silly enough to believe that any thing like fairness was ever intended; and he has been bravely undeceived."[34]

In promoting the concept of the country being beset by a major conspiracy to expand slaveholding, Lincoln was therefore not alone; and Wills confirms that "As for the legal means the cabal would use, Lincoln lists the same moves Parker had—revive the slave trade, introduce slavery in the North, and extend the institution to Cuba and other parts of the Caribbean."[35] For Parker in his 1854 "Rights of Man" sermon, "The restoration of the African slave-trade, which is already seriously proposed and defended in the Southern journals," promises to be furthered by the fact that "the Senate Committee on Foreign Relations recommend the first step towards it—the withdrawal of our fleet from the coast of Africa" (Rights of Man, 389–90). The logic involved was ineluctable: "You cannot escape the consequence of your first principle: if slavery is right, then the slave-trade is right; the traffic between Guinea and New Orleans is no worse than between Virginia and New Orleans; it is no worse to kidnap in Timbuctoo than in Boston" (Rights of Man, 390). In 1858 Lincoln casts a similar net in his effort to entangle Douglas in the same odious commerce:

> A leading Douglas Democratic newspaper thinks Douglas' superior talent will be needed to resist the revival of the African slave trade.
>
> Does Douglas believe an effort to revive that trade is approaching? He has not said so. Does he *really* think so? But if it is, how can he resist it? For years he has labored to prove it a *sacred right* of white men to take negro slaves into the new territories. Can he possibly show that it is *less* a sacred right to *buy* them where they can be bought cheapest? And, unquestionably they can be bought *cheaper* in *Africa* than in *Virginia.* (House Divided, 379–80)

And where Parker points out that "there is one kind of property which is not safe just now:—property in men. It is the only kind of property which is purely the creature of violence and law; it has no root in itself" (Rights of Man, 373), Lincoln again extends the issue to embrace Douglas: "He has done all in his power to reduce the whole question of slavery to one of a mere *right of property*" (House Divided, 380).

Lincoln, when attacking Douglas in his House Divided speech, also follows the approach Parker had employed against the senator as recently as January 29, 1858. In his sermon of that date Parker declares it would be nothing short of folly to place any trust in Douglas or his "care not" policy. Lincoln follows the minister in turning Douglas's words "I care not whether [the slavery clause] is voted down or voted up," spoken in the Senate on December 9, 1857, against the Little Giant. Parker twists the "care not" phrase back on Douglas in the following manner: "He is fighting against our foes—that is an accident; he is not fighting for us, but only for Stephen A. Douglas, and if he wins that battle, he cares not who his allies are, nor who his foes."[36]

Lincoln mounts a more direct and heavily ironic assault on Douglas's phrase: "I do not understand his declaration that he cares not whether slavery be voted down or voted up, to be intended by him other than as an *apt definition* of the *policy* he would impress upon the public mind—the *principle* for which he declares he has suffered much, and is ready to suffer to the end" (House Divided, 375). Lincoln subsequently disparages "Senator

Douglas' 'care not' policy," linked with "the several points of the Dred Scott decision," as constituting "the piece of machinery, in its *present* state of advancement" (375). The pleasure Lincoln takes in skewering the senator on his own words is emphasized by the fact that he flings the phrase at Douglas once again toward the end of his speech (in a manner more akin to Parker's), with the unmistakable purpose of excluding Douglas from any further consideration for support by members of the Republican party: "Our cause, then, must be intrusted to, and conducted by its own undoubted friends—those whose hands are free, whose hearts are in the work—who *do care* for the result" (380).

Lincoln's treatment of Douglas's "care not" phrase is thus no gentler than Parker's, and it is not surprising that Parker would thank Herndon on July 1, 1858, for sending along the House Divided speech, which he praises as *"the admirable speech of Mr. Lincoln."* Cross-pollination was clearly proving effective, since Lincoln was demonstrating an awareness of the content of even the freshest of Parker's productions. But we know from Herndon's letter to Parker of March 4, 1858, that he had received the January 29 sermon only that morning, had "read it with pleasure," and was "instructed by it." Herndon felt that Parker had "hit Doug[las] hard, yet [did] him justice."[37] Given Herndon's reaction, it would seem that the recently arrived sermon, with its sharp and focused attack on Douglas, might well have occupied a prominent place in Lincoln's thinking as he undertook the writing of his House Divided speech that same spring, shortly before being nominated by the Republicans of Illinois to run against the Little Giant.

Supporting this contention is information provided by the same man whose underscoring of the connection between the opening sentence of the House Divided speech and Lincoln's reading of Webster's Reply to Hayne has influenced and colored the accounts of so many successive historians. Once again, Herndon is the person best positioned to describe Lincoln's preparation for the momentous presentation, and his report, though written many years afterward and therefore subject to certain reservations, cannot be ignored. Herndon recalls that "Mr. Lincoln was a good while preparing his house-divided-against-itself speech: he was at it off and on about one month."[38]

> This speech he wrote on stray envelopes and scraps of paper, as ideas suggested themselves, putting them into that miscellaneous

> and convenient receptacle, his hat. As the convention drew near he copied the whole on connected sheets, carefully revising every line and sentence, and fastened them together, for reference during the delivery of the speech, and for publication. The former precaution, however, was unnecessary, for he had studied and read over what he had written so long and carefully that he was able to deliver it without the least hesitation or difficulty.[39]

If accurate, this report indicates that Lincoln was conscious of ideas and phrasing stemming from more than Webster's Reply to Hayne, and that he gathered the various strands together slowly. This would open the door to the possibility of his having used even that most recently acquired Parker sermon, while not excluding older but still pertinent sources of ideas. From Herndon's colorful description, the effort seems to have been marked by an approach that can perhaps best be characterized as eclectic.

It may also be observed that, while Lincoln was apparently privy to Parker's most recent thinking, his memory seems to have been capable of recalling many aspects of the "Rights of Man" sermon, as a glance at the closing lines of the House Divided Speech appears to confirm: "The result is not doubtful. We shall not fail—if we stand firm, we shall not fail. *Wise councils* may *accelerate* or *mistakes delay* it, but, sooner or later the victory is *sure* to come" (House Divided, 381). Parker, too, had used double formulations of "We shall not fail" to encourage his audience not to waver before the coming challenge. He told the listeners of his "Rights of Man" sermon delivered that Sunday in 1854:

> But we shall not fail! I look into your eyes—young men and women, thousands of you, and men and women far enough from young! I look into the eyes of fifty thousand other men and women, whom, in the last eight months, I have spoken to, face to face, and they say, "No! America shall not fail!"
>
> I remember the women who were never found faithless when a sacrifice was to be offered to great principles; I look up to my God, and I look into my own heart, and I say, "We shall not fail! We shall not fail!" (Rights of Man, 394–95)

Like the "house divided" metaphor, the doubled use of "We shall not fail!" is employed by Parker uniquely in his "Rights of Man" sermon; and, considering the similarity of their contexts, it would appear difficult to put such precise parallels between the words of Parker and Lincoln down to mere happenstance.

❧ Thus, when one considers how closely Lincoln's thought in the House Divided speech parallels Parker's, as well as the strength of the link between the two men that Herndon provided, it would not seem unwarranted to speak of influence by the Boston minister on the Illinois lawyer. Whereas Daniel Webster clearly inspired the first sentence of Lincoln's speech, apparently provided some vocabulary for Lincoln's closing section, suggested rhetorical or stylistic flourishes, and contributed courage of conviction with regard to preserving the Union, thereafter it was Parker's ideas that took precedence. Lincoln absorbed each detail of the minister's argument, eliminated the excess verbiage, and methodically followed Parker's philosophical lead in the critical opening portion of his presentation. He subsequently adopted all facets of the preacher's conception of a conspiracy within the highest levels of government; pursued Douglas with fervor and arguments similar in nature to those of Parker; and lastly, closed with repeated, Parker-like, "We shall not fail!" phrasing.

The possibility that Parker may have played at least a part in suggesting to Lincoln the use of the "house divided" image also cannot be completely discounted. And if indeed this is the case, it could help throw light on what Fehrenbacher characterizes as "a mystery that has never been satisfactorily resolved": the question of why Lincoln stubbornly held to this divisive metaphor despite advice to the contrary from his closest advisors. "Why," Fehrenbacher asks, "did Lincoln choose this moment for the most provocative utterance of his career?"[40]

One explanation warranting consideration is that there was a precedent for Lincoln's action. During the Mexican War he had not hesitated to repeatedly pose his controversial "spot" question, despite the potential risk to his career, and it is possible he now reckoned the time had come once again to step to the fore and demonstrate he was the courageous leader required by his party. Another conceivable reason, not unconnected with this possibility, is that Lincoln's use of the "provocative utterance" largely meshed with his thinking at the time—thinking that in many ways correlated with and may have received succor from that found in Parker's 1854 "Rights of Man" sermon. This answer does not establish that Parker's use of the phrase was indispensable in influencing Lincoln to take this decision, but it could help explain why Lincoln might have thought the moment again propitious to use a phrase he had employed without repercussions in 1843. This view could be further strengthened by the fact that even Daniel Webster, the man abolitionists considered a pariah, had used the metaphor in a somewhat freer fashion in 1851.

Lincoln could well have had other grounds for employing the phrase, but the fact that he chose to make use of it also raises the question of whether he had stepped unwarily onto abolitionist ice, since, as Fehrenbacher points out: "his language in the House Divided speech contained echoes of old-line abolitionism, he was adapting Garrisonian rhetoric to a more conservative purpose."[41] It is thus conceivable that Lincoln's regular contact with the abolitionist thinking and writings of men such as Owen Lovejoy and Theodore Parker led him to underestimate the explosiveness of what, at the time, may have seemed to him merely one biblical phrase among others. Intent on his attempt to expand the parameters of the discussion, in order to force the divisiveness of the slavery issue into wider public consciousness, and in spite of his usual political shrewdness, Lincoln could have simply misjudged the political mood of the electorate at that moment. And if that was indeed the case, it would certainly merit considering to what extent Parker's influence may have been instrumental in inspiring Lincoln to run the risk involved in drawing such a definite line in the sand.

CHAPTER FIVE

What Lincoln Took to Gettysburg

❧ There is little doubt that Lincoln consulted Webster's work before writing the House Divided speech, as Herndon tells us he did. It would also appear undeniable that, whether or not he had Parker's writings in front of him as he drafted his speech, Lincoln had imbibed the minister's message and had it at his mental fingertips when it was most needed. And if the lawyer was as deeply indebted to Parker's "Rights of Man" sermon as it appears he was, it would seem only logical to expect further traces of the influence of such a powerful document to be visible elsewhere in his writings. The Gettysburg Address does, indeed, reveal such influence; and, to better comprehend the grounds for this, it will first prove helpful to briefly review Lincoln's political thinking and activity during the years leading up to 1863.

When Stephen Douglas's Kansas-Nebraska bill of 1854 ripped open the nation's slavery scar, partially healed over since 1820 by the Missouri Compromise and again by the compromise measures of 1850, Lincoln, in the speech he gave at Peoria, Illinois, on October 16, 1854, recalled that he and many others who had felt that, with time, slavery would die a natural death were "thunderstruck and stunned; and we reeled and fell in utter confusion." A rally was not long in coming, however. Although the opponents of Douglas's initiative were drawn from widely different political factions, Lincoln affirms "we rose each fighting, grasping whatever he could first reach—a scythe—a pitchfork—a chopping axe or a butcher's cleaver. We struck in the direction of the sound; and we are rapidly closing in on him. He must not think to divert us from our purpose, by showing us that our drill, our dress, and our weapons, are not entirely perfect and uniform." Adopting this image of a poorly clad and inadequately armed band, united only by an ideal, allows Lincoln to dramatize his conviction that Douglas's efforts to divide the heterogeneous opposition will fail—and to draw his troops even more tightly together by emphasizing, inclusively, that "When the storm shall be past, he shall find us still Americans; no less devoted to the continued Union and prosperity of the country than heretofore."[1]

Lincoln then proceeds to explain his willingness to draw on any source that will help restore the Missouri Compromise. He does not promise that when "the storm shall be past" he or his collaborators will necessarily see eye to eye on other issues, but that on the question of preserving the Union they will continue to agree. For the present, however, he ventures to offer advice to those, "mostly whigs, who condemn the repeal of the Missouri compromise" but "hesitate to go for its restoration, lest they be thrown in company with the abolitionist." Calling their position "very silly," Lincoln advances the idea that they should "Stand with anybody that stands RIGHT. Stand with him while he is right and PART with him when he goes wrong. Stand WITH the abolitionist in restoring the Missouri Compromise; and stand AGAINST him when he attempts to repeal the fugitive slave law. . . . In both cases you are right. In both cases you oppose [expose?] the dangerous extremes." Lincoln's lack of reluctance at standing "WITH the abolitionist" was nevertheless stronger than he revealed in these lines, and his personal repugnance at applying the Fugitive Slave Law may have contributed to this. In addition (as we have now seen), the willingness of this accomplished politician to stand spiritually close to the thinking, phrasing, and philosophy of the Boston abolitionist Theodore Parker would be made manifest in the House Divided speech, and the minister's hand would once again rest on the president's shoulder during the somber scene at Gettysburg.[2]

Meanwhile, however, Lincoln's even-handed political advice to his cohorts to "Stand with anybody that stands RIGHT" was promoting the realpolitik of seeking support from any quarter in striving to attain objectives. Viewed in this light his friendship with the Illinois abolitionist Owen Lovejoy, which had its beginnings during this same year, seems less surprising. But this does not mean it was uncomplicated. For, although the two men's interests converged on the Kansas-Nebraska Act, such was not always the case. When Lovejoy defeated Lincoln's close political associate Leonard Swett for the Republican nomination for Congress in 1856, for instance, Lincoln confided to a friend: "It turned me blind when I first heard Swett was beaten, and Lovejoy nominated; but after much anxious reflection, I really believe it is best to let it stand. This, of course, I wish to be confidential."[3] And two years later (only a few weeks following his supportive letter to Lovejoy cited in Chapter 1), Lincoln warns Ward H. Lamon of the possible risks involved if an inappropriate campaign strategy is adopted in connection with the radical abolitionist: "running an independent candidate against Lovejoy, will not do—that will result in nothing but disaster all round. . . . I shall be held responsible for it, and Republican members of the Legislature, who are partial to Lovejoy, will, for that, oppose me."[4]

It is therefore evident that Abraham Lincoln was possessed of political tolerance of an extraordinary breadth and would do his utmost to avoid alienating anyone who might consider voting with or for him (as Lovejoy indeed did during Lincoln's unsuccessful bid for the Senate in 1855).[5] Considering this fact Lincoln's attitude concerning the Kansas-Nebraska Act is not inconsistent with the position he had staked out in his Lyceum speech so many years before. In 1838 he had opposed those on either side of the abolition issue who would break the law, sharply rejecting extremism from any quarter. In asking his associates in the present case to "stand AGAINST" the abolitionist "when he attempts to repeal the fugitive slave law," Lincoln again rejects extreme measures, but it should not be assumed that he sees the Fugitive Slave law as a positive good. He regards it, rather, as an expedient that can, for a time, contribute to helping preserve a peaceful state of affairs between the slave and the nonslave states; it is a necessary interim evil in a gradual but steady progression toward the ultimate goal of eliminating slavery in America. But since it is embodied in the Constitution, it must consequently be respected as legally binding despite personal antislavery convictions.

The shattering of the Missouri Compromise, on the other hand, represents distinct violence done to precisely the type of status quo to which the Fugitive Slave law makes an indispensable contribution. As in 1838 Lincoln encourages only the use of legal means in striving to rectify what he regards as an aberration of the law. Restoring Compromise calm by peaceful methods is his objective, and knowing how abolitionists will vote on the Kansas-Nebraska question, he exhibits few qualms about joining hands with them in what he considers a just cause. There was nevertheless a serious drawback to this approach. It opened the door to allowing Douglas to repeatedly charge his opponent with being an undercover abolitionist and led abolitionists early on to see Lincoln as a comrade in arms. The situation demanded delicate diplomacy, and although Lincoln did not wish to alienate the abolitionists and their potential votes, he pulled back from what might strike other supporters as too snug an embrace.

For instance, when in October 1854 a convention was held in his hometown of Springfield for the purpose of forming a Republican party favoring the abolition of slavery and a repeal of the Fugitive Slave law, Lincoln, perhaps feeling that his presence at such a gathering might compromise him with more moderate voters, did not attend.[6] And when the noted antislavery activist Ichabod Codding invited him in November 1854 to attend a party committee meeting to be chaired by Codding and Owen Lovejoy, Lincoln unhesitatingly and somewhat impatiently declined: "I suppose my opposition to the principle of slavery is as strong as that of any member of the Republican party," he told Codding, "but I had also supposed that the *extent* to which I feel authorized to carry that opposition, practically; was not at all satisfactory to that party. The leading men who organized that party, were present, on the 4th of Oct. at the discussion between Douglas and myself at Springfield and had full oppertunity [*sic*] to not misunderstand my position. Do I misunderstand theirs?"[7]

Almost a year after this Lincoln's position had not wavered. On August 24, 1855, he offers the following explanation of his posture to his Kentucky slaveholding friend Joshua Speed, who recognizes that he and Lincoln are drifting apart over the issue of slavery: "You enquire where I now stand. That is a disputed point. I think I am a whig; but others say there are no whigs, and that I am an abolitionist. When I was in Washington I voted for the Wilmot Proviso as good as forty times, and I never heard of any one attempting to unwhig me for that. I now do no more than oppose the *extension* of slavery." Lincoln also expressed to Speed his irritation at the Know-Nothing faction of voters who opposed both catholics and foreigners: "I am not a Know-Nothing. That is certain. How could I be? How can any one who abhors the oppression of negroes, be in favor of degrading classes of white people? . . . As a nation we began by declaring that '*all men are created equal.*' We now practically read it 'all men are created equal, *except negroes*.' When the Know-Nothings get control, it will read 'all men are created equal, except negroes *and foreigners and catholics.*'"[8]

Less than two weeks prior to this, in a more practical political vein, Lincoln had written Owen Lovejoy regarding the strategy necessary to corral the vote of this splinter movement:

> Not even *you* are more anxious to prevent the extension of slavery than I; and yet the political atmosphere is such, just now, that I fear to do any thing, lest I do wrong. Know-nothingism has not yet entirely tumbled to pieces—nay it is even a little encouraged by the late elections in Tennessee, Kentucky & Alabama. Until we can get the elements of this organization, there is not sufficient materials to successfully combat the Nebraska democracy with. We can not get them so long as they cling to a hope of success under their own organization; and I fear an open push by us now, may offend them, and tend to prevent our ever getting them.

Lincoln was thus taking his own advice on standing "with anybody that stands RIGHT" and showed, in his letter to Lovejoy, "no objection to 'fuse' with any body provided I can fuse on ground which I think is right; and I believe the opponents of slavery extension could now do this, if it were not for this K.N.ism." He was also aware, as Fehrenbacher notes, "It is plainly Lovejoy, not Speed, with whom he expects to act in the future."[9]

Lincoln did not attempt to keep this fact from Speed, telling him, "I do oppose the extension of slavery, because my judgment and feelings so prompt me; and I am under no obligation to the contrary. If for this you and I must differ, differ we must." Courteously but candidly he then revealed his reasons: "In your assumption that there may be a *fair* decision of the slavery question in Kansas, I plainly see you and I would differ about the Nebraska-law. I look upon that enactment not as a *law,* but as a violence from the beginning. It was conceived in violence . . . because the destruction of the Missouri Compromise, under the circumstances, was nothing less than violence." And despite Speed's liberal private views, Lincoln harbors no illusions about how his friend will vote when the moment of truth arrives: "You say if Kansas fairly votes herself a free state, as a christian you will rather rejoice at it. All decent slave-holders *talk* that way; and I do not doubt their candor. But they never *vote* that way. Although in a private letter, or conversation, you will express your preference that Kansas shall be free, you would vote for no man for Congress who would say the same thing publicly."[10]

Only nine days before writing this, Lincoln had also clarified facets of his thinking to another Kentuckian, George Robertson:

> When we were the political slaves of King George, and wanted to be free, we called the maxim that "all men are created equal" a self evident truth; but now when we have grown fat, and have lost all dread of being slaves ourselves, we have become so greedy to be *masters* that we call the same maxim "a self evident lie." The fourth of July has not quite dwindled away; it is still a great day—*for burning fire-crackers*!!!
>
> That spirit which desired the peaceful extinction of slavery, has itself become extinct, with the *occasion*, and the *men* of the Revolution.

Lincoln expressed to Robertson, in addition, the belief that would be underscored in the House Divided speech three years later: "Our political problem now is 'Can we, as a nation, continue together *permanently—forever*—half slave, and half free?'"[11] By 1858 Lincoln would have decided to answer that question in the negative.

❧ For Lincoln there were two key concepts connected with the slavery issue, always present in his thinking and speeches. In his Peoria speech of October 16, 1854, he phrased them in the following terms: "I particularly object to the NEW position which the avowed principle of this Nebraska law gives to slavery in the body politic. I object to it because it assumes that there CAN be a MORAL RIGHT in the enslaving of one man by another. . . . I object to it because the fathers of the republic eschewed, and rejected it."[12] Ever careful to avoid the taint of abolitionism, this consummate politician was in a bind. He wanted the slaves to be freed, as he believed the fathers of the country had desired, and he felt slavery to be morally wrong. He had said as much in his Lyceum speech and did not deviate from this policy as the years pulled ever tighter the cords constraining him. At the same time, however, he needed the support of both antislavery and antiabolition voters in order to be elected to office. Maintaining a balanced posture in this situation posed a continual challenge; but one he had to meet if he were to eventually have any chance of slowing the wheels of slavery.

Lincoln therefore clung for as long as possible to the option of seeing America's slaves colonized somewhere outside the United States. This permitted him to support an antislavery position without appearing to call for abolition. Like Thomas Jefferson and Henry Clay, he saw colonization as the safety valve that would one day allow the country to rid itself of its black burden. So as long as that safety valve maintained its promise, Lincoln was willing to see the country attempt to accommodate itself to whatever difficulties were entailed in the present situation. This meant that he, too, was required to adapt himself to the same circumstances and was often obliged to accept terms or conditions with which he was morally uncomfortable. One of these was the Fugitive Slave Law. In his final debate with Douglas on October 15, 1858, at Alton, Illinois, he lucidly delineated the repugnant position he felt compelled to adopt with regard to that law:

> I suppose most of us, (I know it of myself,) believe that the people of the Southern States are entitled to a congressional fugitive slave law—that it is a right fixed in the Constitution. . . . And as the right is constitutional I agree that the legislation shall be granted to it—and that not that we like the institution of slavery. We profess to have no taste for running and catching niggers—at least I profess no taste for that job at all. Why then do I yield support to a fugitive slave law? Because I do not understand that the Constitution, which guarantees that right, can be supported without it.[13]

It also troubled Lincoln that the obligation he felt to adjust to the status quo provided Douglas with an easy opportunity to publicly try to shove him beyond the bounds of the politically imposed *"extent"* of his opposition to slavery he had attempted to make clear to Ichabod Codding. One of Douglas's goals in the 1858 debates with Lincoln was to situate his opponent—in the eyes of the voters—in the extreme abolitionist camp. And Lincoln's seemingly rigid posture on "a house divided against itself" was tailor-made for that purpose. It was vulnerable to being interpreted as threatening to involve the nation in civil war, and Douglas seized upon this interpretation with alacrity. Nor did the senator hesitate to employ the house divided metaphor in the service of rabble-rousing, as may be seen from the following passage where he pretends to discover in Lincoln's "ultimate extinction" phrase a cruel intention neither meant nor suggested:

> How then does Lincoln propose to save the Union, unless by compelling all the States to become free, so that the house shall not be divided against itself? . . . How is he going to bring it about? Why, he will agitate, he will induce the North to agitate until the South shall be worried out, and forced to abolish slavery. . . . He first tells you that he would prohibit slavery everywhere in the territories. He would thus confine slavery within its present limits. When he thus gets it confined, and surrounded, so that it cannot spread, the natural laws of increase will go on until the negroes will be so plenty that they cannot live on the soil. He will hem them in until starvation seizes them, and by starving them to death, he will put slavery in the course of ultimate extinction. . . . This is the humane and Christian remedy that he proposes for the great crime of slavery.[14]

Despite such manifest misrepresentation, Lincoln chose to maintain the high ground on the immorality of treating another human being as property. As he made clear on October 15, 1858, this was the central concern of the debates: "That is the real issue. That is the issue that will continue in this country when these poor tongues of Judge Douglas and myself shall be silent. It is the eternal struggle between these two principles—right and wrong—throughout the world. . . . The one is the common right of humanity and the other the divine right of kings. . . . It is the same spirit that says, 'You work and toil and earn bread, and I'll eat it.'"[15] Nonetheless, Lincoln did not feel he could safely ignore Douglas's barbs about proposing racial "amalgamation"; he had publicly avowed on June 26, 1857, "that the separation of the races is the only perfect preventive of amalgamation," and that "Such separation, if ever effected at all, must be effected by colonization."[16] In his debate with Douglas over a year later at Ottawa, he therefore quoted a long passage from his own 1854 Peoria speech, indicating thereby that over the intervening years he had not modified his position on the Missouri Compromise, colonization, or slavery. But still he felt obliged to tender the following exculpating declaration:

> I will say here, while upon this subject, that I have no purpose directly or indirectly to interfere with the institution of slavery in the States where it exists. . . . I have no purpose to introduce political and social equality between the white and the black races. There is a physical difference between the two, which in my judgment will

> probably forever forbid their living together upon the footing of perfect equality, and inasmuch as it becomes a necessity that there must be a difference, I, as well as Judge Douglas, am in favor of the race to which I belong having the superior position. I have never said anything to the contrary, but I hold that notwithstanding all this, there is no reason in the world why the negro is not entitled to all the natural rights enumerated in the Declaration of Independence, the right to life, liberty and the pursuit of happiness. . . . I agree with Judge Douglas he is not my equal in many respects—certainly not in color, perhaps not in moral or intellectual endowment. But in the right to eat the bread, without leave of anybody else, which his own hand earns, *he is my equal and the equal of Judge Douglas, and the equal of every living man.*[17]

Douglas wisely quoted to his audience only the central section of this statement before declaring: "that is a good doctrine, but Mr. Lincoln is afraid to advocate it in the latitude of Chicago where he hopes to get his votes. (Cheers.) It is a good doctrine in the anti-abolition counties for him, and his Chicago speech is good doctrine in the abolition counties."[18] To the charge that he tailored his speeches in the areas where he was speaking to suit his audiences' views on the abolition of slavery, Lincoln's response was firm: "Judge Douglas had said I had made a speech at Charleston that I would not make up north, and I turned around and answered by showing I *had* made that same speech up north—had made it at Ottawa—made it in his hearing—made it in *the* Abolition District—in Lovejoy's District—in the personal presence of Lovejoy himself—in the same atmosphere exactly in which I had made my Chicago speech of which he complains so much."[19] Although there was truth in Douglas's charge, since the Chicago speech and the Charleston speech did indeed differ, Lincoln had earlier ventured onto the same fragile limb in defending speeches delivered at Ottawa, Freeport, and Jonesboro. He stated: "I will not charge upon Judge Douglas that he willfully misrepresents me, but I call upon every fair-minded man to take these speeches and read them, *and I dare him to point out any difference between my printed speeches north and south.*"[20]

Notwithstanding his wish to garner the abolitionists' votes, Lincoln steadfastly declined to heed their insistent appeal for direct action to put an immediate end to slavery. With no attempt to blur the issue he firmly declared, "if there be a man amongst us who is so impatient of [slavery] as a wrong as to disregard its actual presence among us and the difficulty of getting rid of it suddenly in a satisfactory way, and to disregard the constitutional obligations thrown about it, that man is misplaced if he is on our platform. We disclaim sympathy with him in practical action."[21] In saying this the future president was carving out a position that would allow him to maintain a well-defined moral posture on equality while not overly exposing himself to the charge of intending to demolish the Union over the question of slavery.

By July 6, 1859, Lincoln was also prodding Schuyler Colfax, U.S. Representative from Indiana, to join him in laying politic groundwork for the 1860 election. As Lincoln saw it:

> The point of danger is the temptation in different localities to *"platform"* for something which will be popular just there, but which, nevertheless, will be a firebrand elsewhere, and especially in a National convention. As instances, the movement against foreigners in Massachusetts; in New-Hampshire, to make obedience to the Fugitive Slave law, punishable as a crime; in Ohio, to repeal the Fugitive Slave law; and squatter sovereignty in Kansas. In these things there is explosive matter enough to blow up half a dozen national conventions, if it gets into them; and what gets very rife outside of conventions is very likely to find it's [*sic*] way into them. . . .
>
> I write this for your eye only; hoping however that if you see danger as I think I do, you will do what you can to avert it. Could not suggestions be made to the leading men in the State and congressional conventions; and so avoid, to some extent at least, these apples of discord?[22]

In his own way Lincoln had already taken steps to avoid one of those "apples of discord" through trying to put a damper on the activity of Salmon P. Chase, the antislavery senator from Ohio. Chase had been planning to press for a repeal of the Fugitive Slave law at the upcoming Republican National Convention, but Lincoln firmly advised him that "the introduction of a proposition for repeal of the Fugitive Slave law, into the next Republican National convention, will explode the convention and the party."[23]

On the eve of the 1860 elections, therefore, Lincoln maintained virtually the same position on the slavery question as he had adopted in his Lyceum speech over two decades earlier. As seen in connection with the House Divided speech, the Senate race of 1858 had found the lawyer voluntarily adopting a rhetoric that could offer a clear challenge to Stephen Douglas, but his fundamental positions remained substantially unchanged. The debates with Douglas revealed clearly that, without openly faulting the South, Lincoln still condemned the immorality of enslaving another human being of any color; that he felt supported on this issue by the founders of the country; that he was still hopeful long-term opposition to slavery would one day result in its "extinction"; and that he thought removing the black population of the United States to a foreign "colony" was what the founders originally had in mind. But although he favored "ultimate extinction" as the best method for finally resolving the slavery issue, Lincoln expressed no urgency on the matter. As a matter of fact, in his September 18, 1858, debate with Douglas at Charleston he sought to smooth the feathers of pro-slavery voters by pushing the problem off into the distant future. Somewhat enigmatically, he predicted: "I do not suppose that in the most peaceful way ultimate extinction would occur in less than a hundred years at the least; but that it will occur in the best way for both races in God's own good time, I have no doubt."[24] However, as J. David Greenstone points out, Lincoln's fundamental and unwavering position continued to be "that, regardless of other considerations, the Union must adopt 'practices and policies' that would both stigmatize slavery as immoral and eventually end it"; consequently, "although some delay was acceptable, retrogression was not."[25]

For the present, therefore, all laws were to be adhered to, even the Fugitive Slave Law and the Dred Scott decision. The last two, however, were to be opposed by every legal means since, in Lincoln's judgment, they broke faith with the intention of the founding fathers. In addition, all persons in the land, slaveholders and nonslaveholders alike, were to be fully respected, since "the Southern people," he professed, "are just what we would be in their situation. If slavery did not now exist amongst them, they would not introduce it. If it did now exist amongst us, we should not instantly give it up."[26] The distant objective Lincoln nevertheless set for the country was to one day achieve equivalent respect for its enslaved members. In the meantime, his shorter-term goal was to reverse the "tendency" represented by the Dred Scott decision and the repeal of the Missouri Compromise. Difficult as that task promised to be (and Douglas scoffed openly at Lincoln's chances of success),[27] it had to be undertaken if the nation were once again to be placed on the path toward the ultimate elimination of slavery. Otherwise, Lincoln's—and, in his view, the fathers'—intention of rectifying a major moral wrong would be thwarted and the country allowed to become permanently stained.

There was a strong religious element in this attitude, and Lincoln, not unlike Parker, frequently resorted to biblical language and metaphors in his struggle to right the wrong of slavery. The concept of a sin present at the founding of the country, and thus one day to be eradicated, surfaced often. In his 1854 Peoria speech, Lincoln spoke of repurifying the "soiled" republican robe, of washing "it white, in the spirit, if not the blood, of the Revolution."[28] From the perspective of the future president, the presence of slavery was a thing "hid away, in the constitution, just as an afflicted man hides away a wen or a cancer, which he dares not cut out at once, lest he bleed to death; with the promise, nevertheless, that the cutting may begin at the end of a given time." But Lincoln absolved the founders of the original crime of having planted the evil in the land themselves. He affirmed that the fathers "found the institution existing among us, which they could not help; and they cast blame upon the British King for having permitted its introduction."[29] In his October 13, 1858, debate with Douglas, he further absolved the fathers of any guilt for not having resolved the problem at the founding:

> Judge Douglas asks you "why cannot the institution of slavery, or rather, why cannot the nation, part slave and part free, continue as our fathers made it *forever*?" In the first place, I insist that our fathers did not make this nation half slave or half free, or part slave and part free. [Applause, and "That's so."] I insist that they found the institution of slavery existing here. They did not make it so, but they left it so because they knew of no way to get rid of it at that time.[30]

Nor in the years following his election to the presidency did Abraham Lincoln himself know quite what to do in order to rid the country of the curse of slavery. The secession of Southern states shortly after he took office brought about a crisis in the Union, and in time Lincoln would adopt the public position that it was the Union and not slavery that took priority. In the midst of the war that followed hard upon the heels of the secessionists' action, Lincoln explained to Horace Greeley, in response to criticism from the *New York Tribune* editor:

> I would save the Union. I would save it the shortest way under the Constitution. . . . My paramount object in this struggle *is* to save the Union, and is *not* either to save or destroy slavery. If I could save the Union without freeing *any* slave I would do it, and if I could save it by freeing *all* the slaves I would do it; and if I could save it by freeing some and leaving others alone I would also do that. What I do about slavery, and the colored race, I do because I believe it helps to save the Union; and what I forbear, I forbear because I do *not* believe it would help to save the Union.[31]

At the time he wrote this, on August 22, 1862, the president was being pulled by powerful forces in two directions at once and was straining to find a solution to resolve both the war and the slavery issue, while at the same time preserving the Union. In his annual message to Congress on December 3, 1861, he explained that the slaves liberated by the war "are already dependent on the United States, and must be provided for in some way"; he suggested remunerating slaveholders in states that freed their slaves voluntarily. He further proposed that "steps be taken for colonizing both classes . . . at some place, or places, in a climate congenial to them," submitting that "It might be well to consider, too,—whether the free colored people already in the United States could not, so far as individuals may desire, be included in such colonization."[32]

On April 16 and July 16, 1862, bills providing funds for colonization became law. The colonization plan, which had been underway for several months, called for a purchase of land "at the Isthmus of Chiriqui" in Panama, where "captured Africans" could be settled. And it could be "a measure of great economy to direct there negroes to some of the unoccupied lands of Central America, and . . . an equally desirable measure to secure the removal of negroes from this country."[33] But while the president was working on this plan, he was also feeling compelled by the onerous pressures engendered by the war to consider emancipating slaves in those areas in open rebellion against the United States. By July 22, 1862, he had already completed a first draft for a proclamation to that effect. This—and the fact that on April 16 he had already signed the act to liberate the slaves in the District of Columbia—did not mean he had relinquished hope with regard to some form of colonization, however. On August 14, 1862, only three weeks after drafting an emancipation proclamation, he received a delegation of free blacks for the purpose of convincing them of the viability of the colonization plan. He announced his views bluntly:

> You and we are different races. We have between us a broader difference than exists between almost any other two races. Whether it is right or wrong I need not discuss, but this physical difference is a great disadvantage to us both, as I think your race suffer very greatly, many of them by living among us, while ours suffer from your presence. In a word we suffer on each side. If this is admitted, it affords a reason at least why we should be separated.

Lincoln attempted to make clear, moreover, that freedom in and of itself would not lead to their happiness, maintaining that

> even when you cease to be slaves, you are yet far removed from being placed on an equality with the white race. You are cut off from many of the advantages which the other race enjoy. The aspiration of men is to enjoy equality with the best when free, but on this broad continent, not a single man of your race is made the equal of a single man of ours. Go where you are treated the best, and the ban is still upon you.

Nor did the president withhold from the group his view of the connection he saw existing between slavery and the war. He explained: "But for your race among us there could not be war, although many men engaged on either side do not care for you one way or the other. Nevertheless, I repeat, without the institution of Slavery and the colored race as a basis, the war could not have an existence."[34]

If we consider that the drafting of an emancipation proclamation, the discussion on colonization with the delegation of free blacks, and the writing of the letter to Horace Greeley purporting to indicate Lincoln's attitude concerning the primacy of the Union all took place between July 22 and August 22, the complexity of the president's situation becomes evident. Lincoln was clearly juggling several balls at the same time, and as Fehrenbacher points out with regard to the Greeley letter, "Although Lincoln gave the impression that options were still open, he had in fact already made up his mind, had committed himself to a number of persons, had drafted the Proclamation."[35] It is nevertheless evident that even on the eve of proclaiming slaves free, the idea of colonizing them in another land apparently still maintained a powerful hold on Lincoln. If this was indeed the case, he can be seen as still trying to follow the guideline he felt had been laid down by the founders.

Within a year all this had changed. Lincoln was finally driven to emancipate the slaves in the states in open rebellion in order to help preserve the Union. What he termed "this fit and necessary war measure" he saw as imperative, whereas efforts at colonization had to be put on a back burner, or indeed forgotten, since despite the president's appeal America's free blacks did not favor that solution.[36] Lincoln was thus obliged to take the measure that had so long been advocated by proponents of abolition such as Theodore Parker and Parker's friend Charles Sumner. It was a difficult step, but it conformed with his firm belief in what he judged to be the founders' principle of equality for all, which contrasted sharply with Douglas's interpretation of the founders' concept as referring only to whites. The decision on emancipation was construed by Lincoln as a military measure, but it accorded with his interpretation of the phrase "all men are created equal" and answered his wish to see an immoral institution removed from the country that had undertaken to set a new moral standard for government.

In this his hopes coincided with Parker's, and it should come as no surprise to find Lincoln recalling in November 1863 some of the minister's perceptions and phrases that William Herndon had shared with him back in their Illinois law office. The president had gone through a baptism by fire in attempting to deal justly with the moral issue of human enslavement, and at Gettysburg he would assess the cost the country was paying in order to remain unified while simultaneously striving to excise the evil represented by slavery. To better understand why Lincoln might look to Parker at such a moment, we must turn again to 1854 and Parker's "Sermon of the Dangers which Threaten the Rights of Man in America." As this is the only one of the minister's efforts in which parallels to the Gettysburg Address of phrasing and political philosophy are so consistent and striking, the sermon merits reexamination; in this instance from a different point of view than that taken in connection with Lincoln's House Divided speech.

❧ When Theodore Parker addressed his listeners on the first Sunday of July 1854, it was as one of the most renowned preachers of the era to the largest congregation in the city of Boston.[37]

Since he spoke each week before an audience of around three thousand, his opportunity for influencing the Boston public was considerable. According to John White Chadwick, "There were chairs [in the Music Hall] for 1500 on the main floor and for 500 more upon the stage, and 700 more in the two narrow galleries or balconies which ran along the sides and rear. There was standing room for some 300 more, making a total capacity of 3000, which on special occasions was exhausted by the multitude who came to hear 'the great American Preacher'."[38] This particular morning Parker took as his theme "The Dangers which Threaten the Rights of Man in America," explaining to his congregation that he believed the nation had arrived at a crossroads in its history.

With this in mind, he dedicated the main thrust of his message to a thorough treatment of the slavery question, and a reference to the founding of the American nation did not prevent him from beginning on a somber note: "Next Tuesday will be the seventy-eighth anniversary of American Independence. The day suggests a national subject as theme for meditation this morning. The condition of America makes it a dark and sad meditation" (Rights of Man, 333). The fundamental question to be considered was whether American democracy was to live or die: "The human race is permanent as the Mississippi, and like that is fed from springs which never dry," affirmed Parker, "but the several nations are fleeting as its waves. In the great tide of humanity, States come up, one after the other, a wave or a bubble; each lasts its moment, then dies—passed off, forgot" (333). He pointed out that "The family of ephemera, permanent amid the fleeting, is yet as old as that of elephants, and will last as long. But free governments have commonly been brief" (334). Then, reflecting on the fate of nations that had fallen by the wayside in the past, he painted an unpromising picture for his listeners:

> The historic period of Greece begins 776 B.C.; her independence was all over in six hundred and thirty years. . . . Her tree of freedom grew in a narrow field of time and briefly bore its age-outlasting fruit of science, literature and art. Now the tree is dead; its fragments are only curious Athenian stone. The Grecian colonies in the East, Aetolian, Dorian, Ionian—how fair they flourished in the despotic waste of Asia! how soon those liberal blossoms died! Even her colonies in the advancing West had no long independent life. . . . The Roman commonwealth could not endure five hundred years. . . . The

> republics of Italy in the middle ages were no more fortunate . . . [and] even the Teutonic towns, where freedom ever wore a sober dress, were only spots of sunshine in a day of wintry storm. Swiss, German, Dutch, they were brief as fair. In Novogorod and in Poland, how soon was Slavonian freedom lost! (335–37)

But Parker detected a clear ray of hope in the fact that, in America, a thoroughly new kind of free government was being attempted. The United States was "making the greatest political experiment which the sun ever looked down upon" in aspiring to found an industrial State "ruled by the constable, not by the soldier" (Rights of Man, 341). And key to the success of the endeavor would be the fact that "the national theory of government is a democracy—the government of all, by all, for all. All officers depend on election, none are foreordained. There are to be no special privileges, only natural, universal rights" (342). The minister judged that the United States was blessed with "many elements of national success. Our territory for quantity and quality is all we could ask; our origin is of the Caucasian's best. No nation ever had so fair a beginning as we. The Anglo-Saxon is a good hardy stock for national welfare to grow on. To my American eye, it seems that human nature had never anything so good for popular liberty to be grafted into" (342).

But Parker was also convinced that not since the American Revolution had the peril to the nation been greater. States crumbled, he declared, when outward violence, inward moral or political vice, or general decay made them too weak to carry on the disciplined battle required to secure to themselves their continued existence. Since he considered that the American nation needed "to fear nothing from any foreign power" ("The violent cannot take us by force. No nation is our enemy" [342]), the primary foreseeable danger lay within America's borders. Hence, it was "for America, for this generation of Americans" (343) to decide whether the country was to survive the present crisis—whether America was "to live or to die" (342).

Parker nevertheless felt it mandatory to warn his congregation that "No fate holds us up, our character is our destiny" (Rights of Man, 343), and he expressed the belief that it would not be easy to make it through the difficult years that lay ahead: "since '76 our success was never so doubtful as at this time" (343). After weighing the threats posed by "our exclusive devotion to riches," by "the Roman Catholic Church established in the midst of us," and by the "danger from the idea that there is no higher law above the statutes which men make," Parker turned his attention to slavery, "the child of violence and atheism" (362). In the minister's view, "Brute material force is its father: the atheistic idea that there is no law of God above the passions of men—that is the mother of it" (362). Parker regarded all four threats to America as inseparable elements of a destructive matrix: slavery, the worst of the dangers, was nurtured by greed for money, a corrupt sense of what could be treated as property, and atheistic or jesuitical approaches to life, morality, and politics. Given such an analysis, it was inevitable that the preacher would expend far more energy on excoriating slavery than on attacking the other three perceived threats, and he approached the issue by first setting forth the ideals upon which the government in 1776 had been founded. His sermon called upon his congregation to reconsider these ideals in the light of the present state of American affairs:

> The idea of freedom first got a national expression seventy-eight years ago next Tuesday. Here it is. . . . First. All men are endowed by their Creator with certain natural rights, amongst which is the right to life, liberty, and the pursuit of happiness. Second. These rights are inalienable; . . . Third. In respect to these all men are equal; . . . Fourth. It is the function of government to secure these natural, inalienable, and equal rights to every man. . . . Fifth. Government derives all its divine right from its conformity with these ideas, all its human sanction from the consent of the governed. (362–63)

Following this summary of his understanding of the spirit of the Declaration of Independence and of 1776, Parker went on to explain his perception of the religious nature of the democratic principles upon which this form of government was based:

> Now this government, just in its substance, in its form must be democratic: that is to say, the government of all, by all, and for all. You see what consequences must follow from such an idea, and the attempt to re-enact the law of God into political institutions. There will follow the freedom of the people, respect for every natural right of all men, the rights of their body, and of their spirit—the rights of mind and conscience, heart and soul. (363)

From Parker's perspective, the significance of the American experiment with Jefferson's "idea of freedom" lay in the incorporation of the "law of God" into a political governing system. The minister maintained that this "is a religious idea; and when men pray for the 'reign of justice' and the 'kingdom of heaven,' to come on earth politically, I suppose they mean that there may be a commonwealth where every man has his natural rights of mind, body, and estate" (364).

This was precisely the definition favored by Lincoln, as Jaffa carefully explains:

> Although Abraham Lincoln did not belong to any church, he constantly appealed to the Bible—along with the Declaration—as a source of moral authority, and never more so than when he said, "As I would not be a *slave,* so I would not be a *master.* This expresses my idea of democracy. Whatever differs from this, to the extent of the difference, is not democracy." The first sentence is clearly an application of that Golden Rule that, according to Jesus, was the sum of the law and the prophets. The second and third sentences indicate that the ethical core of biblical religion is identical with the rational principle of popular government—that is to say, of the Declaration. Lincoln's axiom assumes the coincidence of equality, rightly understood, as the principle of Christianity and of free government.[39]

It is also clear from Lincoln's words that his "idea of democracy" correlates completely with Parker's "idea of freedom."

Opposed to this "idea of freedom" was what Parker characterized "in a philosophic form" as "the idea of slavery"—where "There are no natural, inalienable, and equal rights, wherewith men are endowed by their Creator; no natural, inalienable, and equal right to life, liberty, and the pursuit of happiness. . . . There is no natural law of God to forbid the strong to oppress the weak, and enslave and ruin the weak" (Rights of Man, 364). The minister maintained that "It has never got a national expression in America; it has never been laid down as a principle in any act of the American people, nor in any single State, so far as I know. All profess the opposite; but it is involved in the measures of both State and nation. This idea is founded in the selfishness of man; it is atheistic" (364). And because of the un-American, atheistic selfishness embodied in the "idea of slavery," Parker was convinced that no good could be derived from its continued existence. Moreover, he regarded it as a major threat to democracy, feeling that "The idea must lead to a corresponding government; that will be unjust in its substance—for it will depend not on natural right, but on personal force; not on the constitution of the universe, but on the compact of men. It is the abnegation of God in the universe and of conscience in man. Its form will be despotism—the government of all by a part, for the sake of a part" (364–65).

As Parker saw it, this "idea of slavery" represented the total negation of the concepts put forward in the Declaration of Independence concerning natural rights and Christian principle. It led to the fact that "Mr. [John C.] Calhoun denied the self-evident truths of the Declaration of Independence; denied the natural, inalienable, and equal rights of man" (Rights of Man, 365). Goading his audience, the preacher strove to enliven his assault by quoting offensive statements culled from Southern newspapers: "Rome and Greece owed their literary and national greatness exclusively to the institution of slavery"; "Free society is a sad and signal failure"; "There is no moral wrong in slavery"; "We belong to that society of which slavery is the distinguishing element, and we are not ashamed of it. We find it marked by every evidence of Divine approval" (366).

Then, his words and logic rolling inexorably onward as the waves of the mighty Atlantic against the jagged Massachusetts coastline, the preacher posed the difficult question confronting the country in terms similar to those that had faced the Philadelphia gathering in 1776:

> The question before the nation to-day is, Which shall prevail—the idea and fact of freedom, or the idea and fact of slavery; freedom exclusive and universal, or slavery, exclusive and universal? The question is not merely, Shall the African be bond or free? but, Shall America be a democracy or a despotism? For nothing is so remorseless as an idea, and no logic is so strong as the historical development of a national idea by millions of men. A measure is nothing without its principle. The idea which allows slavery in South Carolina will establish it also in New England. The bondage of a black man in Alexandria imperils every white woman's daughter in Boston. You cannot escape the consequences of a first principle more than you can "take the leap of Niagara and stop when halfway down." (Rights of Man, 367–68)

Should slavery gain the upper hand in the United States, Parker was persuaded that its despotic character would swiftly lead to the annihilation of the essential liberties of the individual. And at the moment Parker was writing, the "tendency" Lincoln would later describe seemed only too evident; the menace seemed to be increasing with every passing day. "Ten years more like the ten years past," declared Parker, "and it will be all over with the liberties of America. Everything must go down, and the heel of the tyrant will be on our neck. It will be all over with the rights of man in America, and you and I must go to Austria, to Italy, or to Siberia for our freedom; or perish with the liberty which our fathers fought for and secured to themselves—not to their faithless sons!" (390–91).

For Lincoln and many others, Parker's prediction would probably have sounded exaggerated at the time it was made, but we would do well to remember that in fewer years than the minister had foreseen the country would indeed be involved in a civil war testing the Union; slaves would already have been proclaimed free; and Lincoln would be delivering his Gettysburg Address. In the "Rights of Man" sermon that Parker gave only two days before the 1854 Fourth of July Independence Day celebrations, however, he showed no inclination to relinquish hope without a struggle. The preacher was attempting to stir the dormant patriotism of his listeners, seeking to challenge their latent idealism; he called upon his audience to throw off the hobbles of lethargy in order to save what their forefathers had sacrificed precious blood on so many battlefields to create and preserve. Shall our fathers have died in vain? he asked, in essence. Was it "for this that our fathers fought—the Adamses, Washington, Hancock? for this that there was an eight years' war, and a thousand battle-fields? for this the little monument at Acton, Concord, Lexington, West Cambridge, Danvers, and the great one over there on the spot which our fathers' blood made so red?" (Rights of Man, 392). Was America to go the way of Athens, the Hebrew commonwealth, the Teutonic free cities, and fall before the scythe of time and despotism? "Shall America thus perish?" he asked (393).

Even if, in the worst case, this should actually come to pass, however, Parker felt that America's ideals would survive. Never one to yield to despair, and with conviction born of strong religious faith, the minister strove to cheer his flock by instilling the belief that, in the end, "Truth shall triumph, justice shall be law! And, if America fail, though she is one fortieth of God's family, and it is a great loss, there are other nations behind us; our truth shall not perish, even if we go down" (Rights of Man, 394). But Parker did not want to believe America could falter under the burden of her responsibility to her past, and he challenged his audience not only to sustain hope but to endeavor to successfully defend a glorious heritage. "We shall not fail!" he insisted. "Boston only sleeps; one day she will wake! Massachusetts will stir again! New England will rise and walk! the vanished North be found once more queenly and majestic! Then it will be seen that slavery is weak and powerless in itself, only a phantom of the night" (394–95). Meanwhile, however, the battle remained to be fought; and in the closing portion of his sermon Parker enjoined his listeners not to abandon the struggle in the face of seemingly crushing odds. "Each one of you," he urged, "take heed that the Republic receive no harm!" (396).

❧ Over nine years after Parker delivered his "Rights of Man" sermon, Lincoln presented the following brief speech in Gettysburg, Pennsylvania, at the dedication of a cemetery created to honor the Union soldiers who had fallen there in one of the most bitter battles of the Civil War:

The Gettysburg Address
November 19, 1863

Four score and seven years ago our fathers brought forth on this continent, a new nation, conceived in Liberty, and dedicated to the proposition that all men are created equal.

Now we are engaged in a great civil war, testing whether that nation, or any nation so conceived and so dedicated, can long endure. We are met on a great battlefield of that war. We have come to dedicate a portion of that field, as a final resting place for those who here gave their lives that that nation might live. It is altogether fitting and proper that we should do this.

But, in a larger sense, we can not dedicate—we can not consecrate—we can not hallow—this ground. The brave men, living and dead, who struggled here, have consecrated it, far above our poor power to add or detract. The world will little note, nor long remember what we say here, but it can never forget what they did here. It is for us the living, rather, to be dedicated here to the unfinished

> work which they who fought here have thus far so nobly advanced. It is rather for us to be here dedicated to the great task remaining before us—that from these honored dead we take increased devotion to that cause for which they gave the last full measure of devotion—that we here highly resolve that these dead shall not have died in vain—that this nation, under God, shall have a new birth of freedom—and that government of the people, by the people, for the people, shall not perish from the earth.[40]

It will be noted that the theme of Lincoln's address is precisely that of Parker's "Rights of Man" sermon: the question of whether the United States "or any nation" dedicated to preserving the rights of the individual, dedicated to maintaining a government "of the people, by the people, for the people," can rise above internal conflict and not only hold to the ideals of its founders but continue the struggle for existence in spite of serious threats to those ideals. For Lincoln the question was certainly in order. As president of the United States of America on November 19, 1863, he found himself the leader of a nation committed to high principles but embroiled in one of the bloodiest internecine wars the world had ever witnessed. The danger to America's democratic form of government was only too real, and it was with conscious intent that he reminded his listeners in the opening lines of his speech—as had Parker—of the ideals upon which the men of 1776 had founded "a new nation." The gravity of the conflict upon which the nation had embarked made it imperative for Lincoln to make clear to his audience the direction in which the compass needle of the ship of state needed to point if the vessel were to reach its destination. The dedication of a portion of the Gettysburg battlefield as a cemetery offered a fitting moment to do this.

Parker had spoken in a time of peace and felt it appropriate to recall to his listeners the battlefields that the United States had known on its own territory. But Massachusetts had a long history, and his audience knew only too well to what he was referring when he asked, "Was it for this that our fathers fought—the Adamses, Washington, Hancock? for this there was an eight years' war, and a thousand battle-fields? for this the little monument at Acton, Concord, Lexington, West Cambridge, and the great one over there on the spot which our fathers' blood made so red?" (Rights of Man, 392). Lincoln, echoing a similar hope "that these dead shall not have died in vain," had no need to jog the memory of his audience; his battlefield lay before him with the blood hardly dry.

Infused with the importance of the occasion, Lincoln challenged Americans with the notion that this was not merely the moment to recall the great deeds of the men who had founded "a new nation" eighty-seven years before but this was also the time "for us the living, rather, to be dedicated here to the unfinished work which they who fought here have thus far so nobly advanced." Parker, too, had chosen a historically meaningful moment prior to the Fourth of July celebration to tell his listeners that it was "for America, for this generation of Americans" (Rights of Man, 343), to decide if America was "to live or to die" (342) and to urge them to "take heed that the Republic receive no harm" (396). Both men asked of their audience continued commitment to the cause, but it is significant that Lincoln called on the members of the throng gathered at Gettysburg to rededicate themselves to the ideals for which the men had died, not to the dead themselves. He asked his audience to look beyond death, in order that "this nation, under God, shall have a new birth of freedom—and that government of the people, by the people, for the people, shall not perish from the earth." Nor had Parker neglected to stipulate the need for God's assistance in working toward an ideal government, promising that, once slavery had been eliminated, "we shall have a commonwealth based on righteousness, which is the strength of any people, and shall stand longer than Egypt,—national fidelity to God our age-outlasting pyramid!" (396). To the question of whether the American government itself would fall, Parker had responded that "We shall not fail!" and that "Boston only sleeps" (394). The minister had nevertheless felt it prudent to assure his audience that even if the government *should* fail, even if the United States of America should go the way of all other nations, "our truth shall not perish, even if we go down" (394).

Parker used the word "perish" fourteen times in his sermon, and he asked thrice "Shall America thus perish?" But that Lincoln employed the exact expression utilized by Parker would not be so striking were it not for the fact that it appears in precisely the same context as Parker's and echoes exactly the preacher's doubt concerning whether the United States would continue to carry the torch to the end. Parker made explicit that "even if we go down," even if the United States should fall, its ideals would continue to light the human race out of the darkness of the past: "*our truth* shall not perish" (Rights of Man, 394; emphasis added).

Lincoln, too, was careful not to specify whether it would be *this* government that would continue to lead the fight for justice, dignity, and equal rights for all members of humanity. His prudent words asked only that "this nation, under God, have a new birth of freedom—and that government of the people, by the people, for the people shall not perish from the earth." When he turned to the word "government," he judiciously refrained from qualifying it with an easy "this." And that Lincoln's choice was a conscious one may be deduced from the fact that he deliberately substituted "this" for "the" prior to "nation" in the last sentence of all copies of the speech following the first and saw fit to insert "this" before "government" in the second draft, or Hay copy, only to delete the word entirely in subsequent copies.[41]

Each man thus hoped that democratic government would continue to exist, but neither ventured to predict the future of the United States itself. Parker reminded his audience that all previous democracies had fallen, and he outlined the very real dangers facing this one if it wandered away from its ideals. Lincoln, through a cautious choice of words, also left the door of doubt open to his listeners regarding the continued survival of the American nation as they had known it. If anything, he was slightly more circumspect than Parker on this point. Neither man, however, could bring himself to envision the complete disappearance of democracy as government "of all, by all and for all." Each stressed that democracy required strong resolve on the part of its participants if it were to weather the violent storms by which it was continually being buffeted.

In beginning his Gettysburg Address with a reference to the founding of the United States and the Declaration of Independence; in considering whether any nation founded on such ideals could endure; in referring to the ideals for which dead Americans had given their lives; in asking his audience, in the name of those dead and the ideals for which they had died, to shoulder the responsibility for preserving those ideals; in asking that the United States under God's guidance might not falter; and in hoping that democracy's light would burn forever in human hearts, Lincoln parallels in form, thought, and often in specific phrasing Parker's "Sermon of the Dangers which Threaten the Rights of Man in America." The country's chief executive eliminated the lengthy references to the lessons taught by history about how nations fall; he eliminated the careful compilation of facts concerning the immediate dangers threatening the United States; but he followed step by careful step the political philosophy methodically set forth by the minister. No aspect of Parker's logical progression is omitted or altered. Lincoln was laconic but not careless. That his words and phrasing are often similar or identical to those of Parker only serves to underscore to what extent the political philosophy elaborated in the Gettysburg Address had been molded by that of the minister. An American historian once declared:

> Lincoln is remembered as the "Great Emancipator" and remains universally a symbol of Union. Yet the martyred President might more appropriately and consistently be honored first as America's prophet of democracy. For it was on the great battlefield at Gettysburg, on November 19, 1863, that this giant amongst men taught that he had struck the chains of bondage from the slaves and had preserved his beloved Union, only to the end that "government of the people, by the people, for the people, shall not perish from the earth."[42]

If Lincoln should be so honored, what, one might ask, should be the place of Theodore Parker, who seems not only to have provided Lincoln with the essential elements of his prophecy but to have preceded him by many years in the preaching of it?

CHAPTER SIX

The Gettysburg Phrase

❧ The most widely recognized feature of Lincoln's Gettysburg Address, aside from the opening words of that speech, is undoubtedly the Gettysburg Phrase, "government of the people, by the people, for the people." This ten-word formulation has received much attention over the years, with many fine minds laboring to discover the origin of the idea and its expression. And though Lincoln made the phrase the common property of the world, that it was not original with him has long been recognized. But it was not original with Webster or Parker either. The honor of being the first to couch the idea in a form approximating the one adopted by Lincoln seems to belong to the Englishman Thomas Cooper, who, in the process of moving permanently to America, wished to explain his reasons for doing so to compatriots back home in Great Britain.

At a meeting held by the Massachusetts Historical Society on May 9, 1901, Samuel A. Green pointed out that Cooper, in a work titled *Some Information Respecting America, Collected by Thomas Cooper* and published in 1794, defines the government of the United States in the following terms: "The government is the government *of* the people, and *for* the people."[1] Cooper's underlining of the two prepositions draws attention to the concept, while the repetition of the words "government" and "people" helps to make the double formulation memorable, even though it occurs in the middle of a long paragraph listing "general inducements to people to quit England for America."[2] The construction employed by Cooper is both concise and catchy, and it would not be surprising if the combination of these qualities served to make it the inspiration for later writers, thinkers, and speakers. The book did, after all, help Cooper's own countrymen as well as Americans understand many attractive features of the New World; and the general significance of the work is pointed to by its being chosen by Augustus M. Kelley Publishers, in 1969, to be one of their "Reprints of Economic Classics."

The next appearance of a construction approximating the Gettysburg Phrase seems to have taken place only four years following the publication of Cooper's work and could conceivably have received inspiration from it, although there is no specific evidence that it did. The following triple formulation is included in an address sent on June 30, 1798, by the Citizens of Westmoreland County, Virginia, to and in support of President John Adams during what has been called "The Quasi-War" with France:[3] "The Declaration that our People are hostile to a Government made by themselves, for themselves, and conducted by themselves, is an Insult."[4] That Adams appreciated the citizens' commitment as well as their phrasing may be gathered from the fact that, in replying to the address less than two weeks later, he echoes their words: "The declaration that our People are hostile to a Government, made by themselves, for themselves, and conducted by themselves, if it were true, would be a demonstration that the people despise and hate themselves."[5]

In the years since Lincoln made the Gettysburg Phrase famous, there have also been less well founded claims as to its origin. Green, for instance, mentions in passing that Samuel Sewall, a judge at the Salem witchcraft trials, once employed a similar construction. Sewall's use of the structure had nothing to do with government, however. What he wrote in his private diary for November 8, 1690, was "Jn*o* Hoar comes into the Lobby and sais [*sic*] he comes from the Lord, by the Lord, to speak for the Lord."[6] If the word "Lord" is replaced by "people," the phrasing does acquire a democratic political dimension and—even without such an alteration—might still have proved influential in connection with the Gettysburg Phrase. But there is an awkward particular linked with Sewall's use of the phrase that Green fails to note, and which cannot easily be modified or disregarded. The quote from Sewall's diary did not become available to the general public until fifteen years after Lincoln delivered his Gettysburg Address: its first publication took place in 1878, nearly two hundred years after it was written.

As the earliest known source for a formulation similar to Lincoln's, a line allegedly located in a preface to the Wycliffe translation of the Bible has also been mentioned by more than one author. Stuart P. Garver, for instance, tells the following undocumented story:

> John Wycliffe was exhausted beyond description. Banished as Oxford's Professor of Divinity, branded "an instrument of the Devil . . . the author of schism," he was destined to win world acclaim for his masterful translation of the Scriptures into the English vernacular. That translation not only infused a new depth and beauty into the English language but imparted to all who read it, the Good News of God's saving grace.
>
> Having been driven into virtual exile by the hypocritical alliance of church and state authorities, he knew full well they would now unite to destroy his translation of the Bible. Therefore, with a bold defiance of all their threats and evil imaginings against him, Wycliffe wrote in the fly-leaf of this Bible: *"This Bible is translated and shall make possible a Government of the people, by the people, and for the people."*
>
> Little did he know that five hundred years later his words would be immortalized by the President of a new Government, founded on the shores of a new continent, as he arose to dedicate a blood-drenched battle field, saying "Fourscore and seven years ago our forefathers brought forth upon this continent, a new Nation,. . . and we are here highly resolved that this Nation under God shall have a new birth of freedom, and that government of the people, and for the people, and by the people shall not perish from the earth [*sic*]."[7]

William Barton attributes the origin of such a notion to "Sir Hall Caine, the distinguished English novelist," but maintains that "as far as I am aware, Sir Hall Caine is the sole and only man who has ever been able to find that phrase there."[8] Barton requested librarians at the Library of Congress, the New York Public Library, and the Congregational Library in Boston to search their copies of the Wycliffe Bible for the sentence, only to have these searches turn up no evidence of its presence.[9]

On Wycliffe's side of the Atlantic, Claire Breay, curator in the Department of Manuscripts at the British Library, states, "according to *The Oxford Dictionary of the Christian Church* (3rd edn, 1997), p. 1770, 'Though he [Wycliffe] wrote in English, probably none of the English works attributed to him is really his. He apparently played no direct part in the translation of the Bible undertaken by his disciples (c. 1380–92) though he undoubtedly inspired the project.'"[10] Anne Hudson, a Wycliffe Bible specialist, further declares:

> The story was not known to me . . . and I have not been able to find it in various sources about the history of the Wycliffites and

> their translation activities. So far as I can see the formulation does not appear in the so-called General Prologue to the translation, or in the standard prefaces; the latter are found in most copies of the translation, the former in only a few copies. It is now generally agreed that the process of translation, as described in the last chapter of the General Prologue, must have involved a collaborative effort over a fairly long period of time; Wyclif was probably the inspirer of the translation, but there is disagreement about whether he played any part in the work himself—it is almost certain that it was finished and revised after his death.[11]

Conrad Lindberg, another Wycliffite scholar, adds: "I have not come across any such reference in the course of my work on this bible."[12] The claim made by Caine, Garver, and others thus seems dubious, if for no other reason than that it would have been difficult for Wycliffe to write on the flyleaf of a work apparently completed only after his death. My own examination of several copies of the Wycliffe Bible has led me to the same conclusion as Barton, Breay, Hudson, and Lindberg, and I must agree with F. Lauriston Bullard's assessment of the story that "Probably it is apocryphal."[13]

In *"A Few Appropriate Remarks": Lincoln's Gettysburg Address* Bullard, often following in the footsteps of Green and Barton, attempts to trace possible sources for the Gettysburg Phrase and manages to gather together a significant number. Several of these sources predated both Webster's and Parker's earliest use but, given Lincoln's evident dependence upon the writings of these two men, may probably be discounted as having been of more than indirect influence, if that. Some of the less likely candidates mentioned are Cleon of Athens; a Swiss judge by the name of Schinz; Alphonse de Lamartine; the American naval officer and scientist Matthew Fontaine Maury; and Joel Parker of Cambridge, Massachusetts. Of this group Cleon, the political opponent of Pericles, would seem to have had one of the better chances of having his words (assuming they ever existed) seen by Lincoln, but neither Barton nor Bullard offer more than rumor to bolster their contention regarding the Greek general. Nor have I been able to confirm their claim.

The Schinz suggestion, probably the most interesting of the lot, was first brought to public attention in 1895 by Ward Hill Lamon, Lincoln's friend and former bodyguard, who gave the following report:

> A distinguished diplomat has acquainted me with the singular fact that almost the identical phrase employed by Mr. Lincoln was used in another language by a person whose existence even was not probably known to Mr. Webster, the Parkers [Theodore and Joel], or to Mr. Lincoln. On the thirty-first page of a work entitled "Geschichte der Schweizerischen Regeneration von 1830 bis 1848, von P. Feddersen," appears an account of a public meeting held at Olten, Switzerland, in May, 1830. On that occasion a speaker named Schinz used the following language, as translated by my friend just referred to: "All the governments of Switzerland [referring to the cantons] must acknowledge that they are simply from *all the people, by all the people, and for all the people.*"[14]

The original German "aus dem Volke, durch das Volk und für das Volk" would probably translate more exactly as "from the people, through the people and for the people,"[15] but since Feddersen's work was not published until four years following the Gettysburg Address (in 1867, with the translation apparently done after that) the by-then-famous Gettysburg Phrase could easily have suggested itself to Lamon's diplomat-translator friend. In what appears to be a serendipitous turn of fate, Feddersen himself found the quotation from Schinz in a Swiss history work published the same year, 1863, in which Lincoln delivered his famous address.[16] In addition the 1830 date of Schinz's statement places it in the same year as Daniel Webster's use of a similar construction in his Reply to Hayne and thus makes it one of the earlier appearances of such a formulation. But as Lamon indicates, there is little likelihood that the words of Schinz could have been known or of aid to Lincoln. I have discovered, for instance, no evidence that the meeting in Olten was reported on in the United States prior to 1867, and Lamon neglects to tell us when the translation was carried out, when he was apprised of it, if he was actually shown it, or if it was ever published. Lincoln is not known to have been proficient in German.[17] Nor, at this stage of his career, could he any longer draw on Herndon's wide-ranging and up-to-date library, or (more important) their joint discussions of fresh acquisitions. It would therefore seem that much more evidence than Lamon provides would be needed to demonstrate that the Illinois lawyer could have seen or heard of Schinz's statement.

Turning from German to French, one finds the following quotation from an 1848 translation of Alphonse de Lamartine's *His-*

toire des Girondins to be another Gettysburg Phrase precursor, albeit a more tardy one:

> This end was the representative sovereignty of all the citizens, concentrated in an election as extensive as the people themselves, and acting by the people, and for the people, in an elective council, which should be all the government.[18]

Aside from the fact that the original French term "puisée" would more accurately be rendered as "derived from" than "concentrated in," this translation is faithful to the original.[19] It arrives rather late on the scene, however, and this plus the infelicitous phrasing almost certainly prevents this source from being of more than curiosity importance. There is a chance that, in the course of Parker's omnivorous reading, he encountered either Lamartine's original (published in 1847) or the subsequent translation.[20] But, as the minister's earliest public use of such a phrase occurred in 1847 and he had already employed a similar formula in a private letter in 1846, neither the original French work nor its translation can be considered to have appeared early enough to exert any meaningful influence.

Another latecomer to the use of words bearing a similarity to those Lincoln would subsequently make famous is Matthew Maury, author of *The Physical Geography of the Sea,* the first textbook on modern oceanography. In 1851 in a report to Congress on the military defense capabilities of the United States, Maury loftily declared:

> Unlike Europe, the armed occupation of a capitol here, would be no more than the occupation of any other town by an enemy—unlike Europe, there are no disaffected people in this country for a foe to tamper with. The Government is by the people, for the people, and with the people. It is the people.[21]

This formulation clearly fits within the pattern set by several of Maury's predecessors, yet the late date of its presentation, together with the fact that it is buried in a congressional report of relatively minor importance, would appear to seriously diminish its chances of having been of influential importance for Lincoln. A paradoxical sidelight is that Maury, a Virginian, had himself become "disaffected" by the time Lincoln delivered the Gettysburg Address and, as an agent of the Confederacy, was safely ensconced in England attempting to curry favor with potential foes of the fragile Union.[22]

An even later use of "Gettysburg" phrasing has been attributed to Joel Parker, a Massachusetts politician whom Lamon mentions as having used "substantially the same phrase" as Lincoln's at the Massachusetts Constitutional Convention of 1853.[23] Parker's closest parallel to Lincoln's formulation occurs in a passage explaining what the citizens of Massachusetts had striven to achieve in drawing up their original constitution:

> They undertook to solve the problem of self-government, to establish a government, not distinct from, and adverse to, the people, but a government of the people themselves, to be administered by and through the people; acting, of course, not in their collective and primary capacity, because that was impossible, but as they could only act, through agents appointed to do their work, their bidding, their will.[24]

The 1853 date would indicate that Joel Parker could easily have received the idea for his formulation from many another before him—in particular, and closest to home, Theodore Parker or Daniel Webster. It is also somewhat doubtful that, even if Lincoln had taken time from his busy schedule in that period of his life to familiarize himself with the proceedings of the Massachusetts convention, he would have been impressed by Joel Parker's pale phrasing. For although the politician's language was perhaps inspired by Theodore Parker or Daniel Webster, it certainly is no match in form or rhythm for that of either of those predecessors, with whose works Lincoln was unquestionably well acquainted.

Taking his lead from Barton, Bullard finds firmer footing in pointing out: "If Lincoln had read the annual message of [President] James Monroe for 1820 he would have found in the introductory portion a characterization of ours as 'a government which is founded by, administered for, and supported by the people'."[25] The phraseology is more limping and less lyrical than Cooper's, but it is indeed a triple formulation using a series of prepositional phrases. Furthermore, it is situated within a document with which Lincoln, Webster, and Parker were more than likely to have been familiar.[26]

Another person who used a phrase similar to Lincoln's—and prior to Webster, Parker, and Monroe—was Chief Justice John

Marshall. Green points to the relevance of the following passage from Marshall's famous opinion in the *McCulloch v. Maryland* case of March 6, 1819: "The government of the Union, then, (whatever may be the influence of this fact on the case,) is, emphatically, and truly, a government of the people. In form and substance it emanates from them. Its powers are granted by them, and are to be exercised directly on them, and for their benefit." In addition to this passage, it is worth noting the following lines of Marshall's decision, which precede that quote:

> But when, "in order to form a more perfect union," it was deemed necessary to change this alliance [of the states] into an effective government, possessing great and sovereign powers, and acting directly on the people, the necessity of referring it to the people, and of deriving its powers directly from them, was felt and acknowledged by all.[27]

The chief justice's phrasing acquires greater significance when we realize that Daniel Webster was one of the lawyers who argued *McCulloch v. Maryland* before the U.S. Supreme Court. Consequently, Webster was clearly conversant with the wording of the decision long before he employed a construction similar to Marshall's. Hence, the following passages may well have resounded in his ear:

> The government proceeds directly from the people; is "ordained and established" in the name of the people; and is declared to be ordained, "in order to form a more perfect union, establish justice, ensure domestic tranquillity, and secure the blessings of liberty to themselves and to their posterity." . . .
>
> It is the government of all; its powers are delegated by all; it represents all; and acts for all. . . .
>
> Those means [that the people of a state grant to their government to tax themselves and their property] are not given by the constituents of the legislature, which claim the right to tax them but by the people of all the States. They are given by all, for the benefit of all—and upon theory, should be subjected to that government only which belongs to all.[28]

Each of these excerpts contains repetitions of the kind seen in the variations on the Gettysburg Phrase to be found in works of Webster,

Parker, and Lincoln, and all three men would have been sensitive to the musical balance created by such repetition. Marshall's reiteration of his concept within the same document further contributes to helping it echo in the mind of the reader. And despite Webster's familiarity with the *McCulloch v. Maryland* case and its final disposition, it is unlikely he alone would have been aware of the content of Marshall's decision. Lincoln the lawyer would have been expected to know the details of such a landmark legal opinion, while Parker's wide-ranging interest in matters relating to the history and content of the founding documents of the United States would suggest that he, too, was acquainted with Marshall's words.

Another plausible origin for the Gettysburg Phrase, one that preceded its use by Webster and Parker and that would also have been accessible to Lincoln, is suggested by Bullard:

> In Scotland there was published about 1820 a book by one James Douglas with the title, "The Advancement of Society in Knowledge and Religion", an American edition of which was issued in Hartford ten years later. The following year the president of Andover Theological Seminary, Ebenezer Porter, got out, for the training of his students in the art of preaching, a "Rhetorical Reader" in which he included a chapter from Douglas on "A New Social Order in America." The chapter is short and eloquent as this excerpt will indicate: "America . . . is the land of aspirations and dreams, a country of daring enterprise, and the asylum of misfortune, which receives alike the exile and the adventurer, the discontented and the aspiring, and promises to all a freer life and a fresher nature . . . in a government where all power is from the people, and in the people, and for the people." Both the American editions of Douglas and Porter's "Reader" had an extensive circulation in this country, and Lincoln may have seen both of them.[29]

Nor is it inconceivable that Webster, or Parker, or both might have found such a work of more than passing interest.

❧ Nonetheless, and in spite of these and other possible sources that could have been available to Lincoln prior to writing the Gettysburg Address, Green, Barton, and Bullard all come to the conclusion that it was Theodore Parker whose phrasing was closest to Lincoln's and who was the most probable candidate for the honor of having inspired the Gettysburg Phrase. This view finds substantial support in an account by Jesse W. Weik, published in *The Outlook* of July 12, 1913, relating how he and Herndon, in cleaning out the latter's law office "Some years ago, when Herndon had decided to retire from the practice of law," happened upon

> one package on the top of which, underneath the string, was a strip of paper, about two by five inches in size, which bore this brief and suggestive indorsement in Mr. Lincoln's handwriting:
>
> "When you can't find it anywhere else, look into this."
>
> I called Mr. Herndon and, at his direction cut the string. When the papers fell apart—for it comprised a varied assortment of letters, canceled checks, newspapers, and other like material—two of Theodore Parker's printed addresses appeared, both of which Mr. Herndon promptly identified as pamphlets given by him to Mr. Lincoln, and which plainly showed the creases made while folded in the latter's pocket. One, entitled "The Relation of Slavery to a Republican Form of Government," was a speech delivered at the New England Anti-Slavery Convention, May 26, 1858. On page 5 was the following:
>
> "III. Democracy—The All-Men Power; government over all, by all, and for the sake of all."
>
> Evidently this expression had caught Mr. Lincoln's attention, for the paragraph in which it occurs he had encircled with pencil marks—an indication of his approval, or, at least, his deep interest in it.
>
> The other pamphlet was a sermon delivered by Mr. Parker at Music Hall, Boston, July 4, 1858, on "The Effect of Slavery on the American People." On page 5 occurs this, which Mr. Lincoln had also marked:
>
> "Democracy is Direct Self-Government, over all the people, for all the people, by all the people."
>
> And on page 14 he had marked this:
>
> "Slavery is in flagrant violation of the institutions of America—Direct Government—over all the people, by all the people, for all the people."
>
> Whether this expression so frequently used by Mr. Parker was original with him does not require investigation here. It probably was not, for it is said Daniel Webster and James Douglas, a Scotchman, made use of it before Parker's day. Even as late as 1851 George Thompson, the English reformer, and a member of parliament . . . [alluded to]

> "the government of all, by all, for all" . . . But without delving deeper into the question of the real origin of this noble sentiment, this wholesome tribute to the efficacy and enduring value of popular government, it is fair to conclude, in view of the circumstances above narrated, that the repeated use of it by Mr. Parker was not without its effect on Abraham Lincoln; that it found welcome lodgment in the latter's great mind and heart, and that it inspired the exalted and memorable prophecy uttered that crisp November morning in 1863 over the graves of the heroic dead sleeping at Gettysburg:
>
> "Government of the people, by the people, for the people, shall not perish from the earth."[30]

Weik's account was written for the fiftieth anniversary of the Gettysburg Address and is of decided interest, being a firsthand description of the discovery of the documents in question. From the distinctive details described, it also appears that Weik had before him as he wrote the same copy of Parker's July 4 sermon, "The Effect of Slavery on the American People," to which Herndon referred in the biography of Lincoln written roughly twenty-five years before. That copy (now located in the Herndon-Weik Collection in the Library of Congress) does indeed possess all of the indications pointed to by Weik, if we interpret his description of "encircled" to mean a single, vertical, parenthesis-shaped pencil marking in the margin. It bears the precise page numbers on which the quotes occur, the signs of having been folded, and betrays damaged corners from having possibly been carried in a coat pocket.

In recounting the same story nine years afterward, Weik essentially repeats what he wrote earlier, but with some noteworthy modifications. He informs his readers that

> the item which awakened [Herndon's] deepest interest was a couple of printed sermons, opposing the extension of slavery, delivered by Theodore Parker of Boston in the summer of 1858. Herndon told me that these pamphlets were sent to him by Parker and that he was so deeply impressed by them that he turned them over to Lincoln. The latter folded and carried them in his pocket to read. "That he did read them," said Herndon after he had opened the package, "is shown by the fact that he endorsed them by marking several paragraphs with his pen." He then called my attention to two paragraphs around which Lincoln had drawn his pen. In one of them Parker said: "Democracy is direct self-government, over all the peo-

> ple, for all the people, by all the people." In another place which Lincoln had underscored he said, "Slavery is in flagrant violation of the institutions of America—direct government, over all the people, by all the people, for all the people." Herndon insisted it was from this source that Lincoln drew the inspiration for the closing paragraph of his famous Gettysburg Address.[31]

In this 1922 version of the event, it should be observed that Herndon is reported to have affirmed that he did *not* bring back from his 1858 trip east Parker's "The Effect of Slavery on the American People," as he states in the Lincoln biography, but that he was sent it by the minister. This would correlate with the evidence presented earlier in this study, but only on this single occasion was such a claim ever made. Whether Weik fully realized that he was placing Herndon in contradiction with himself would seem doubtful, but such is the case. Further confusion results from Weik's changing the writing instrument from a pencil to a pen. Why he did this can only be guessed at since the rest of his description is relatively faithful to the 1913 account, and, as mentioned earlier, the markings on the two sermons in the Herndon-Weik collection are not in pen but in pencil. Nor, it may be noted, does any actual underscoring occur. Such inconsistencies are the historian's nightmare and may be chalked up to Weik's failing memory or any number of other causes; but, whatever importance may be ascribed to them, they exist, and until now have gone unremarked and are so far unexplained.

As with Herndon's description in the Lincoln biography of the origin of the Gettysburg Phrase, certain other questions arise concerning Weik's accounts of the discovery of the two sermons. Why, for example, did neither he nor Herndon mention this engaging story in the biography? The evidence would point to the event having taken place prior to the publication of that joint work. In fact, the incident seems to have occurred in November 1882, many years before either the writing or the publication of the book.[32] It also appears from Herndon's detailed description of the Parker sermon he regarded as the source of the Gettysburg Phrase that, while writing his account, he was almost certainly working with a copy of that sermon before him, most probably this particular one. We can only speculate as to the reason for his neglecting to mention its discovery, but there is one possible explanation that, despite its apparent simplicity, should not be overlooked.

The incident could easily have seemed much more memorable to the young and enthusiastic Weik than to the aging Herndon, more taken up at that moment with closing down a career than with concentrating on his old friend Parker's possible influence on Lincoln. After all, Herndon had been used to seeing Parker's works lying about the law office, once telling Weik, "I was the abolitionist and kept on my table such speeches as Theo Parker's—Gidding's, Phillips', Sumners—Sewards, etc. [*sic*]."[33] The discovery of a couple of pamphlet-sized sermons in one of Lincoln's boxes, therefore, would probably not have seemed of earth-shaking significance. Such an accounting could also help to explain why, in subsequently referring to Parker's sermon during his writing of the Lincoln biography, Herndon would mistake the sermon's date and place of acquisition and fail to notice the second appearance of the Gettysburg Phrase near its close.

A further complication arises from the fact that, whereas in the Lincoln biography Herndon refers to only one sermon as the probable source for the Gettysburg Phrase, Weik mentions finding two. As might reasonably be expected from Weik's account of the discovery of the Parker sermons, a copy of each can be found in the Herndon-Weik Collection, the only works of the minister located there. And, as with "The Effect of Slavery" sermon to which Weik and Herndon both refer, the copy of Parker's "The Relation of Slavery to a Republican Form of Government" also displays all the features mentioned by Weik.[34] These include central fold–creasing, to the point where the pamphlet in places is split in two; worn-down corners; and a single, vertical, parenthesis-style pencil marking at the point where the lines "Democracy—The All-Men Power; government over all, by all, and for the sake of all" appear on page 5.

Once again, however, there is no handwriting to indicate that Lincoln himself made the mark. We have only Weik's firsthand accounts of the discovery—and of Herndon's confirmation to him of the origin of the sermons—as proof for the source of that mark. Why, then, did Herndon himself not notice—or if he noticed, why did he not make use of—this meaningful piece of evidence at the time he was writing the biography of Lincoln? One may wonder as well why Weik, his co-author, did not make certain Herndon mentioned the second sermon or the discovery itself in the biography. Whatever answers may be suggested for these and other related questions, the pencil marks in the margins of the two sermons (assuming Weik's 1913 account and Herndon's explanation in that version of the discovery to be accurate and true) would, as Weik concludes, clearly point to Lincoln's conscious awareness of Parker's repeated use of the triple formulation, which in the president's sensitive and poetic hands would eventually gain lasting fame as the Gettysburg Phrase.

Nonetheless, there are still other features of Weik's story that deserve considering. One is Weik's assertion that he played a central role in the discovery of the marked Parker sermons. This claim is significant, for it is known that a certain tension existed between Herndon and Weik with regard to the relative importance of each to the authorship of the biography; and Weik was a jealous custodian of his right to receive more credit for his work than Herndon seemed willing to bestow.[35] By 1913, however, with Herndon safely in his grave, this problem no longer existed. Weik could finally take what he may have seen as a fair share of the glory connected with the discovery of the sermons: glory that Herndon had refrained from conferring on him in the Lincoln biography's account of the origin of the Gettysburg Phrase. It is also possible that Weik felt his action justified by the fact that Herndon had by no means been bashful about drawing attention to his own importance as a contributing participant at the inception of more than one of Lincoln's celebrated speeches (see Chapter 2).

A further curious and possibly germane detail relating to Weik's story is the astonishing claim by the Editors, contained in the biographical introduction to the 1913 article, that "Mr. Weik studied law with Lincoln for over a year." This pronouncement would add considerable weight to Weik's claim to authority were it not that the author was not born until 1857. This would mean the year of study would have had to have been within the three years immediately following Weik's birth, and prior to Lincoln's departure from Springfield to take on the responsibilities of the presidency. Since the other facts in the Editors' introductory remarks about Weik are accurate, one may be permitted to wonder where they discovered this detail, which placed the author in a closer relationship to Lincoln than was physically or logically possible. Could it conceivably have been Weik himself who was in some way responsible for this serious slip? Was he consciously or unconsciously attributing to himself more credit than he might otherwise receive? Definitive answers to these questions will probably never be found, but here again, as with the discovery of the sermons, Jesse Weik would appear, intentionally or not, to infringe on territory previously the exclusive purview of William Herndon.[36]

Whatever undercurrents of ego may have been active in the relations between the two biographers, both Herndon and Weik attribute ultimate recognition to Theodore Parker for providing Lincoln with the famous formula that closes the Gettysburg Address. Weik is more circumspect and less simplistic in presenting his case than Herndon, but he, too, comes to the conclusion that Parker's repeated use of the Gettysburg Phrase produced a more profound effect on Lincoln's "mind and heart" than any other possible source, and there seems little reason to dissent from this view. Before turning to other questions, however, there is an ancillary piece of information regarding the relationship of Lincoln's Gettysburg Phrase to Parker's formulations that warrants noting. Bullard mentions that

> in connection with the Sanitary Fair at Baltimore for which Lincoln wrote the final copy of the address there was circulated what nowadays would be called a daily tabloid, named *The New Era* and devoted to the exploitation of that philanthropy. In the thirteenth issue, dated May 2, 1864, less than six months after the consecration ceremonies, there was printed an item entitled "Parallel Thoughts." There were two brief paragraphs. The first merely quoted from Parker the passage just cited ["a government of all the people, by all the people, for all the people"]; the second repeated the final lines of the Gettysburg Address.[37] Surely it is probable that some of Lincoln's hearers in 1863, and many who read his "remarks" as quoted in the newspaper reports, must have noticed the similarity between Lincoln's words and Parker's definition of "democracy."[38]

This would appear to indicate that, despite Herndon's familiarity with Parker's works and ideas, he may not have been the first to notice his friend's probable connection with the Gettysburg Phrase. Unless additional evidence comes to light, however, the question as to when it initially dawned on Herndon that the phrase could have been borrowed from Parker must remain unanswered.

The latest this could have occurred would seem to have been toward the end of 1866, when Herndon received a letter from the Boston native Daniel W. Wilder, stating:

> By the way, Lincoln's greatest speech, Gettysburg, has two ideas—self-consecration and a "government of the people, for the people and by the people." This last is word for word from Theodore Parker (unconsciously, of course, to Lincoln at the time, his mind having assimilatied [*sic*] it) and you must give him the credit for it. I can find the Sermon where it occurs.—[39]

Wilder's quote inverts two of the prepositional phrases, and he never seems to have sent Herndon the sermon to which he refers. But in wishing Parker to receive due credit for the Gettysburg Phrase, Wilder is not off the mark. For Lincoln certainly seems to have incurred a debt in that respect. Yet although it is clear that the Gettysburg Phrase could have found its way into Lincoln's consciousness via a number of different avenues, the significance of the question concerning the ultimate origin of this single phrase pales in the light of the evidence thus far presented of Parker's far deeper influence on Lincoln's speech than either William H. Herndon or Jesse W. Weik suggest.

❧ To understand why the story of Parker's influence should not end here, it is necessary to realize that Parker had once been a serious admirer of Daniel Webster, having as a boy of ten first heard Webster speak at Plymouth Rock in 1820, and again four years after that.[40] In spite of this early adulation the minister became one of the senator's most virulent critics following the passage of the Fugitive Slave Bill in 1850. On this occasion, and again upon Webster's death in 1852, Parker wrote long sermons dealing with Webster's career. The minister's disciplined, deep-delving approach to the writing of his sermons presupposed serious research, and it is conceivable that one of the things he did by way of preparation was to thoroughly familiarize himself with Webster's works—if, as is more than likely, he were not already imbued with the words of that famous son of Massachusetts.[41] In either case, it would seem that some of Webster's ringing rhetoric could easily have worked its way into Parker's own; and what would become the Gettysburg Phrase is one line that Parker may well have borrowed from Webster and honed to a finer, more effective edge before it was adopted by Lincoln.

Although Herndon confidently and with well-founded justification claimed Parker as the source for the Gettysburg Phrase, there is a possibility that Lincoln also found inspiration for that phrase in Webster's celebrated Reply to Hayne. In this speech Webster speaks at one point of "the people's Constitution, the people's government, made for the people, made by the people, and answerable to the people" (Reply, 321). Since Lincoln was familiar with Webster's writings and, according to Herndon's account of the genesis of the House Divided speech, had consulted the Reply to Hayne prior to drafting his own speech, there is no reason to dismiss the possibility that, when writing the Gettysburg Address, the president might have recalled Webster's formulation just as readily as, or in addition to, Parker's. On the other hand, since Parker employed a triple formulation much closer in form, order, and rhythm to Lincoln's and did so twice in his "Rights of Man" sermon as well as in a number of other speeches and sermons that, according to Herndon, were also known to the president, simple percentages point toward the Boston preacher as the most direct and probable source. Even then, there may be still more depths to this story.

For instance, the possibility exists that Webster's influence on Parker was not confined to the Gettysburg Phrase, and that some of the formulations used by Parker in his sermon on the "Rights of Man," and later by Lincoln in the Gettysburg Address, could be directly or indirectly attributable to Webster.[42] A line discussed earlier in relation to Lincoln's House Divided speech (for which, as a minister, Parker would have also known the biblical origin) is, in Webster's phrasing, "If a house be divided against itself, it will fall, and crush every body in it."[43] It is conceivable, however, that it was Webster who recalled this sentence to the minister's attention—particularly if one considers that the senator's speech was delivered in the fall of 1851, little more than a year before his death, in connection with the slavery issue and that Parker may have reacquainted himself with it while preparing his funeral sermon on "the Great Daniel."

With regard to Lincoln's Gettysburg Address, it may further be observed that in "An Address delivered at the Laying of the Cornerstone of the Bunker Hill Monument at Charlestown, Massachusetts, on the 17th of June, 1825"—on the fiftieth anniversary of the battle that had taken place there, and in the presence of the aging General Lafayette—Webster spoke "among the sepulchres of our fathers" in praise of, and in memory of the service of, the early friends of "American Independence."[44] Lauding General

Joseph Warren, who had fallen in the battle, Webster heightened the drama by addressing the defunct hero directly: "Our poor work may perish; but thine shall endure! This monument may moulder away; the solid ground it rests upon may sink down to a level with the sea; but thy memory shall not fail!" (Bunker Hill, 65). Here, in close proximity, we find the words "our poor work," "perish," and "endure," words that would appear in Lincoln's Address, while "shall not fail" (as mentioned earlier) appears in the House Divided speech. It should also be noted that, together with "our fathers" and "sepulchers," all save "our poor work" are to be found in Parker's "Rights of Man" sermon.

The primary distinction between Parker's and Webster's use of the same words and phrasing is that Webster is speaking in memory of an individual hero whereas Parker (and Lincoln after him) is concerned with the survival of an entire system of government. The close conjunction of these specific features in Webster's speech, in a context differing only slightly from Parker's and Lincoln's, thus opens the door to speculation about their possible appropriation by Parker, and thereafter by Lincoln. From the above examples it would seem evident that a direct line, flowing from Webster through Parker to Lincoln, exists in the use of language. For this reason, careful attention should be paid to the closing lines of Webster's Bunker Hill speech, where the senator challenges his listeners to take on the responsibility of defending, preserving, and improving what the fathers of the country have created and handed down to them:

> Let us endeavor to comprehend in all its magnitude, and to feel in all its importance, the part assigned to us in the great drama of human affairs. We are placed at the head of the system of representative and popular governments. Thus far our example shows that such governments are compatible, not only with respectability and power, but with repose, with peace, with security of personal rights, with good laws, and a just administration. . . . If, in our case, the representative system ultimately fail, popular governments must be pronounced impossible. No combination of circumstances more favorable to the experiment can ever be expected to occur. The last hopes of mankind, therefore, rest with us; and if it should be proclaimed, that our example had become an argument against the experiment, the knell of popular liberty would be sounded throughout the earth.

These are excitements to duty; but they are not suggestions of doubt. Our history and our condition, all that is gone before us, and all that surrounds us, authorize the belief, that popular governments, though subject to occasional variations, in form perhaps not always for the better, may yet, in their general character, be as durable and permanent as other systems. We know, indeed, that in our country any other is impossible. The *principle* of free governments adheres to the American soil. It is bedded in it, immovable as its mountains.

And let the sacred obligations which have devolved on this generation, and on us, sink deep into our hearts. Those who established our liberty and our government are daily dropping from among us. The great trust now descends to new hands. Let us apply ourselves to that which is presented to us, as our appropriate object. We can win no laurels in a war for independence. Earlier and worthier hands have gathered them all. Nor are there places for us by the side of Solon, and Alfred, and other founders of states. Our fathers have filled them. But there remains to us a great duty of defence and preservation; and there is opened to us, also, a noble pursuit to which the spirit of the times strongly invites us. Our proper business is improvement. Let our age be the age of improvement. In a day of peace, let us advance the arts of peace and the works of peace. Let us develop the resources of our land, call forth its powers, build up its institutions, promote all its great interests and see whether we also, in our day and generation, may not perform something worthy to be remembered. Let us cultivate a true spirit of union and harmony. In pursuing the great objects which our condition points out to us, let us act under a settled conviction, and an habitual feeling, that these twenty-four States are one country. Let our conceptions be enlarged to the circle of our duties. Let us extend our ideas over the whole of the vast field in which we are called to act. Let our object be, OUR COUNTRY, OUR WHOLE COUNTRY, AND NOTHING BUT OUR COUNTRY. And by the blessing of God, may that country itself become a vast and splendid monument, not of oppression and terror, but of Wisdom, of Peace, and of Liberty, upon which the world may gaze with admiration for ever! (76–78)

In Webster's words we find a number of features that would later be found both in Parker's "Rights of Man" sermon and in Lincoln's Gettysburg Address. The most salient of these is perhaps the notion that America and its system of government are being tested. For Webster, America is the last best hope, and if America fails, then "popular governments must be pronounced impossible" (Bunker Hill, 77). Parker was not this exclusive, taking a more hopeful view in declaring that, in the worst case, "our truth shall not perish, even if we go down" (Rights of Man, 394). And it would seem that Lincoln followed Parker's lead.

Rather than limit himself to the democratic system of government existing in his own country, Lincoln generalizes—hoping "that government of the people, by the people, for the people shall not perish from the earth" (Gettysburg). It is difficult to divine from his final paragraph, however, whether he felt as Webster did: that if American democracy were to wither and die democracy itself would vanish from the face of the earth as a viable form of government. The president asks only "for us to be here dedicated to the great task remaining before us . . . that we here highly resolve that these dead shall not have died in vain; that this nation shall have a new birth of freedom" (Gettysburg). Determining Lincoln's precise thinking on the subject is further complicated by the fact mentioned earlier that only in the second draft of his speech does the word "this" appear preceding "government"; and in the "newspaper version," the plural "governments" is reported to have been used (possibly, according to Roy Basler, an error of transcription).[45] But if we draw our conclusions on the basis of Lincoln's final rendering of his speech, where "this" no longer precedes "government," his thinking would appear to lean toward the broader vision limned by Parker.

When Daniel Webster proclaims in his speech, "These are excitements to duty; but they are not suggestions of doubt" (Bunker Hill, 77), he and Theodore Parker seem quite close. For although the minister states unambiguously, "We shall not fail!" (Rights of Man, 394), it should be noted that in attempting to stir the faith of his congregation, he follows Webster in not categorically excluding the possibility of failure. Lincoln, too, avoids an unequivocal promise of success, while exhorting the members of his audience to clearly "resolve" to strive toward attaining the goals he sets for them. All three men draw attention as well to the responsibility the living need to assume in committing themselves to the cause of freedom, through honoring both the dead as well as those still alive who fought for the country. For Webster, the weight falls on "this generation"; Parker speaks of "this generation of Americans"; and Lincoln calls on "us the living."

In 1825, at the time he delivered his speech, Webster was conscious that the heroes of the American Revolution were becoming ever fewer, and he pointed this out to his listeners. Stressing the need for continued support of the ideals espoused by the founders, the senator urged his audience to accept the challenge: "Those who established our liberty and our government are daily dropping from among us. The great trust now descends to new hands. Let us apply ourselves to that which is presented to us, as our appropriate object" (Bunker Hill, 77). Thirteen years later, in his Lyceum speech, Lincoln too would refer to the heroes of the Revolution—by then even fewer—and also speak of their passing the torch of responsibility to their successors:

> They *were* a forest of strength; but, what invading foemen could *never do,* the silent artillery of time *has done;* . . . They *were* a forest of giant oaks; but the all-resistless hurricane has swept over them, and left only, here and there, a lonely trunk, despoiled of its verdure, shorn of its foliage; unshading and unshaded, to murmur in a few more gentle breezes, and to combat with its mutilated limbs, a few more ruder storms, then to sink, and be no more.
>
> They *were* the pillars of the temple of liberty; and now, that they have crumbled away, that temple must fall, unless we, their descendants, supply their places with other pillars, hewn from the solid quarry of sober reason. (Lyceum, 115)

Considering the powerful imagery with which Lincoln clothed this concept in 1838, it is not surprising to find him adopting a similar tone twenty-five years later in the Gettysburg Address, suggesting to his listeners that, "It is for us the living, rather, to be dedicated here to the unfinished work which they who fought here have thus far so nobly advanced."

Another revealing parallel between Webster, Lincoln, and Parker lies in their use of triple formulations at the close of their speeches. Evidently appreciating the power of such a construction to continue reverberating in the ears of listeners long after its actual delivery, Lincoln employed only one; Webster in this instance resorts to two. By substituting the word "country" for "truth" in the traditional law court oath administered to formal witnesses, the senator amplifies the force of his admonition to "Let our object be, OUR COUNTRY, OUR WHOLE COUNTRY, AND NOTHING BUT OUR COUNTRY. And by the blessing of

God, may that country itself become a vast and splendid monument, not of oppression and terror, but of Wisdom, of Peace, and of Liberty, upon which the world may gaze with admiration for ever!" (Bunker Hill, 78). Parker, on the other hand, is satisfied with less grandiloquence, utilizing simply three names ("a Luther, a Paul, a Jesus") rather than a series of prepositional phrases. It should not be forgotten, however, that he had employed such a series within the body of his sermon in speaking of democracy as "the government of all, by all, and for all," as had Webster, in his Reply to Hayne, in speaking of "the people's government, made for the people, made by the people, and answerable to the people" (Reply to Hayne, 321). Lincoln, in asking that "government of the people, by the people, for the people shall not perish from the earth," appears to profit from moderating Webster's orotund approach, while inclining toward Parker's taut phrasing.

In Webster's closing sentence he, like many other orators of the period, asks the "blessing of God" in the hope that the country may become a "vast and splendid monument." Lincoln, too, calls on God to grant the nation "a new birth of freedom." Parker, as might be expected of a man of the cloth, also invokes God near the end of his sermon, paralleling Webster in holding up for admiration a vision of what the republic can one day become: "We shall have a commonwealth based on righteousness, which is the strength of any people, and shall stand longer than Egypt,—national fidelity to God our age-outlasting pyramid!" (Rights of Man, 396). Still another correlation between Webster and Parker may be seen in their appealing to similar images of strength: Webster to the country as a "monument"; Parker to God as a "pyramid." In all three speeches, references can also be found to "our fathers." In addition, Webster speaks of a "noble pursuit," Parker inspires his listeners with the courage of "nobler" and "noblest" biblical figures, and Lincoln employs the word "noble" in adverbial form in "so nobly advanced."

Of more profound significance is Webster's assertion that "We can win no laurels in a war for independence. Earlier and worthier hands have gathered them all. Nor are there places for us by the side of Solon, and Alfred, and other founders of states. Our fathers have filled them" (Bunker Hill, 77). Lincoln, perhaps influenced by Webster's 1825 oration, had noted the same fact in his 1838 Lyceum speech, declaring that "This field of glory is harvested, and the crop is already appropriated." He nevertheless realized that "new reapers will arise, and *they,* too, will seek a field" (Lyceum, 113). On the occasions when Webster and Lincoln were expressing their views, the nation was under no threat to its existence, however, and whereas Webster saw the primary effort being to maintain continuity, Lincoln questioned whether "gratification" for those "reapers" possessed of "Towering genius" could "be found in supporting and maintaining an edifice that has been erected by others?" (Lyceum, 114). A fresh war, on the other hand, created new possibilities for such "reapers" to achieve recognition, and in a measure satisfactory to them.

Thus, one might well ask whether this concept was perhaps lurking somewhere in Lincoln's consciousness as he wrote the words "this nation shall have a new birth of freedom." For although Webster at Bunker Hill and Lincoln in the Lyceum speech had spoken during periods of peace, the civil war in which Lincoln and the country were currently engaged did, in fact, present the chance to win new "laurels" in the cause of freedom. A "new birth of freedom" offered those who would be privileged to serve as midwives to it the chance to win glory equivalent to that earned by the patriots of the American Revolution. Lincoln could therefore have conceivably drawn the conclusion that the dawning of this new day promised the kinds of opportunities necessary to "gratifying" the hungers of new "reapers." A democratic form of government had to be preserved, of course, but there were clear advantages to having the "nation" born anew.

In this connection, as in so many others, Theodore Parker seems to have added a critical dimension to Webster's concept that could appeal to and warrant adoption by Lincoln. In speaking, as had Webster, of the grandeur of the nation's "fathers" and their glorious achievements, the minister goes farther than the senator and points the way to future potential, as would Lincoln after him. Where Lincoln speaks of a "new birth of freedom," Parker speaks of a new awakening, a return to nobleness of purpose: "Did our fathers live? are we dead? Even in our ashes live their holy fires! Boston only sleeps; one day she will wake! Massachusetts will stir again! New England will rise and walk! the vanished North be found once more queenly and majestic!" (Rights of Man, 395). Parker, whose grandfather had commanded the Minutemen at the battle of Lexington, understandably places high hopes in the North, whereas both Webster and Lincoln include the entire country in their vision. On the other hand, Webster saw the role of his generation as "a great duty of defence and preservation," maintaining that "Our proper business is improvement" and desiring that "we also, in our day and generation, may . . . perform something worthy to be remembered" (Bunker Hill, 78). For Webster the goal is maintaining and improving the status quo. For Parker, and later Lincoln, a return to the ideals of the founding fathers was considered necessary, to be sure, but not only for the purpose of "defence and preservation."

Seeking guidance with regard to the future, Parker and Lincoln were harking back to the fathers as the best source of direction in confronting the unknown. Faced in their day with what each saw as an untenable situation requiring a major alteration, it was a reawakening or even a rebirth of the founders' original concepts that they felt was called for. Lincoln, like Webster, accorded the founding fathers full honor and respect. But when attempting to penetrate the cold fog of the present in seeking a path to a more clement future, it was to Parker's perception of the importance of a reawakening to the vision of the founders that he turned. It was from this direction and from above this horizon that the requisite rays of hope promised to dawn, and from their warmth that rejuvenating sustenance could potentially be drawn.

Conclusion

❧ On April 14, 1876, at the unveiling in Washington, D.C, of the Freedman's Monument honoring Abraham Lincoln, the ex-slave and abolitionist Frederick Douglass declared:

> Any man can say things that are true of Abraham Lincoln, but no man can say anything that is new of Abraham Lincoln. His personal traits and public acts are better known to the American people than are those of any other man of his age. He was a mystery to no man who saw him and heard him. Though high in position, the humblest could approach him and feel at home in his presence. Though deep, he was transparent; though strong, he was gentle; though decided and pronounced in his convictions, he was tolerant towards those who differed from him, and patient under reproaches. Even those who only knew him through his public utterances obtained a tolerably clear idea of his character and his personality. The image of the man went out with his words, and those who read them, knew him.[1]

Lincoln's words, in Douglass's view, enable us to know much about the thinking and spirit of the sixteenth American president, and this heritage is what succeeding generations have often appealed to when striving, like him, to peer into the future. Just as Lincoln turned to the documents of the founders for guidance, we often turn to the words of Abraham Lincoln. To discover a hitherto almost unremarked source for concepts and language embodied in two of the railsplitter's landmark speeches therefore offers not only the unusual privilege of saying something "that is new of Abraham Lincoln" but also represents a gift of major significance, since it makes possible the exploration of unfathomed dimensions of the mind of a figure central to American political thought. That this opportunity is furnished by the work of an abolitionist clergyman unfolds an exceptional vista with respect to Lincoln's deepest reflections on and moral commitment to ridding the American continent of the scourge of slavery. But that another dedicated abolitionist, a man of the stature of Frederick Douglass, deemed Lincoln "a mystery to no man" and even "transparent" betrays the fact that Lincoln was far less obvious in his approach to resolving the slavery issue than Douglass or anyone else was permitted to perceive.

Inadvertently aiding Lincoln in maintaining an illusion of transparency, as well as in maintaining the strategic secret of his debt to Theodore Parker's "Sermon of the Dangers which Threaten the Rights of Man in America," is William Herndon's categorical account of the origin of the Gettysburg Phrase, an account that seems to have unintentionally diverted most historians from examining the possibility of wider influence by Parker on Lincoln's Gettysburg Address. In an analogous fashion, Herndon's mention of Daniel Webster's Reply to Hayne in connection with Lincoln's House Divided speech has ostensibly prevented those same historians from perceiving that Parker might have had anything to do with Lincoln's thinking or writing on that occasion as well. Nor did Joseph Fort Newton's injudicious editing of the Herndon-Parker letters help matters.

In spite of such stumbling blocks, it now should be apparent that the writings of Parker, Webster, and Lincoln reveal undeniable parallels, which range well beyond questions coupled only with the Gettysburg Phrase. These parallels go deepest between Parker and Lincoln, connecting the two men and their thinking at many levels. Yet Webster's influence on Lincoln's two speeches is also indisputable, though noticeably less extensive and profound than that of Parker. Lincoln plainly was aware of and conversant with Webster's writings, obviously admired the famous senator's use of language and rhetoric, and displayed evidence of that admiration in several key speeches. Parker, moreover, as both an admirer and a reviler of Webster was well positioned, through his use of Webster's concepts and language, to reinforce aspects of the senator's influence on Lincoln.

But Parker's importance to Lincoln was not confined to serving merely as an intermediary for Webster's language and notions. It rested far more on the fact that the minister formulated ideas and insights in a manner to which Lincoln could relate, and that shared views, values, and personal qualities linked the two men in more ways than have generally been understood. With regard to the central issue of slavery, for instance, there are indications that, although Herndon's claim that Lincoln was "our abolition leader" would appear overstated and that the Great Emancipator gave the impression of backing only slowly and haltingly toward emancipation, Lincoln was never deaf to abolitionist voices. Douglass perceived Lincoln's position in the following manner: "Viewed from the genuine abolition ground, Mr. Lincoln seemed tardy, cold, dull, and indifferent; but measuring him by the sentiment of his country, a sentiment he was bound as a statesman to consult, he was swift, zealous, radical, and determined."[2] Lincoln's political savvy, yoked to his personal sense of justice, could not, it seems, permit him to ignore abolitionist voices any more than he could ignore the slaveholder's voice speaking to him through his friend Joshua Speed. And because the voice of Theodore Parker—as heard, for example, in the monumental "Sermon of the Dangers which Threaten the Rights of Man in America"—was continually being relayed to him through Herndon, the possibility of Parker's thinking on the slavery question being reflected in Lincoln's own was far greater than has often been assumed.

Even after Parker's demise in 1860, and even after Lincoln had left Herndon behind in Illinois to move on to Washington and the presidency, echoes of the minister's voice were not to be stilled. Men Parker had long encouraged and influenced such as Senator Charles Sumner and Secretary of State William Seward were present on the national stage, near the country's leader, and could continue to champion his ideas. Just how much the preacher's voice ultimately meant to Lincoln can never be measured in numbers or statistics, but the fact that there were many more decibels sounding in Lincoln's ears than have previously been evident should give historians pause. This should in addition create a challenge to reopen inquiry into the significance of Theodore Parker to the critical period of American history during which he was a conscientiously committed and commanding presence.

What this presence meant to the slave can be gathered from words penned by Douglass following a visit to Parker's grave in Florence, Italy:

> The brave stand taken by Theodore Parker during the antislavery conflict endeared him to my heart, and naturally enough the spot made sacred by his ashes was the first to draw me to its side. He had a voice for the slave when nearly all the pulpits of the land were dumb. . . . It was in his pulpit that I made my first antislavery speech in Roxbury. That its doors opened to me in that dark period was due to him. . . . His character was cast in a mold too large to be pressed

> into a form or reform less broad than humanity. He would shed his blood as quickly for a black fugitive slave pursued by human hounds as for a white President of the United States. He was the friend of the non-voting and non-resistant class of abolitionists, but not less the friend of Henry Wilson, Charles Sumner, Gerrit Smith, and John Brown. He was the large and generous brother of all men, honestly endeavoring to bring about the abolition of Negro slavery.[3]

Considering Douglass's admiration for a minister known at the time as the Great American Preacher, it is not surprising that Herndon would seek to share the wisdom and idealism of such a man and would press upon his partner what he felt he had gleaned. Nor should we any longer find it difficult to comprehend why Lincoln might weigh and subsequently adopt from Parker whatever he believed could help him in his struggle to discover a moral way of delivering America from an immoral institution. That Lincoln absorbed far more than the Gettysburg Phrase should now be clear. How much more is nevertheless difficult to determine. Who can be certain, for example, that on the day Lincoln uttered the now famous phrase at Gettysburg he was not looking forward to the all-encompassing freedom for America's slaves that Parker and other abolitionists had struggled so long to achieve?

For linked with the "new birth of freedom" Lincoln called for on that occasion is the distinct possibility that, many months following the carefully circumscribed Emancipation Proclamation, the president was envisioning the United States' being reborn in what he saw as Thomas Jefferson's broad conception of a land where indeed all—including slaves, and regardless of skin color—were to be considered human, and therefore "created equal." In this sense the entire country required a rebirth, and it was altogether reasonable for the president to accent the idea by employing the word "new." In using this word Lincoln may also have been looking further, looking toward completing the emancipation process he had essentially only initiated with the Proclamation. By emphasizing the equality of "all men," interpreting that equality in a manner Stephen Douglas could never have sanctioned, and asking for a "new birth" of a freedom the slaves had never enjoyed, Abraham Lincoln can be seen as nudging the nation in the direction of a far more comprehensive notion of emancipation than he had delineated in the Proclamation. Viewed from this perspective it is not beyond imagining that the president was looking ahead toward the day when life, at long last, could be breathed into the spirit of Jefferson's original but still unrealized dream: the dream Daniel Webster held high in his Bunker Hill speech; the dream to which Theodore Parker made such a powerful appeal in his "Rights of Man" sermon; the dream to which Lincoln himself was turning at that moment for moral and spiritual support in his Gettysburg Address.

❧ To understand this is to distinguish but one of many possible reverberations resulting from a realization of Abraham Lincoln's strong yet hitherto well-concealed connection to Theodore Parker. Another reverberation might be found in Lincoln's familiarity with Parker's religious notions, which could have disposed Lincoln to perceive the major issues of his day more from the minister's slant than from the analytical and unimpassioned perspective promoted in the Lyceum speech back in 1838. For the man some fondly referred to as Father Abraham was faced in the final decade of his life with personal as well as public stress of major proportions and was perhaps more susceptible to Parker's spiritual support during that period than has generally been recognized.[4]

The minister's emphasis on a humanity common to all could therefore have had a bearing on the humane approach Lincoln took toward the burdensome problems he faced in the final decade of his life. That the dilemma of dealing with the slavery issue benefited from those humane considerations is only too evident; and that Lincoln, however hesitantly, finally aligned himself with Parker's basic position is undeniable. Emancipation on the basis of human equality would nevertheless remain a distasteful notion to many, and not only to Southerners; but Abraham Lincoln finally found it the only road open to him. When he did, he was aided by the fact that Theodore Parker had already cleared a path and left guiding markers. How much Parker's work meant to Lincoln in his struggles is made clear by evidence discernible in the House Divided speech and Gettysburg Address, revealing that the aid received from Parker went well beyond what Webster could provide on those occasions. Hence, as we reorient our thinking with regard to the Great Emancipator's deeper attitudes toward such subjects as abolitionism, political philosophy, practical religion, and the future of America, we need to reevaluate Parker's role with regard to the creative process that engendered Lincoln's vision. For such an undertaking holds out the promise of illuminating and ultimately reconfiguring our perception of the man whose commitment to reuniting a "house" divided by the issue of slavery led inexorably to Gettysburg.

Notes

INTRODUCTION

1. William Safire, "Faithful, Even in Death," *New York Times Magazine,* April 18, 1999, pp. 72–73; Garry Wills, *Lincoln at Gettysburg: The Words that Remade America* (New York: Simon and Schuster, 1992), 40. The significance of the speech for the American people is indicated by the fact that the copy housed in the Library of Congress was singled out a few years ago as one of the key documents to be evacuated by helicopter to a secret safe haven in case of nuclear war. Ted Gup, "Grab that Leonardo," *Time,* August 10, 1992, p. 37.

2. The William H. Herndon–Theodore Parker Correspondence (henceforth HP) is located in the Illinois State Historical Library in Springfield, Illinois.

3. William H. Herndon and Jesse W. Weik, *Herndon's Life of Lincoln: The History and Personal Recollections of Abraham Lincoln as Originally Written by William H. Herndon and Jesse W. Weik,* with a newly revised introduction and notes by Paul M. Angle (1930; Greenwich, Conn.: Fawcett Publications, 1961), 294, 295. For the purposes of this study I shall refer to this edition and not the original three-volume edition, which is not readily available.

4. Abraham Lincoln, "Address at Cooper Institute, New York City," February 27, 1860, in *The Collected Works of Abraham Lincoln,* ed. Roy P. Basler with assistant editors Marion Dolores Pratt and Lloyd A. Dunlap, 9 vols. (New Brunswick, N.J.: Rutgers University Press, 1953), 3:538. Basler's work will be referred to hereafter as Lincoln, *CW.*

5. Herndon and Weik, *Herndon's Life of Lincoln,* 321; Wills, *Lincoln at Gettysburg.* See, in particular, chapter 3, "The Transcendental Declaration," 90–120.

6. Theodore Parker, "A Sermon of the Dangers which Threaten the Rights of Man in America," in *The Works of Theodore Parker,* centenary edition, 15 vols. (Boston: American Unitarian Association, 1907–1911 [henceforth *Works*]), 12:333–96. Further references to this sermon will be cited parenthetically within the text.

7. The version used here is the so-called Bliss copy. According to David C. Mearns and Lloyd A. Dunlap, "it represents Lincoln's last-known revision . . . [and] has become accepted as the standard text . . . . The Bliss

copy is the only one dated and signed by President Lincoln." See *Long Remembered: Facsimiles of the Five Versions of the Gettysburg Address in the Handwriting of Abraham Lincoln,* with notes and comments on the preparation of the address by Mearns and Dunlap (Washington: The Library of Congress, 1963), no page numbering.

8. In their famous debate, Webster replied twice to Hayne's arguments. The first response was delivered on January 20, 1830. The second was delivered on January 26, 1830. It is this second reply, Daniel Webster, "Second Speech on Foot's Resolution," in *The Works of Daniel Webster* (Boston: Little Brown, 1853), vol. 3, that is the most acclaimed, and it is usually referred to simply as "Webster's Reply to Hayne." I shall follow this tradition throughout my work.

9. Wills, *Lincoln at Gettysburg,* 127. Wills's reference (285n. 12) is the following: "Herndon-Weik, pp. 327, 386. Hertz, p. 118." The edition of the Herndon-Weik biography used by Wills is "the Paul M. Angle edition for Da Capo (1942)." The other reference is to Emanuel Hertz, *The Hidden Lincoln: From the Letters and Papers of William H. Herndon* (New York: Viking, 1938).

10. Wills, *Lincoln at Gettysburg,* 127.

11. Although Parker visited Herndon in Springfield, Illinois, in the fall of 1856, there is no evidence he came in contact with Lincoln, whose enemies would have taken full political advantage of finding him in the presence of a well-known abolitionist. It can be assumed that Lincoln and Herndon were fully cognizant of that danger.

12. Thomas Wentworth Higginson, "Theodore Parker," in *Contemporaries* (Boston: Houghton Mifflin, 1899), 38.

13. John Weiss, *Life and Correspondence of Theodore Parker,* 2 vols. (New York: D. Appleton, 1864), 2:99–102.

14. Albert J. Von Frank (the only author to my knowledge to do so) notes the appearance in Parker's "Rights of Man" sermon of the phrases "a house divided against itself" and "government of all, by all, for all," pointing out that "Lincoln must have paid special attention to this sermon." *The Trials of Anthony Burns: Freedom and Slavery in Emerson's Boston* (Cambridge, Mass.: Harvard University Press, 1998), 365n. 4. Frank does not, however, explore any wider implications of this fact.

15. Jefferson made his position quite clear in 1785 in *Notes on the State of Virginia,* in *Basic Writings of Thomas Jefferson,* ed. Philip S. Foner (New York: Halcyon House, 1944), where he proposed to

> emancipate all slaves born after passing the act . . . and further directing, that they should continue with their parents to a certain age, then be brought up, at the public expence, to tillage, arts, or sciences, according to their geniusses, till the females should be eighteen, and the males twenty-one years of age, when they should be colonized to such place as the circumstances of the

> time should render most proper, sending them out with arms, domestic animals, &c. to declare them a free and independant people, and extend to them our alliance and protection till they shall have acquired strength. (144)

For Henry Clay, see George M. Fredrickson, "A Man but Not a Brother: Abraham Lincoln and Racial Equality," *The Journal of Southern History* 41, no. 1 (February 1975): 40–55.

16. Lincoln, "Eulogy on Henry Clay," *CW* 2:130–32.

17. Lincoln to Albert G. Hodges, April 4, 1864, in *CW* 7:281. In "Autobiography Written for John L. Scripps," circa June 1860, Lincoln also recalls that his father moved from Kentucky to Indiana in 1816, "A. then being in his eigth [*sic*] year. This removal was partly on account of slavery; but chiefly on account of land titles in Kentucky" (*CW* 4:61–62).

18. Lincoln to Hodges, *CW* 7:281.

19. See James M. McPherson, *Abraham Lincoln and the Second American Revolution* (New York: Oxford University Press, 1991), 29–37; and LaWanda Cox, "Lincoln and Black Freedom," in *The Historian's Lincoln: Pseudohistory, Psychohistory, and History,* ed. Gabor S. Boritt and Norman A. Fornes (Urbana and Chicago: University of Illinois Press, 1988), 178–85.

20. See Wills, *Lincoln at Gettysburg.*

21. As George P. Fletcher points out, "The word count differs, depending on the draft used and the way of counting such words as 'battle-field'." *Our Secret Constitution: How Lincoln Redefined American Democracy* (Oxford: Oxford University Press, 2001), 264n. 20. Fletcher's own count is 268.

22. J. David Greenstone, *The Lincoln Persuasion: Remaking American Liberalism* (Princeton, N.J.: Princeton University Press, 1993), 263, 265.

23. See, for example, Richard N. Current, "Lincoln and Daniel Webster," *Journal of the Illinois State Historical Society* 48 (1955): 319–20; Wills, *Lincoln at Gettysburg,* 122–32.

CHAPTER 1

1. Lincoln, *CW* 1:420–22.

2. Lincoln, "The War with Mexico," *CW* 1:431–42.

3. Herndon to Weik, October 28, 1885, in the Herndon-Weik Collection, Library of Congress. This collection will subsequently be referred to as HW.

4. At Alton, Illinois, on October 15, 1858, for instance, Douglas declared that when "the American army was surrounded by the enemy in Mexico, he [Lincoln] thought that war was unconstitutional, unnecessary and unjust. ('That's so,' 'you've got him,' 'he voted against it,' &c.) He thought it was not commenced on the right *spot.* (Laughter.)" Cited in Lincoln, *CW* 3:319. For Lincoln's nickname see David Donald, *Lincoln* (New York: Simon and Schuster, 1995), 128.

5. Lincoln to Herndon, February 1, 1848, *CW* 1:446–48.

6. Lincoln to Williamson Durley, Springfield, October 3, 1845, *CW* 1:347.

7. Lincoln, "What General Taylor Ought to Say," (March?) 1848, *CW* 1:454.

8. Lincoln, "Gen: Taylor and the Veto," *CW* 1:505.

9. Stephen B. Oates, *Abraham Lincoln: The Man Behind the Myths* (New York: Meridian, 1985), 61.

10. Lincoln to Hodges, *CW* 7:282.

11. "Theodore Parker's Experience as a Minister," April 19, 1859, in Weiss, *Life and Correspondence,* 2:466.

12. Julia Ward Howe, *Reminiscences of Julia Ward Howe* (Boston: Houghton Mifflin, 1899), 166.

13. Parker, "A Sermon on War," in *Works,* 9:323.

14. Parker, "The Mexican War," in *Works,* 11:21 (taken from the *Liberator* article of February 19, 1847), 28.

15. Jefferson, *Notes,* 160.

16. All references to the William H. Herndon–Theodore Parker Correspondence (HP) will be by date.

17. Herndon and Weik, *Herndon's Life of Lincoln,* 295.

18. Herndon to Weik, October 28, 1885, HW.

19. Lincoln, "Autobiography" included with letter to Jesse W. Fell, December 20, 1859, *CW* 3:512.

20. See Vincent C. Hopkins, *Dred Scott's Case* (New York: Fordham University Press, 1951).

21. Oscar Sherwin, *Prophet of Liberty: The Life and Times of Wendell Phillips* (New York: Bookman, 1958), 223.

22. Herndon to Weik, October 28, 1885, HW.

23. Another whose position may have been noted by Lincoln is Edward Coles, the second governor of Illinois, who had left his home state of Virginia in order to more easily liberate his own slaves. Coles later worked within the American Colonization Society to promote the return to Liberia of America's blacks but, despite his commitment, never managed to convince even one of his former bondsmen to return to Africa or, indeed, to accept a subsidized visit for the purpose of writing a report on prevailing conditions. See Drew R. McCoy, *The Last of the Fathers: James Madison and the Republican Legacy* (Cambridge, England: Cambridge University Press, 1989), 312–17. Coles also failed to persuade James Madison to free his own slaves (318–19) and was unable to induce Thomas Jefferson to head a wider slave-liberation movement. See Thomas Jefferson to Edward Coles, August 25, 1814, in Thomas Jefferson, *Writings* (New York: Library of America, 1984), 1343–46.

24. Parker, "An Anti-Slavery Address," in *Works,* 12:162–63.

25. Lincoln, "Speech at Springfield, Illinois," October 4, 1854, in *CW* 2:245–46.

26. Lincoln, "Speech at Peoria, Illinois," October 16, 1854, *CW* 2:265.

27. Herndon to Weik, October 28, 1885, HW.

28. Herndon and Weik, *Herndon's Life of Lincoln,* 295, 294 (quote).

29. Joseph Fort Newton, *Lincoln and Herndon* (Cedar Rapids, Iowa: Torch Press, 1910), 114. References in the text to letters included in Newton's work will be by date rather than by page number.

30. Herndon and Weik, *Herndon's Life of Lincoln,* 299.

31. Lincoln, *CW* 2:435–36.

32. *Bureau County Republican* (no date) "Extra," containing "Remarks of Mr. Lovejoy on receiving the Nomination at the Convention Held at Joliet, June 30th," as quoted in Edward Magdol, *Owen Lovejoy: Abolitionist in Congress* (New Brunswick, N.J.: Rutgers University Press, 1967), 204.

33. Lincoln, *CW* 7:366.

34. Sherwin, *Prophet of Liberty,* 58–72.

35. Herndon and Weik, *Herndon's Life of Lincoln,* 172.

36. Lincoln, "Address Before the Young Men's Lyceum of Springfield, Illinois," *CW* 1:108–15. All subsequent quotes from this speech are taken from here and will be cited parenthetically in the text.

37. I leave to psychobiographers the question as to whether Lincoln was referring to his own ambition here. Michael Burlingame finds "It is hard to know what to make of this curious remark" but presents an interesting case for the possibility that "Lincoln aimed his barbs about Caesarism at Stephen A. Douglas, who was running for Congress against Lincoln's law partner, friend, and mentor, John T. Stuart." *The Inner World of Abraham Lincoln* (Urbana: University of Illinois Press, 1994), 26, 365–68.

38. James Hurt, "All the Living and the Dead: Lincoln's Imagery," *American Literature* 52.3 (November 1980): 367.

39. Lincoln, *CW* 1:75.

40. In 1841 Lincoln argued against the sale of a free black woman in the case of *Bailey v. Cromwell* before the Illinois Supreme Court and won; but in 1847 he lost a more complex case in which Robert Matson was attempting to recover slaves he had brought into Illinois. Donald, *Lincoln,* 103, 104 (quote).

41. Lincoln made the claim in his "Speech at Peoria" (*CW* 2:252), and on August 24, 1855, in a private letter to his slaveholding friend Joshua F. Speed (*CW* 2:323). Albert J. Beveridge in *Abraham Lincoln: 1809–1858* (London: Victor Gollancz, 1928), 1:480, claims that the first occurrence was campaign exaggeration.

42. Donald, *Lincoln,* 135–37.

43. Lincoln, *CW* 1:75.

44. Donald, *Lincoln,* 135–37; Lincoln, *CW* 2:20n. 3 (quote).

45. See Lincoln, *CW* 2:22n. 4.

46. "A Beacon: Freeing the Slaves in U.S. Capitol," *International Herald Tribune,* April 13, 2000, p. 3.

47. Lincoln, *CW* 5:192.

48. Douglas L. Wilson and Rodney O. Davis, *Herndon's Informants:*

Letters, Interviews, and Statements about Abraham Lincoln (Urbana: University of Illinois Press, 1998), 64. Herndon's quotation marks seem somewhat misleading here, but Lincoln's words are evidently meant to begin with the word "When."

49. Donald, *Lincoln,* 120.

50. Herndon and Weik, *Herndon's Life of Lincoln,* 321.

51. Henry Steele Commager, *Theodore Parker: Yankee Crusader* (1937; Boston: Beacon Press, 1960), 330.

52. Donald, *Lincoln,* 461.

53. Exceptions to the rule do exist. Don E. Fehrenbacher, for example, is skeptical of Herndon as a "psychobiographer"; as a secondary source for information on "Lincoln's childhood, youth, and early manhood"; and as someone who in later years could "confuse what he remembered with what he had conjectured and with gossip that he had heard." But Fehrenbacher acknowledges that the "recollections . . . he recorded in the Herndon-Weik biography and in hundreds of letters written between 1865 and 1891 constitute a primary source for the entire twenty-four years of Lincoln's residence in Springfield—the period of his legal career and of his political rise from the state legislature to the presidency." *Lincoln in Text and Context: Collected Essays* (Stanford: Stanford University Press, 1987), 216. David Donald, in *Lincoln's Herndon: A Biography* (1948; New York: Da Capo Press, 1989), 301, submits that

> Sometimes Herndon's ambiguity was the result of his painful effort to arrive at a balanced judgment. Sometimes he sent his friends a hasty judgment which he later corrected. In any case, the result is a queer hodgepodge of fact and fancy. . . . Events which he himself had witnessed Herndon still remembered distinctly. He could, of course, make mistakes. After thirty years he sometimes confused names, dates, and places. But when one allows for an old man's garrulity, it must be admitted that Herndon's recollection of men whom he had known and of events in which he himself participated remained startlingly accurate.

54. Newton, *Lincoln and Herndon,* 155n. 1.

55. Convers Francis to Theodore Parker, July 7, 1842, in Letterbook 12:161, Theodore Parker Papers, Massachusetts Historical Society. Following Parker's death much of his correspondence was transcribed into what are known as letterbooks, now in the possession of the Massachusetts Historical Society (hereafter MHS). Subsequent references to such transcribed letters will be to Letterbook, followed by volume and page number.

56. Parker to James Freeman Clarke, April 8, 1845 (shelf mark bMS Am 1569.7 [479]), Clarke Papers, by permission of the Houghton Library, Harvard University.

57. James Russell Lowell to Parker, July 28, 1848, quoted in Horace

E. Scudder, *James Russell Lowell, a Biography* (Boston: Houghton Mifflin, 1901), 1:288.

58. Newton, *Lincoln and Herndon,* 124.

CHAPTER 2

1. Herndon and Weik, *Herndon's Life of Lincoln,* 294–95.

2. Ibid., 322–24.

3. Herndon to Weik, October 29, 1885, HW.

4. Donald, *Lincoln's Herndon,* 119.

5. David Zarefsky, *Lincoln, Douglas and Slavery: In the Crucible of Public Debate* (Chicago: University of Chicago Press, 1990), 211.

6. John Armstrong, WHH interview, February 1870, in Wilson and Davis, *Herndon's Informants,* 575.

7. See Donald, *Lincoln's Herndon,* 119n. 32; Armstrong, in Wilson and Davis, *Herndon's Informants,* 574–75.

8. William Jayne, *Abraham Lincoln: Personal Reminiscences of the Martyred President* (Chicago: Grand Army Hall and Memorial Association, 1900).

9. Herndon to Parker, June 18, 1858, HP. Newton cites only the third sentence of this note.

10. Herndon to Parker, July 8, 24, 1858, HP.

11. Herndon to Parker, August 31, 1858; Parker to Herndon, August 28, 1858; Herndon to Parker, November 23, 1858, HP.

12. Herndon to Weik, October 29, 1885, HW.

13. Herndon to Weik, January 1, 1886, HW.

14. Wills, *Lincoln at Gettysburg,* 107.

15. Herndon and Weik, *Herndon's Life of Lincoln,* 321.

16. Newton, *Lincoln and Herndon,* 155.

17. Weiss, *Life and Correspondence,* 2:71.

18. Theodore Parker, *A False and True Revival of Religion: A Sermon, Delivered at Music Hall, Boston, on Sunday, April 4, 1858* (Boston: William L. Kent, 1858).

19. Parker to Hale, April 24, 1858, Letterbook 7:57.

20. Theodore Parker, *The Effect of Slavery on the American People: A Sermon Preached at the Music Hall, Boston, on Sunday, July 4, 1858* (Boston: William L. Kent, 1858), 5.

21. Ibid., 14.

22. "Several writers" include John White Chadwick, *Theodore Parker: Preacher and Reformer* (Boston and New York: Houghton Mifflin, 1900), 322–23; William E. Barton, *Lincoln at Gettysburg* (Indianapolis: Bobbs-Merrill, 1930), 135–36; and Wills, *Lincoln at Gettysburg,* 281. See Parker's sermons "The Slave Power" in 1850 for "a democracy, that is, a government of all the people, by all the people, for all the people" (*Works,* 11:250); "The Progress of America" in 1854 for "government is to be of all the people, by

all the people, and for all the people" (12:214); and "The Present Crisis in American Affairs" in 1856 for "By Democracy I mean a Government over all the people, by all the people, and for the sake of all" (12:436).

23. Parker to Samuel J. May, November 13, 1846, Letterbook 5:137–41. Portions of the letter containing the citation are also to be found in Weiss, *Life and Correspondence,* 1:319, 355–56.

24. Theodore Parker, "Letter to the People of the United States Touching the Matter of Slavery," in *Works,* 11:89 (see p. 390n. concerning its publication). Parker had been thinking about this "Letter" since at least July 15, 1846, when he mentioned in a missive to Samuel J. May, "I have long been intending to write an anonymous 'Letter to the American People touching the Matter of Slavery, by One of the Million.'" Weiss, *Life and Correspondence,* 1:319.

25. Armstrong, in Wilson and Davis, *Herndon's Informants,* 574–75.

26. Ibid., 574n. 1.

27. William Herndon to Ward Hill Lamon, February 25, 1870, quoted from the Ward Hill Lamon Papers, LN 367. This item is reproduced by permission of the Henry E. Huntington Library, San Marino, California. My own research supports Wilson and Davis, who decipher Herndon's handwriting as referring to "Jno Armstrong," thereby rectifying Emanuel Hertz's mistaken reading of the script as "Mrs. Armstrong." Emanuel Hertz, ed., *The Hidden Lincoln: From the Letters and Papers of William H. Herndon* (New York: Viking Press, 1938), 62.

28. Wilson and Davis, *Herndon's Informants,* 574n. 1. Herndon, for instance, quotes exactly from the following two stories (ibid., 575), although he shortens them:

> Mr Lincoln sat still a short moment—rose from his chair—walked backwards & forwards in the Hall—stopt & said—"Friends: I have thought about this matter a great deal—have weighed the question well from all corners; and am thoroughly Convinced the time has come when it should be uttered & if it must be that I must go down because of this speech then let me go down linked to truth—die in the advocacy of what is right & just. This nation cannot live on injustice—a house divided against itself cannot stand &c I say again & again."

> In a few days after the speech had been delivered a gentleman—Doct Long, came into Lincoln's office and said—"well, Lincoln that foolish speech of yours will kill you—will defeat you in this Contest—and probably for all offices for all time to come—am sorry—very sorry. I wish it was wiped out of existence—Don't you now wish so." Mr Lincoln was intently writing while the Doct was loudly lamenting. Lincoln stopped—raised up his spectacles—put the pen down—looked at the Doct one Moment with a peculiar look of insulted dignity—sorrow for a timid soul, & contempt of his weakness—Said—"well Doct—, If I had to draw a pen across and erase my whole life

> from Existence & all I did; and I had one poor gift or choice left, as to what I should Save from the wreck, I should choose that speech and leave it to the world unerased."

29. Newton omits the first sentence and, in a complete misreading, understands "paying me for what I send" as "praising me for what I said." Parker to Herndon, July 1, 1858, HP.

30. Herndon to Parker, August 23, 1858; Parker to Herndon, September 23, 1858, HP.

31. Herndon to Parker, February 20, 1858, HP. (This paragraph is omitted by Newton.) Parker was battling tuberculosis ("that old cat" as he called it), the disease that would ultimately prove fatal to him.

32. Herndon to Parker, July 24, 1858, HP.

33. Theodore Parker, "The Effect of Slavery on the American People," in *Saint Bernard and Other Papers,* ed. with notes by Charles W. Wendte, in *Works,* 14:332, 345 (last two quotations).

34. Herndon, "Abraham Lincoln's Religion," letter of February 18, 1870, to Mr. Abbott in *The Index* 1, no. 14, April 2, 1870, p. 5.

35. Herndon to Parker, December 27, 1856, HP.

36. Herndon and Weik, *Herndon's Life of Lincoln,* 352. A transcription of the complete letter, devoid of Herndon's minor changes, may be found in Wilson and Davis, *Herndon's Informants,* 578–80. A slightly different copy of Fell's letter, which from an examination of the handwriting appears to have been written out by a secretary but emended by Fell, is also located in the Jeremiah Sullivan Black papers in the Library of Congress. The date on that copy is September 26, 1870.

37. Fell to Herndon, September 20, 1870, in Wilson and Davis, *Herndon's Informants,* 578.

38. Herndon to Weik, December 29, 1885, HW.

39. Herndon to Parker, June 11, 1854, HP.

40. See Emerson's journal entry for January 31, 1862, in Ralph Waldo Emerson, *Journals of Ralph Waldo Emerson: 1856–1863,* ed. Edward Waldo Emerson and Waldo Emerson Forbes (Boston: Houghton Mifflin, 1913), 375–76.

41. Theodore Parker, "The Transient and Permanent in Christianity," in *Theodore Parker: An Anthology,* ed. with introduction and notes by Henry Steele Commager (Boston: Beacon Press, 1960), 48, 45, 48, 49. In the interest of accessibility I have chosen to quote here from Commager's easily available anthology rather than from his source: Theodore Parker, *The Collected Works of Theodore Parker,* ed. Frances Power Cobbe (London: Trübner, 1863–1876), 8:1 ff. For a discussion of the problems bearing on the publishing of the text in Parker's day, and a version of the text that incorporates many changes Parker made to the manuscript, see Philip F. Gura, "Theodore Parker and the South Boston Ordination: The Textual

Tangle of *A Discourse on the Transient and Permanent in Christianity," Studies in the American Renaissance,* ed. Joel Myerson (Charlottesville: University Press of Virginia, 1988), 149–78.

42. In a "Handbill Replying to Charges of Infidelity" sent "To the Voters of the Seventh Congressional District" on July 31, 1846, Lincoln defended himself against "infidelity," pointing out "That I am not a member of any Christian Church, is true: but I have never denied the truth of the Scriptures; and I have never spoken with intentional disrespect of religion in general, or of any denomination of Christians in particular" (*CW* 1:382). He did not, it should be noted, assert divine origin for the Scriptures.

43. Parker, "The Transient and Permanent in Christianity," 58–59, 56, 57.

44. For Lincoln, see Allen C. Guelzo, *Abraham Lincoln: Redeemer President* (Grand Rapids, Mich.: William B. Eerdmans, 1999), 149–60.

45. Lincoln, "Reply to Emancipation Memorial Presented by Chicago Christians of All Denominations," September 13, 1862, in *CW* 5:420.

46. See Harry V. Jaffa, *A New Birth of Freedom: Abraham Lincoln and the Coming of the Civil War* (Lanham, Md.: Rowman and Littlefield, 2000), 403.

47. Donald, *Lincoln's Herndon,* 55.

48. Newton, *Lincoln and Herndon,* 98.

49. The note is in Herndon's handwriting but was apparently signed by Post and bears the date November 11, 1856.

50. Parker to Herndon, November 17, 1856, HP.

51. See, for example, Herndon to Parker, June 17, July 4, 29, 1857, also February 24, April 7, 1858, HP.

52. Herndon to Parker, December 27, 1856, HP. Newton, in this instance, seriously muffles the intensity of Herndon's vexation by deleting from the quotation the lawyer's description of annoyance with and flight from Parker's implied criticism, revealed in the lines beginning with "This may" and ending with "situation."

53. Herndon to Weik, December 23, 1885, HW.

54. Herndon and Weik, *Herndon's Life of Lincoln,* 319.

55. Herndon to Weik, December 23, 1885, HW.

56. Herndon to Lincoln, March 24, 1858, in Herndon and Weik, *Herndon's Life of Lincoln,* 320.

57. Herndon to Weik, December 23, 1885, HW.

58. Herndon to Parker, May 29, 1858, HP.

59. Ibid.

60. Herndon to Parker, April 7, 1858, HP.

61. Ibid.

62. Herndon to Weik, December 23, 1885, HW.

63. Herndon to Parker, June 1, 1858, HP.

64. Herndon to Lydia Parker, March 30, 1857; Herndon to Parker, April 17, 1858, HP.

65. Herndon to Parker, August 31, September 20, October 4, November 23, 1858, HP.

66. Herndon to Parker, January 24, 1857, April 23, 1855, HP.

67. Herndon to Parker, March 10, 1857, September 25, 1858, HP.

68. Herndon to Parker, November 23, 24, 1858, HP.

69. Herndon to Parker, September 20, 1858, HP.

70. Parker to Herndon, September 23, November 13, 1858, HP.

71. Herndon to Parker, January 15, 1859, HP.

72. Herndon to Parker, June 29, 1857; the letter from Parker to Herndon has apparently been lost; Herndon to Parker, July 29, 1857, HP.

73. Parker to Herndon, July 1, 1858, HP.

74. Herndon to Parker, December 15, 1859, HP.

75. Brown to Parker, February 2, 1858, in Weiss, *Life and Correspondence,* 2:163–64; F. Sanborn to T. W. Higginson, March 21, 1858 (Ms. E.5.1, p. 13), Higginson Papers, Boston Public Library/Rare Books Department, courtesy of the Trustees; John Brown's private notebook (Ms. Am 1996, vol. 2), Boston Public Library/Rare Books Department, courtesy of the Trustees.

76. An excellent account of the details concerning this threat, as well as of the activities of Parker and the other members of the group, may be found in Edward J. Renehan Jr., *The Secret Six: The True Tale of the Men Who Conspired with John Brown* (New York: Crown, 1995). Brown's letter to Parker of March 7, 1858, the same date as the notebook entry, makes clear that one of the tracts he wished Parker to author was designed to encourage treason. Brown explained to Parker that it was to be distributed to "the officers and soldiers of the United States army," and should therefore be "particularly adapted to the peculiar circumstances we anticipate, and should look to the actual change of service from that of Satan to the service of God" (in Weiss, *Life and Correspondence,* 2:164).

77. Lincoln, "Address at Cooper Institute, New York City," *CW* 3:538.

CHAPTER 3

1. Quotes this paragraph are taken from Thomas Wentworth Higginson, *Cheerful Yesterdays* (Boston: Houghton Mifflin, 1898), 216–17, 219, 221 (last two).

2. Seward to Parker, May 12, 1852, and June 23, 1854, in Letterbook 11:2, 11.

3. Seward to Parker, August 10, 1852, March 11, 1858, December 31, 1855, June 28, 1858, in Letterbook 11:3, 21, 17, 23.

4. Seward to Parker, June 28, 1858, Letterbook 11:23.

5. Parker to John Hale, October 21, 1856, Letterbook 7:52.

6. Parker to Hale, September 1856, Letterbook 7:49.

7. Parker to Charles Sumner, August 17, 1845 (shelf mark bMS Am 1, no. 1), Sumner Collection, by permission of the Houghton Library, Harvard University. For Mexican War and Sims, see David Donald, *Charles Sumner and the Coming of the Civil War* (New York: Alfred A. Knopf, 1961), 183–204.

8. Parker to Sumner, April 26, 1851, Letterbook 6:233.

9. Parker to Howe, August 3, 1852, in Weiss, *Life and Correspondence,* 2:213; Howe to Sumner, July 4, 1852, as quoted in Samuel Gridley Howe, *Letters and Journals,* ed. L. E. Richard (Boston: Estes, 1909–1910), 2:382.

10. Parker, entry of August 24, 1852, in Journal 1851–1856, 311, in the Unitarian Universalist Association Library, Boston, Massachusetts. Sumner's reaction to Parker's charge can be seen in his letter to the minister of August 11, 1852:

> I will not argue the question of past delay. To all that can be said on that head there is this explicit answer. With a heart full of devotion to our cause, in the exercise of my best discretion, and on the advice or with the concurrence of friends, I have waited. It may be that this was unwise, but it was honestly and sincerely adopted, with a view to serve the cause. (Weiss, *Life and Correspondence,* 2:214)

11. Sumner to Howe, August 11, 1852, as quoted in Charles Pierce, *Memoirs and Letters of Charles Sumner, 1845–1860* (London, 1893), 291.

12. Parker to Sumner, September 6, 1852 (shelf mark BMS Am 1, no. 22), Sumner Collection, by permission of the Houghton Library, Harvard University.

13. Parker, entry of August 10, 1852, in Journal 1851–1856, 270, in the Unitarian Universalist Association Library, Boston, Massachusetts.

14. Sumner to Parker, June 12, 13, 1854, Letterbook 10:277.

15. Both Sumner to Parker and Parker to Sumner in Weiss, *Life and Correspondence,* 2:179.

16. For a more extensive treatment of the Sumner-Brooks incident, see Donald, *Charles Sumner,* 278–311.

17. Ibid., 322.

18. Herndon to Parker, January 24, 1855, HP; Donald, *Charles Sumner,* 312–47.

19. Donald, *Lincoln,* 345.

20. Parker's respect for the senator may be seen in the fact that Sumner was the third person mentioned in Parker's will, where he was referred to as "my much valued friend" and was bequeathed "the copy of the 'Parliamentary History of England' in 36 volumes, which is now in my library." Weiss, *Life and Correspondence,* 2:443.

21. Wilson to Parker, May 25, 26, Letterbook 11:148, 149.

22. Wilson to Parker, June 27, 1856, Letterbook 11:150.

23. Parker to Wilson, February 15, 1855, Wilson to Parker, July 23, 1855, in Weiss, *Life and Correspondence,* 2:209–12.

24. Parker to Wilson, July 7, 1855, ibid. 2:210–11.

25. Theodore Parker, "The Present Aspect of the Anti-Slavery Enterprise," in *Works,* 12:426–27.

26. Parker to Samuel Andrews, February 15, 1837, in "Memoir of Theodore Parker," Parker Collection, by permission of the Houghton Library, Harvard University.

27. Jacques Barzun, "Lincoln the Writer," in *On Writing, Editing, and Publishing: Essays Explicative and Hortatory* (1959; Chicago: University of Chicago Press, 1971); Higginson, "Theodore Parker," 34–59. Further references to these works will appear as page numbers cited parenthetically in the text.

28. Higginson relates that "Probably there was no private man in the nation, unless it were Beecher or Greeley, whom personal strangers were so eager to see; while from a transatlantic direction he was sought by visitors to whom the two other names were utterly unknown. Learned men from the continent of Europe always found their way, first or last, to Exeter Place; and it is said that Thackeray, on his voyage to this country, declared that the thing in America which he most desired was to hear Theodore Parker talk" (49–50).

CHAPTER 4

1. Herndon to Weik, October 28, 1885, HW. Webster's Reply to Hayne is Webster, "Second Speech on Foot's Resolution," in *Works of Daniel Webster,* vol. 3. Further references to this work will appear parenthetically in the text.

2. Herndon and Weik, *Herndon's Life of Lincoln,* 324.

3. Current, "Lincoln and Webster," 319; Donald, *Lincoln,* 206.

4. Wills, *Lincoln at Gettysburg,* 285n. 18, 91.

5. Fredrickson, "A Man but Not a Brother," 41 (see pages 40–55 for the exposition of Fredrickson's case); Arthur Lehman Goodhart, "Lincoln and the Law," in *Lincoln and the Gettysburg Address: Commemorative Papers,* ed. Allan Nevins (Urbana: University of Illinois Press, 1964), 57–58.

6. Abraham Lincoln, "A House Divided," in *Abraham Lincoln: His Speeches and Writings,* ed. Roy P. Basler (Cleveland: World Publishing, 1946), 372. I follow Fehrenbacher's *Lincoln in Text and Context,* 275–77, in using Basler's earlier rendering of the speech, since the version in the *Collected Works* is marred by transposed paragraphs. Fehrenbacher credits George B. Forgie with detecting the error, for which Basler assumes ultimate responsibility (see 345–46n. 26). Further references to this work will also appear as page numbers cited parenthetically in the text.

7. Lincoln, debate at Ottawa, Illinois, of August 21, 1858, *CW* 3:16.

8. Herndon to Weik, January 1, 1886, HW.

9. See Fehrenbacher, *Prelude to Greatness: Lincoln in the 1850s* (Stanford: Stanford University Press, 1962), 180n. 11.

10. Daniel Webster, "A Speech Delivered before a Large Assembly of the Citizens of Buffalo and the County of Erie at a Public Reception on the 22d of May, 1851," in *Works of Webster,* 2:545.

11. Ibid., 546.

12. Lincoln, *CW* 1:315. Beveridge points out, "those exact words, applied to slavery in the United States, had been in common use for at least half a century" before Lincoln's use. Beveridge cites several examples, of which only one ("'A house divided against itself cannot stand; neither can a government or Constitution: This is coincident with the present Chief Magistrate's [Jefferson's] opinion in his notes on the State of Virginia,' etc. *Remarks on the Slavery of the Black People;* John Parrish, Philadelphia, 1806") precedes that of Webster or Parker. Beveridge, *Abraham Lincoln,* 2:575n. 2.

13. See Donald, *Lincoln,* 206.

14. Reference here is to Lincoln's seventh and last debate with Douglas, at Alton, Illinois, on October 15, 1858, in *CW* 3:307.

15. Thomas Jefferson to John Holmes, Monticello, April 22, 1820, in *Basic Writings,* 767.

16. Lincoln, *CW* 2:401.

17. Lincoln, *CW* 2:405–6.

18. Stephen A. Douglas, "Kansas, Utah, and the Dred Scott Decision: Remarks Delivered in the State House at Springfield, Illinois, on 12th of June, 1857," 5. A copy of this speech is located in the Illinois State Historical Library, Springfield, Illinois.

19. Lincoln, *CW* 2:406.

20. Lincoln, "Speech at Springfield, Illinois," June 26, 1857, in *CW* 2:405.

21. See Fehrenbacher, *Prelude to Greatness,* 181n. 25; Zarefsky, *Lincoln, Douglas and Slavery,* 169–75; Robert W. Johannsen, *Stephen A. Douglas* (New York: Oxford University Press, 1973), 591.

22. In "Notes for Speeches at Columbus and Cincinnati, Ohio," Lincoln was specific about this point, stating: "Whoever would prevent slavery becoming national and perpetual, yields all when he yields to a policy which treats it either as being *right,* or as being a matter of indifference" (*CW* 3:435). In his "Address at Cooper Institute, New York City," he cautioned his listeners: "Let us be diverted by none of those sophistical contrivances wherewith we are so industriously plied and belabored—contrivances such as groping for some middle ground between the right and the wrong, vain as the search for a man who should be neither a living man nor a dead man—such as a policy of 'don't care' on a question about which all true men do care" (*CW* 3:550).

23. Harry V. Jaffa, *Crisis of the House Divided: An Interpretation of the Issues in the Lincoln-Douglas Debates* (1959; Chicago: University of Chicago Press, 1982), 422n. 10, 278.

24. Don E. Fehrenbacher, *The Dred Scott Case: Its Significance in American Law and Politics* (New York: Oxford University Press, 1978), 487.

25. Fehrenbacher, *Prelude to Greatness,* 85.

26. Theodore Parker, "The Present Crisis in American Affairs" (*Works,* 12:430–90). The subtitle of this sermon was "The Slave-Holders' Attempt to Wrench the Territories from the Working People, and to Spread Bondage Over All the Land." The subtitle is omitted from the centenary edition of Parker's works but may be found in Theodore Parker, *The Collected Works of Theodore Parker,* ed. Frances Power Cobbe (London: Trübner, 1863–1876), 6:242. For Parker's use of the word *crisis,* see Parker, "Reply to Webster," where he uses the following sentence: "A great crisis has occurred in the affairs of the United States" (11:218), or his sermon on "The Slavery Power in America" (*Works,* 11:248–86), where he states: "First, I will speak of the present crisis in our affairs; then of the manner in which this crisis is met" (11:250).

27. Parker, "The Present Crisis in American Affairs," in *Works,* 12:488.

28. Quoted in Herndon and Weik, *Herndon's Life of Lincoln,* 410. A full transcription of this letter is also available in Wilson and Davis, *Herndon's Informants,* 162–68. Herndon quotes Swett as saying "it was saying just the wrong thing" (410) whereas Wilson and Davis read it as "first the wrong thing" (163).

29. Herndon and Weik, *Herndon's Life of Lincoln,* 410–11.

30. Wills, *Lincoln at Gettysburg,* 112.

31. Ibid., 114–15. Wills points out that Lincoln had in his speech spoken of Douglas and those of like mind as *"preparing the public mind"* for "making the institution of slavery perpetual and national":

> "Preparing the public mind" is a thing of great importance in an age of Transcendentalism. To fall silent, or to silence others, on the very notion of equality is the ultimate self-betrayal of a land that was dedicated to a *proposition.* Lincoln does not exaggerate the crisis of the house divided if one accepts his premise—and Parker's—that the only ground of legitimate union for the American nation is the American idea enunciated in the Declaration of Independence. (120)

On the quiet communication occurring between Buchanan and certain members of the Supreme Court, see also Philip Auchampaugh, "James Buchanan, the Court and the Dred Scott Case," *Tennessee Historical Magazine* 9 (January 1926): 231–40; Allan Nevins, *The Emergence of Lincoln* (New York: Charles Scribner's Sons, 1950), 106–12; Hopkins, *Dred Scott's*

Case, 53–60; and Kenneth M. Stampp, *America in 1857: A Nation on the Brink* (New York: Oxford University Press, 1990), 91–93.

32. Jaffa, *Birth of Freedom,* 305.

33. In *Lincoln at Gettysburg,* Wills sees the following statement from Parker's sermon "An Anti-Slavery Address," of May 12, 1854, as also suggesting that a conspiracy was taking shape: "The Slave Power controls the President, and fills all the offices. Out of twelve elected Presidents, four have been from the North, and the last of them might just as well have been taken by lot at the South anywhere. Mr. Pierce, I just now said, was Texan in his latitude. His conscience is Texan; only his cradle was New Hampshire. Of the nine judges of the Supreme Court, five are from the slave states—the Chief Justice [Taney] from the slave States" (113). This citation may be found in Parker, *Works,* 12:172.

34. Parker, "The Present Aspect of the Anti-Slavery Enterprise," in *Works,* 12:473, 474; Lincoln, *CW* 2:321.

35. Wills, *Lincoln at Gettysburg,* 113–14. It should be noted that in the House Divided speech Lincoln mentions only the first two of these moves.

36. Parker, "The Present Aspect of Slavery in America," in *Works,* 14:313.

37. Herndon to Parker, March 4, 1858, HP.

38. Herndon to Weik, October 29, 1885, HW.

39. Herndon and Weik, *Herndon's Life of Lincoln,* 321–22.

40. Fehrenbacher, *Prelude to Greatness,* 71.

41. Ibid., 94.

CHAPTER 5

1. All quotations this paragraph from Lincoln, "Speech at Peoria," *CW* 2:282.

2. All quotations from ibid., 273.

3. Lincoln to Henry C. Whitney, Springfield, July 9, 1856, *CW* 2:347.

4. Lincoln to Ward H. Lamon, Springfield, June 11, 1858, *CW* 2:458–59.

5. Newton, *Lincoln and Herndon,* 63.

6. Herndon claims to having warned Lincoln away from the meeting, worrying that

> If he had endorsed the resolutions passed at the meeting, or spoken simply in favor of freedom that night, he would have been identified with all the rancor and extremes of Abolitionism. If, on the contrary, he had been invited to join them, and then had refused to take a position as advanced as them, he would have lost their support. In either event he was in great danger; and so he who was aspiring to succeed his old rival, James Shields,

> in the United States Senate was forced to avoid the issue by driving hastily in his one horse buggy to the court in Tazewell County. (*Herndon's Life of Lincoln,* 300–301)

Donald, while conceding that Herndon's account is not necessarily "a falsehood," calls the story into question on the grounds that "it is out of character for both Lincoln and Herndon, it is supported by no contemporary evidence, and it is on the surface improbable" (*Lincoln's Herndon,* 77–78). Fehrenbacher is also skeptical: "It is an amusing picture—the future Emancipator scurrying away in his buggy to escape contamination from a little group of abolitionists—but scarcely a credible one" (*Prelude to Greatness,* 35). And there is no question but that Lincoln's own description of the incident, presented during his debate with Douglas at Ottawa on August 21, 1858, is less vivid than Herndon's:

> There was a call for a Convention to form a Republican party at Springfield, and I think my friend Mr. Lovejoy, who is here upon this stand, had a hand in it. I think this is true, and I think if he will remember accurately, he will be able to recollect that he tried to get me into it, and I would not go in. [Cheers and laughter.] I believe it is also true, that I went away from Springfield when the Convention was in session, to attend court in Tazewell County. It is true they did place my name, though without authority, upon the Committee, and afterwards wrote me to attend the meeting of the Committee, but I refused to do so, and I never had anything to do with that organization. (*CW* 3:13)

Lincoln's acknowledgment that he left "Springfield when the Convention was in session" would nevertheless imply that he was aware of the convention at the moment he made his decision to leave, and that his departure was not serendipitous. The possible accuracy of Herndon's report cannot, therefore, be dismissed.

7. Lincoln to Ichabod Codding, November 27, 1854, *CW* 2:288.

8. Lincoln to Joshua F. Speed, August 24, 1855, *CW* 2:322–23.

9. Lincoln to Owen Lovejoy, August 11, 1855, *CW* 2:316; Fehrenbacher, *Prelude to Greatness,* 42.

10. Lincoln to Speed, August 24, 1855, *CW* 2:320, 321, 322.

11. Lincoln to George Robertson, Springfield, August 15, 1855, *CW* 2:318.

12. Lincoln, "Speech at Peoria," *CW* 2:274.

13. Lincoln, *CW* 3:317.

14. Douglas's Reply to Lincoln in the debate at Quincy, Illinois, of October 13, 1858, cited in Lincoln, *CW* 3:266.

15. Lincoln, *CW* 3:315.

16. Lincoln, *CW* 2:409.

17. Lincoln, *CW* 3:16. It merits noting here that, although Lincoln's declaration rings sharply, his position on America's blacks was much milder than that of Douglas, or even of Thomas Jefferson, who once asserted—in a statement with which Douglas could no doubt fully agree—"Their amalgamation with the other color produces a degradation to which no lover of his country, no lover of excellence in the human character can innocently consent" (Thomas Jefferson to Edward Coles, August 25, 1814, in Jefferson, *Writings,* 1345).

18. Douglas, Reply to Lincoln at Quincy, Illinois, cited in Lincoln, *CW* 3:264.

19. Lincoln, debate at Quincy, Illinois, *CW* 3:280.

20. Ibid., 179. For the differences between the two speeches, see Zarefsky, *Lincoln, Douglas and Slavery,* 190–94.

21. Lincoln, debate at Alton, Illinois, of October 15, 1858, *CW* 3:313.

22. Lincoln to Schuyler Colfax, July 6, 1859, *CW* 3:390–91.

23. Lincoln to Salmon P. Chase, June 20, 1859, *CW* 3:386.

24. Lincoln, *CW* 3:181.

25. Greenstone, *The Lincoln Persuasion,* 280, 257.

26. Lincoln, "Speech at Peoria," *CW* 2:255.

27. In the debate of October 13, 1858, Douglas declared:

> The Dred Scott decision was pronounced by the highest tribunal on earth. From that decision there is no appeal this side of Heaven. Yet, Mr. Lincoln says he is going to reverse that decision. By what tribunal will he reverse it? Will he appeal to a mob? Does he intend to appeal to violence, to Lynch law? Will he stir up strife and rebellion in the land and overthrow the court by violence? He does not deign to tell you how he will reverse the Dred Scott decision, but keeps appealing each day from the Supreme Court of the United States to political meetings in the country (Laughter). (cited in Lincoln, *CW* 3:267)

28. Lincoln, "Speech at Peoria," *CW* 2:276.

29. Ibid., 274.

30. Lincoln, *CW* 3:276.

31. Lincoln to Horace Greeley, August 22, 1862, *CW* 5:388.

32. Ibid., 48.

33. Lincoln to Caleb B. Smith, October [23?] 1861, *CW* 4:561.

34. Lincoln, "Address on Colonization to a Deputation of Negroes," August 14, 1862, *CW* 5:371–72.

35. Fehrenbacher, *Lincoln in Text and Context,* 109.

36. Lincoln, *CW* 5:370–71n. 1. The quotation is from "Emancipation Proclamation," January 1, 1863, in Lincoln, *CW* 6:29.

37. Chadwick informs us "there were 7000 (!) names upon his parish register." *Theodore Parker,* 201.

38. Ibid., 210.

39. Jaffa, *Birth of Freedom,* 155. Jaffa's source for the Lincoln quote is "Fragment: On Slavery [August 1, 1858?]," in Lincoln, *Speeches and Writings,* 427.

40. Lincoln, Gettysburg Address, Bliss Copy, in Mearns and Dunlap, *Long Remembered.*

41. Lincoln's tinkering with the last sentence of his speech extended also to the words "under God," which are not to be found in the first two drafts but which the Associated Press version of the speech, prepared by Joseph L. Gilbert shortly after the Gettysburg event, has him uttering, and which Lincoln added to the final three copies. See *CW* 7:17–23.

42. Richard D. Heffner, *A Documentary History of the United States* (New York: Indiana University Press, 1952), 149.

CHAPTER 6

1. See Samuel Abbott Green, "President Lincoln's Speech at Gettysburg, November 19, 1863: Remarks presented at a Massachusetts Historical Society meeting of Thursday, May 9, 1901," in Boston, Massachusetts. Document located in the Boston Public Library. This paper was published in *Proceedings of the Massachusetts Historical Society,* 2d ser., vol. 15, 1901, 1902 (Boston: Published by the Society, 1902), 92–94. The quote from Cooper may be found in Thomas Cooper, *Some Information Respecting America, Collected by Thomas Cooper* (1794; New York: Reprints of Economic Classics, Augustus M. Kelley, 1969), 53.

2. Cooper, *Some Information,* 52.

3. See Alexander DeConde, *The Quasi-War: The Politics and Diplomacy of the Undeclared War with France, 1797–1801* (New York: Charles Scribner's, 1966). For specific details of the XYZ affair, which involved demands by the Talleyrand Directory for money and an apology from Adams for comments made in his speech to Congress of May 16, 1797, see *The Debates and Proceedings in the Congress of the United States with an Appendix, Containing Important State Papers and Public Documents, and all the Laws of a Public Nature; with a Copious Index, Fifth Congress, Comprising the Period from May 15, 1797, to March 3, 1799* (Washington, D.C.: Gales and Seaton, 1851), 3336–50, 3447–54.

4. Address sent "To John Adams, President of the United States from Your fellow Citizens of the County of Westmoreland," June 30, 1798, Adams Family Papers, MHS. William Barton mistakenly attributes this quote to John Adams, in *Lincoln at Gettysburg,* 134. George F. Hoar drew attention to the origin of the quote when he presented the original document to the American Antiquarian Society on October 24, 1894. See *Proceedings* for the annual meeting "at the hall of the society in Worcester," n.s. 9 (October 1894): 321–28.

5. John Adams, "To my Fellow Citizens of the County of Westmoreland in the State of Virginia," July 11, 1798, George Frisbie Hoar Autograph Collection, MHS. George F. Hoar presented this document to the American Antiquarian Society at the same time as the address from the citizens of the county of Westmoreland.

6. Green, "Lincoln's Speech," 94. Samuel Sewall, *Diary of Samuel Sewall,* in *Collections of the Massachusetts Historical Society, Vol. V.—Fifth Series* (Boston: Published by the Society, 1878), 333–34.

7. Stuart P. Garver, *Our Christian Heritage* (Hackensack, N.J.: Christ's Mission, 1973), 59–60.

8. Barton, *Lincoln at Gettysburg,* 152–53.

9. Ibid., 132–33.

10. Claire Breay to Carl Wieck, personal correspondence of August 4, 2000.

11. Anne Hudson to Carl Wieck, personal correspondence of August 2, 2000.

12. Conrad Lindberg to Carl Wieck, personal correspondence of August 2000.

13. F. Lauriston Bullard, *"A Few Appropriate Remarks": Lincoln's Gettysburg Address* (Harrogate, Tenn.: Lincoln Memorial University, 1944), 59. Hudson also states: "I would agree with you that the story is probably apocryphal, but am afraid I cannot provide any further confirmation of that" (Hudson to Wieck, August 2, 2000).

14. Ward Hill Lamon, *Recollections of Abraham Lincoln, 1847–1865* (1895; Lincoln: University of Nebraska Press, 1994), 178.

15. The entire sentence reads, "alle Regierungen der Schweiz müssen es erkennen, dass sie blos [*sic*] aus dem Volke, durch das Volk und für das Volk da sind." Peter Feddersen, *Geschichte der Schweizerischen Regeneration von 1830 bis 1848* (Zurich: Verlags-Magazin, 1867), 31–32.

16. According to an unnumbered Feddersen footnote (ibid., 32), the quote from Schinz is taken from "*Die Helvetische Gesellschaft* von Karl Morell (Winterthur, Verlag von Gustav Lücke, 1863), 398." Morrell's source was "Ueber die gegenwärtige Lage unsers Vaterlandes in ihrer Licht- und Schattenseite von Herrn Dr. und Oberrichter Schinz, Vorgelesen in der Helvetischen Gesellschaft, 1830," in *Verhandlungen der Helvetischen Gesellschaft zu Olten im Jahr 1830* (Zurich: Friedrich Schulthess), 107. Claudia Engler of the Stadt- und Universitäts-Bibliothek of Bern, Switzerland, assumes that although no publication date appears on the document, this work was most probably published in 1830, the same year the speech was given (personal correspondence of September 25, 1998).

17. See Newton, *Lincoln and Herndon,* 41.

18. Alphonse de Lamartine, *History of the Girondists; or, Personal Memoirs of the Patriots of the French Revolution,* trans. H. T. Ryde (London:

Henry G. Bohn, 1848), 3:104, from A. de Lamartine, *Histoire des Girondins* (Paris: Furne et Cie—W. Coquebert, 1847), 6:297.

19. The original reads: "Ce but, c'était la souveraineté représentative de tous les citoyens, puisée dans une élection aussi large que le peuple lui-même, et agissant par le peuple et pour le peuple dans un conseil électif qui serait tout le gouvernement."

20. Neither is to be found in his personal library, which was bequeathed to and is presently located in the Boston Public Library.

21. Thirty-Second Congress, 1st sess., H.R. exec. doc. no. 5, 190.

22. Biographical information in this paragraph is drawn from *Webster's New Biographical Dictionary* (Springfield, Mass.: Merriam-Webster, 1988), 667.

23. Lamon, *Recollections,* 172.

24. Intervention of Joel Parker, Monday, May 16, 1853, in *Official Report of the Debates and Proceedings in The State Convention Assembled May 4th, 1853 to Revise and Amend the Constitution of the Commonwealth of Massachusetts* (Boston: White and Potter, 1853), 150.

25. Bullard, *Remarks,* 57. See also Barton, *Lincoln at Gettysburg,* 132, 134–35.

26. James Monroe, "Fourth Annual Message," in *The State of the Union Messages of the Presidents, 1790–1966,* vol. 1, *1790–1860* (New York: Chelsea House, 1967), 175.

27. Green, "Lincoln's Speech," 93; John Marshall, *John Marshall's Defense of "McCulloch v. Maryland,"* ed. and with introduction by Gerald Gunther (Stanford: Stanford University Press, 1969), 26.

28. Marshall, *Defense,* 25, 27, 44.

29. Bullard, *Remarks,* 57–58. Bullard, *Remarks,* 75n. 68, reads: "In the American Edition, p. 71; in the Porter Reader, p. 196." Complete references should be to James Douglas, *The Advancement of Society in Knowledge and Religion,* first American edition, from the second Edinburgh edition (Hartford: Cook and Co. and Packard and Butler, 1840), 71; Ebenezer Porter, *The Rhetorical Reader: Consisting of Instructions for Regulating the Voice* (Andover, Mass.: Flagg and Gould; New York: J. Leavitt, 1831), 196.

30. Jesse W. Weik, "Lincoln's Gettysburg Address," *The Outlook,* 12 July 1913, 573–74.

31. Jesse W. Weik, *The Real Lincoln: A Portrait* (Boston: Houghton Mifflin, 1922), 8–9.

32. See Donald, *Lincoln's Herndon,* 298.

33. Herndon to Weik, October 28, 1885, HW.

34. Theodore Parker, *The Relation of Slavery to a Republican Form of Government: A Speech Delivered at the New England Anti-Slavery Convention, May 26, 1858* (Boston: William L. Kent, 1858).

35. See Donald, *Lincoln's Herndon,* 326–28.

36. The possibility that the Editors mistakenly wrote "Lincoln" instead of "Herndon" must also be discounted since Weik did not study law with Herndon either.

37. See Bullard, *Remarks,* 75n. 73 ("Original in Author's possession").

38. Ibid., 61–62.

39. Wilson and Davis, *Herndon's Informants,* letter of November 24, 1866. As the editors' footnote correctly points out: "AL's phraseology is not identical but apparently owes much to Parker's" (ibid., 420).

40. Mentioned by Parker in "A Discourse on the Death of Daniel Webster," in *Works,* 7:356.

41. Evidence of this may be seen, for example, in Parker's 1850 sermon "Reply to Webster" where Parker states: "Mr. Webster has spoken noble words—at Plymouth, standing on the altar-stone of New England; at Bunker Hill, the spot so early reddened with the blood of our fathers" (*Works,* 11:246–47).

42. Barton, *Lincoln at Gettysburg,* 131–32.

43. Webster, "Speech Delivered before a Large Assembly of the Citizens of Buffalo and the County of Erie, at a Public Reception on the 22nd of May 1851," *Works of Webster,* 2:546.

44. Daniel Webster, "An Address delivered at the Laying of the Cornerstone of the Bunker Hill Monument at Charlestown, Massachusetts, on the 17th of June, 1825" in *Works of Webster,* 2:59. Further references to this work will be cited parenthetically within the text.

45. Basler cited from Lincoln, *CW* 7:21n. 24.

CONCLUSION

1. Frederick Douglass, *Life and Times of Frederick Douglass: Written by Himself* (1892; New York: Collier Macmillan, 1962), 488.

2. Ibid., 489.

3. Ibid., 588–89. The visit took place during Douglass's 1886–1887 tour of Europe.

4. In the private sphere, the death of his beloved son Willie on February 20, 1862, was perhaps the event that touched Lincoln most deeply. See Donald, *Lincoln,* 336–37. Tensions with his wife, Mary, were also public knowledge. See Guelzo, *Redeemer President,* 387–88.

Bibliography

PRIMARY SOURCES

Adams, John. Papers. Massachusetts Historical Society, Boston, Massachusetts.

Black, Jeremiah Sullivan. Papers. Library of Congress, Washington, D.C.

Brown, John. Papers. Boston Public Library, Boston, Massachusetts.

Clarke, James Freeman. Papers. Houghton Library, Harvard University, Cambridge, Massachusetts.

Herndon, William H., and Jesse W. Weik. *Herndon's Life of Lincoln: The History and Personal Recollections of Abraham Lincoln as Originally Written by William H. Herndon and Jesse W. Weik.* Introduction and notes by Paul M. Angle. 1930. Greenwich, Conn.: Fawcett Publications, 1961.

Herndon, William H.–Theodore Parker Correspondence. Illinois State Historical Library, Springfield.

Herndon-Weik Collection of Lincolniana. Library of Congress, Washington, D.C.

Higginson, Thomas Wentworth. Papers. Boston Public Library, Boston, Massachusetts.

Hoar, George Frisbie. Papers. Massachusetts Historical Society, Boston, Massachusetts.

Lamon, Ward Hill. Papers. Henry E. Huntington Library, San Marino, California. (Letters are coded LN and numbered.)

Lincoln, Abraham. *Abraham Lincoln: His Speeches and Writings.* Edited by Roy P. Basler. Cleveland: World Publishing, 1946.

———. *The Collected Works of Abraham Lincoln.* 9 vols. Edited by Roy P. Basler, with assistant editors Marion Dolores Pratt and Lloyd A. Dunlap. New Brunswick, N.J.: Rutgers University Press, 1953–1955.

———. "A House Divided." In Lincoln, *His Speeches and Writings,* ed. Basler, 372–81.

Parker, Theodore. *The Collected Works of Theodore Parker.* 14 vols. Edited by Frances Power Cobbe. London: Trübner, 1863–1876.

———. *The Effect of Slavery on the American People: A Sermon Preached at the Music Hall, Boston, on Sunday, July 4, 1858.* Boston: William L. Kent, 1858.

———. *A False and True Revival of Religion: A Sermon, Delivered at Music Hall, Boston, on Sunday, April 4, 1858*. Boston: William L. Kent, 1858.

———. "The Letter from Santa Cruz, called 'Theodore Parker's Experience as a Minister': Letter to the Members of the Twenty-Eighth Congregational Society of Boston." In Weiss, *Life and Correspondence,* app. 2, 447–515.

———. Papers. Houghton Library, Harvard University, Cambridge, Massachusetts.

———. Papers. Massachusetts Historical Society. Boston, Massachusetts.

———. Papers. Unitarian Universalist Association, Boston, Massachusetts.

———. *The Relation of Slavery to a Republican Form of Government: A Speech Delivered at the New England Anti-Slavery Convention, May 26, 1858*. Boston: William L. Kent, 1858.

———. "The Transient and Permanent in Christianity." In *Theodore Parker: An Anthology,* edited by and with introduction and notes by Henry Steele Commager. Boston: Beacon Press, 1960.

———. *The Works of Theodore Parker.* 15 vols. Centenary Edition. Boston: American Unitarian Association, 1907–1911.

Sumner, Charles. Papers. Houghton Library, Harvard University, Cambridge, Massachusetts.

Webster, Daniel. *The Works of Daniel Webster.* 6 vols. Boston: Little Brown, 1853.

SECONDARY SOURCES

American Antiquarian Society. *Proceedings,* n.s. 9 (October 1894).

Auchampaugh, Philip. "James Buchanan, the Court and the Dred Scott Case." *Tennessee Historical Magazine* 9 (January 1926): 231–40.

Barton, William E. *Lincoln at Gettysburg*. Indianapolis: Bobbs-Merrill, 1930.

Barzun, Jacques. "Lincoln the Writer." In *On Writing, Editing, and Publishing: Essays Explicative and Hortatory,* 57–73. 1959. Chicago: University of Chicago Press, 1971.

"A Beacon: Freeing the Slaves in U.S. Capitol." *International Herald Tribune,* 13 April 2000, 3.

Beveridge, Albert J. *Abraham Lincoln: 1809–1858*. 2 vols. London: Victor Gollancz, 1928.

Bullard, F. Lauriston. *"A Few Appropriate Remarks": Lincoln's Gettysburg Address*. Harrogate, Tenn.: Lincoln Memorial University, 1944.

Burlingame, Michael. *The Inner World of Abraham Lincoln*. Urbana: University of Illinois Press, 1994.

Chadwick, John White. *Theodore Parker: Preacher and Reformer.* Boston and New York: Houghton Mifflin, 1900.

Commager, Henry Steele. *Theodore Parker: Yankee Crusader.* 1937. Boston: Beacon Press, 1960.

Cooper, Thomas. *Some Information Respecting America, Collected by Thomas Cooper.* 1794. New York: Reprints of Economic Classics, Augustus M. Kelley, 1969.

Cox, LaWanda. "Lincoln and Black Freedom." In *The Historian's Lincoln: Pseudohistory, Psychohistory, and History,* edited by Gabor S. Boritt and Norman A. Fornes, 175–96. Urbana and Chicago: University of Illinois Press, 1988.

Current, Richard N. "Lincoln and Daniel Webster." *Journal of the Illinois State Historical Society* 48 (1955): 307–21. Reprinted in Richard Nelson Current, *Speaking of Abraham Lincoln: The Man and His Meaning for Our Times,* 1–15. Urbana and Chicago: University of Illinois Press, 1983.

The Debates and Proceedings in the Congress of the United States with an Appendix, Containing Important State Papers and Public Documents, and all the Laws of a Public Nature; with a Copious Index, Fifth Congress, Comprising the Period from May 15, 1797, to March 3, 1799. Washington, D.C.: Gales and Seaton, 1851.

DeConde, Alexander. *The Quasi-War: The Politics and Diplomacy of the Undeclared War with France, 1797–1801.* New York: Charles Scribner's, 1966.

Donald, David. *Charles Sumner and the Coming of the Civil War.* New York: Alfred A. Knopf, 1961.

———. *Lincoln.* New York: Simon and Schuster, 1995.

———. *Lincoln's Herndon: A Biography.* 1948. New York: Da Capo Press, 1989.

Douglas, James. *The Advancement of Society in Knowledge and Religion.* Hartford: Cook and Co. and Packard and Butler, 1840.

Douglas, Stephen A. "Kansas, Utah, and the Dred Scott Decision: Remarks Delivered in the State House at Springfield, Illinois, on 12th of June, 1857," 1–8. Illinois State Historical Library, Springfield.

Douglass, Frederick. *Life and Times of Frederick Douglass: Written by Himself.* 1892. New York: Collier Macmillan, 1962.

Emerson, Ralph Waldo. *Journals of Ralph Waldo Emerson, 1856–1863.* Edited by Edward Waldo Emerson and Waldo Emerson Forbes. Boston: Houghton Mifflin, 1913.

Feddersen, Peter. *Geschichte der Schweizerischen Regeneration von 1830 bis 1848.* Zurich: Verlags-Magazin, 1867.

Fehrenbacher, Don E. *The Dred Scott Case: Its Significance in American Law and Politics.* New York: Oxford University Press, 1978.

———. *Lincoln in Text and Context: Collected Essays.* Stanford: Stanford University Press, 1987.

———. *Prelude to Greatness: Lincoln in the 1850s.* Stanford: Stanford University Press, 1962.

Fletcher, George P. *Our Secret Constitution: How Lincoln Redefined American Democracy.* Oxford: Oxford University Press, 2001.

Fredrickson, George M. "A Man but Not a Brother: Abraham Lincoln and Racial Equality." *The Journal of Southern History* 41.1 (February 1975): 39–58.

Garver, Stuart P. *Our Christian Heritage.* Hackensack, N.J.: Christ's Mission, 1973.

Goodhart, Arthur Lehman. "Lincoln and the Law." In *Lincoln and the Gettysburg Address: Commemorative Papers,* edited by Allan Nevins, 38–71. Urbana: University of Illinois Press, 1964.

Green, Samuel Abbott. "President Lincoln's Speech at Gettysburg, November 19, 1863: Remarks presented at a Massachusetts Historical Society meeting of Thursday, May 9, 1901." In *Proceedings of the Massachusetts Historical Society,* 2d ser., vol. 15, 92–94. 1901, 1902. Boston: Published by the Society, 1902.

Greenstone, J. David. *The Lincoln Persuasion: Remaking American Liberalism.* Princeton, N.J.: Princeton University Press, 1993.

Guelzo, Allen C. *Abraham Lincoln: Redeemer President.* Grand Rapids, Mich.: William B. Eerdmans, 1999.

Gup, Ted. "Grab that Leonardo." *Time,* 10 August 1992, 37.

Gura, Philip F. "Theodore Parker and the South Boston Ordination: The Textual Tangle of *A Discourse on the Transient and Permanent in Christianity.*" In *Studies in the American Renaissance,* edited by Joel Myerson, 149–78. Charlottesville: University Press of Virginia, 1988.

Heffner, Richard D. *A Documentary History of the United States.* New York: Indiana University Press, 1952.

Herndon, William H. "Abraham Lincoln's Religion." Letter of February 18, 1870, in *The Index,* vol. 1, no. 14, 2 April 1870, 5–6.

Hertz, Emanuel, ed. *The Hidden Lincoln: From the Letters and Papers of William H. Herndon.* New York: Viking Press, 1938.

Higginson, Thomas Wentworth. *Cheerful Yesterdays.* Boston: Houghton Mifflin, 1898.

———. "Theodore Parker." In *Contemporaries,* 34–59. Boston: Houghton Mifflin, 1899.

Hopkins, Vincent C. *Dred Scott's Case.* New York: Fordham University Press, 1951.

Howe, Julia Ward. *Reminiscences of Julia Ward Howe.* Boston: Houghton Mifflin, 1899.

Howe, Samuel Gridley. *Letters and Journals.* Edited by L. E. Richard. Boston: Estes, 1909–1910.

Hurt, James. "All the Living and the Dead: Lincoln's Imagery." *American Literature* 52.3 (November 1980): 351–80.

Jaffa, Harry V. *Crisis of the House Divided: An Interpretation of the Issues in the Lincoln-Douglas Debates.* 1959. Chicago: University of Chicago Press, 1982.

———. *A New Birth of Freedom: Abraham Lincoln and the Coming of the Civil War.* Lanham, Md.: Rowman and Littlefield, 2000.

Jayne, William. *Abraham Lincoln: Personal Reminiscences of the Martyred President.* Chicago: Grand Army Hall and Memorial Association, 1900.

Jefferson, Thomas. *Notes on the State of Virginia.* In *Basic Writings of Thomas Jefferson,* edited by Philip S. Foner. New York: Halcyon House, 1944.

———. *Writings.* New York: Library of America, 1984.

Johannsen, Robert W. *Stephen A. Douglas.* New York: Oxford University Press, 1973.

Lamartine, Alphonse de. *Histoire des Girondins.* Paris: Furne et Cie—W. Coquebert, 1847.

———. *History of the Girondists; or, Personal Memoirs of the Patriots of the French Revolution.* Translated by H. T. Ryde. London: Henry G. Bohn, 1848.

Lamon, Ward Hill. *Recollections of Abraham Lincoln, 1847–1865.* 1895. Lincoln: University of Nebraska Press, 1994.

Lincoln, Abraham. *Long Remembered: Facsimiles of the Five Versions of The Gettysburg Address in the Handwriting of Abraham Lincoln.* Notes and comments on the preparation of the address by David C. Mearns and Lloyd A. Dunlap. Washington, D.C.: Library of Congress, 1963.

Magdol, Edward. *Owen Lovejoy: Abolitionist in Congress.* New Brunswick, N.J.: Rutgers University Press, 1967.

Marshall, John. *John Marshall's Defense of "McCulloch v. Maryland."* Edited by and with an introduction by Gerald Gunther. Stanford: Stanford University Press, 1969.

McCoy, Drew R. *The Last of the Fathers: James Madison and the Republican Legacy.* Cambridge, England: Cambridge University Press, 1989.

McPherson, James M. *Abraham Lincoln and the Second American Revolution.* New York: Oxford University Press, 1991.

Monroe, James. "Fourth Annual Message." In *The State of the Union Messages of the Presidents 1790–1966,* vol. 1, *1790–1860,* 174–81. New York: Chelsea House, 1967.

Nevins, Allan. *The Emergence of Lincoln.* New York: Charles Scribner's Sons, 1950.

Newton, Joseph Fort. *Lincoln and Herndon.* Cedar Rapids, Iowa: Torch Press, 1910.

Oates, Stephen B. *Abraham Lincoln: The Man behind the Myths.* New York: Meridian, 1985.

Official Report of the Debates and Proceedings in The State Convention Assembled May 4th, 1853 to Revise and Amend the Constitution of the Commonwealth of Massachusetts. Boston: White and Potter, 1853.

Pierce, Charles. *Memoirs and Letters of Charles Sumner, 1845–1860*. London, 1893.

Porter, Ebenezer. *The Rhetorical Reader: Consisting of Instructions for Regulating the Voice*. Andover, Mass.: Flagg and Gould; New York: J. Leavitt, 1831.

Renehan, Edward J., Jr. *The Secret Six: The True Tale of the Men Who Conspired with John Brown*. New York: Crown, 1995.

Safire, William. "Faithful, Even in Death." *New York Times Magazine,* 18 April 1999, 72–73.

Schinz, Herrn Dr. und Oberrichter. "Ueber die gegenwärtige Lage unsers Vaterlandes in ihrer Licht- und Schattenseite von Herrn Dr. und Oberrichter Schinz, Vorgelesen in der Helvetischen Gesellschaft, 1830." In *Verhandlungen der Helvetischen Gesellschaft zu Olten im Jahr 1830,* 85–110. Zurich: Friedrich Schulthess, 1830.

Scudder, Horace E. *James Russell Lowell, a Biography*. 2 vols. Boston: Houghton Mifflin, 1901.

Sewall, Samuel. *Diary of Samuel Sewall*. In *Collections of the Massachusetts Historical Society,* vol. 5, fifth series. Boston: Published by the Society, 1878.

Sherwin, Oscar. *Prophet of Liberty: The Life and Times of Wendell Phillips*. New York: Bookman, 1958.

Stampp, Kenneth M. *America in 1857: A Nation on the Brink*. New York: Oxford University Press, 1990.

Thirty-Second Congress, 1st session, H.R. executive document no. 5.

Von Frank, Albert J. *The Trials of Anthony Burns: Freedom and Slavery in Emerson's Boston*. Cambridge, Mass.: Harvard University Press, 1998.

Webster's New Biographical Dictionary. Springfield, Mass.: Merriam-Webster, 1988.

Weik, Jesse W. "Lincoln's Gettysburg Address." *The Outlook,* 12 July 1913, 572–74.

———. *The Real Lincoln: A Portrait*. Boston: Houghton Mifflin, 1922.

Weiss, John. *Life and Correspondence of Theodore Parker*. 2 vols. New York: D. Appleton, 1864.

Wills, Garry. *Lincoln at Gettysburg: The Words that Remade America*. New York: Simon and Schuster, 1992.

Wilson, Douglas L., and Rodney O. Davis. *Herndon's Informants: Letters, Interviews, and Statements about Abraham Lincoln*. Urbana: University of Illinois Press, 1998.

Zarefsky, David. *Lincoln, Douglas and Slavery: In the Crucible of Public Debate*. Chicago: University of Chicago Press, 1990.

Index

abolition societies, 33
Abraham Lincoln: Personal Reminiscences of the Martyred President (Jayne), 43
Adams, John, 144; and address from Citizens of Westmoreland County, 151, 197n.4
Adams, John Quincy, 115, 144
Agassiz, Louis: as "Swiss of Slavery," 23
amalgamation (racial): Douglas on, 131; Jefferson on, 196n.17; Lincoln on, 131–32
American Colonization Society, 9, 182n.23. *See also* Clay; colonizing slaves abroad; Lincoln
annual message to Congress, December 3, 1861, (Lincoln), 136
"An Anti-Slavery Address" (Parker), 194n.33
Anti-Slavery Standard, 24, 41
Armstrong, John, 43, 53
Ashmun, George, 12, 13

Banks, Governor, 63
Barton, William, 152–53, 156, 158
Barzun, Jacques, 82–88
Basler, Roy, 169
Beecher, Henry Ward, 60, 191n.28
Blair, Frank, 26
Blairs (Frank Sr., Frank Jr., Montgomery), 82
Breay, Claire, 152–53
British Library, 152
Brooks, Preston S., 78
Brown, Antoinette L., 16
Brown, John: description of, 72; encourages treason, 189n.76; failed raid of, 4, 69; and links to Parker, 69–73; plan of, 73; private notebooks of, 70
Bryant, John H., 27
Bryant, William Cullen, 84
Buchanan, James, 107–8, 118; communication with Supreme Court and, 117, 193n.31; election of, 105, 108–9; inaugural address of, 105; Parker on, 76, 118; as proslavery, 105, 108–9, 117
Buffalo speech of May 22, 1851, (Webster): Lincoln and, 99–101
Bullard, F. Lauriston, 153, 156, 158, 164
Bunker Hill speech of June 17, 1825, (Webster): and importance to Lincoln and Parker, 166–73, 178
Burns, Anthony: returned to slavery, 21
Butler, Andrew, 78

Caine, Sir Hall, 152–53
Calhoun, John C., 143; as threat to Constitution and Union, 93
Carlyle, Thomas, 57
Cass, Lewis, 14
Chadwick, John White, 139
Channing, William Ellery, 84, 89
Charleston *Mercury,* 24, 41
Chase, Salmon P., 81–83, 133
Chicago *Tribune,* 24, 41
civil war, 130; Parker and, 75–76, 144
Civil War, U. S., 40, 75, 145; John Brown and, 73; Lincoln and, 145
Clarke, James Freeman, 48
Clay, Henry: admired by Lincoln, 9, 20; colonizing of slaves and, 9, 22, 130; Compromise of 1850 and, 18, 20; death of, 20, 22; Lincoln's borrowing from, 92; Missouri Compromise and, 10, 18, 20, 103; 1850 speech of, 46
Cleon of Athens, 153
Codding, Ichabod, 127, 130

Coles, Edward: and emancipation, 182n.23
Colfax, Schuyler, 133
colonizing slaves abroad, 8–9, 130, 134; plan for 136–37; opposed by free blacks, 138. *See also* Clay; Jefferson; Lincoln
Commager, Henry Steele, 36
Compromise of 1850, 18, 20, 124
Congregational Library, Boston, 152
Constitution, U.S., 46; blacks not mentioned in, 105; Lincoln and, 9, 30–31, 130; Webster's support of, 95, 97–100, 114–15; word *slavery* omitted from, 102–3. *See also* Calhoun
"The Constitution Not a Compact" (Webster): Wills on, 92
Cooper, Thomas, 150
crisis: word favored by Parker, 112, 193n.26
Current, Richard N., credits Webster, 92
Curtis, Benjamin R., 109

D.C. Emancipation Act, 34, 136
Declaration of Independence, 5–6, 114; blacks not mentioned in, 105; Douglas on, 106; importance to Lincoln of, 5–6, 11, 30–31, 59; Lincoln on, 106; Parker on, 141, 143. *See also* Lincoln; slavery
"Defense" (Parker), 21–22
The Dial, 48
"A Discourse on the Transient and Permanent in Christianity" (Parker). *See* "The Transient and Permanent in Christianity"
Donald, David, 33, 43, 60; credits Parker, 36; credits Webster, 92; on Herndon's reliability, 184n.53, 194n.6
doubled "X," 61–62
Douglas, James, 158–59
Douglas, Stephen A.: attacked by Sumner, 78; attacks Lincoln, 13, 26, 99, 126–27, 130–32, 134, 181n.4, 196n.27; and "Caesarism," 183n.37; on Declaration of Independence and white race, 106; and "don't care" phrase, 107–8, 110, 120, 192n.22; Lincoln and, 54, 91, 102–112, 117, 119–20, 124–25, 134; and Lovejoy letter, 26; Parker on, 117, 119; and secret Chicago meeting, 67; as senatorial candidate, 44–45; and slave trade, 119; sends speech to Parker, 69; as threat to Union, 99; as traitor to cause, 20; as villain of House Divided speech, 107; visited by Herndon, 62. *See also* Dred Scott decision; Compromise of 1850; Kansas-Nebraska Act; Kansas-Nebraska Bill; Missouri Compromise
Douglass, Frederick, 26; on Lincoln, 174; on Parker, 176–77. *See also* Dred Scott decision
Dred Scott decision, 21, 102; "deferred," 105; and denial of citizenship to blacks, 105; Douglas mocks Lincoln on, 196n.27; Douglas's support of, 105–8, 196n.27; opposed by Lincoln, 104–9, 116–17, 134

"The Effect of Slavery on the American People" (Parker), 35–36, 47–52, 55–56, 159–61
Emancipation Proclamation, 9, 137, 177; draft of, 136; as war measure, 138
Emancipator, 41
Emerson, Ralph Waldo, 19, 57, 84–86
Engler, Claudia, 198n.16
equality, 6, 178; Lincoln and, 3, 18, 59, 106, 127–28, 132–34, 137–38, 145, 148, 177–78; Parker on, 18, 141
Euclid, 58
"The Excellence of Goodness" (Parker), 48
Exclusion amendment, 108; Douglas and, 105

"A False and True Revival of Religion" (Parker), 48
Fedderson, P., 154, 198n.16
Fehrenbacher, Don E., 110–11,

122–23, 128; on reliability of Herndon, 184n.53, 194n.6
Fell, Jesse W., 20; on Lincoln's religion, 56
"A Few Appropriate Remarks": Lincoln's Gettysburg Address (Bullard), 153
First Inaugural Address (Lincoln), 6, 46, 92; Webster and, 5–6; Wills on, 92
Forgie, George B., 191n.6
Founding Fathers, 102–5; Lincoln and, 3, 30–31, 129, 134–35, 138, 145, 147, 167, 171, 174; Parker and, 114, 144, 146, 171–73, 200n.41; reawakening of vision of, 172–73; ultimate goal of, 102–4
"Fourth of July Oration" (Parker). *See* "The Effect of Slavery on the American People"
Francis, Convers, 37
Frederickson, George M., 92
Freedman's Monument, Washington, D. C.: unveiling of, 174
Fugitive Slave Bill, 165
Fugitive Slave Law, 21, 125–27, 130, 133–34

Garrison, William Lloyd, 59, 62–3, 65, 81
Garver, Stuart P., 151, 153
Gettysburg Address, 3–7, 9–10, 28, 36, 47–48, 52, 90, 138, 144–46, 150, 155, 166, 168–73, 175, 178; importance of, 179n.1; Parker and, 3–7, 9–10, 36, 47–48, 90, 124, 138, 145–49 160–61, 165–73, 175, 178; second draft of (Hay copy), 148; standard text of, 145–46, 179n.7; Webster and, 166–73, 175
Gettysburg Phrase, 4, 7–8, 11, 25, 36, 47, 52, 55–56, 140–41, 148, 150–51, 153–55, 164, 166, 169, 171, 175, 177; Herndon and, 49–51, 165; Herndon errs on, 36–37, 47–49, 51–52, 55–56; on origin of, 150–66, 175, 177; Parker and, 4, 7, 11, 51–52, 155–66, 171; praise for, 3; Webster and, 36, 150, 154–159, 165–66, 171. *See also* Weik
Giddings, Joshua R., 22, 26, 34–5, 41, 162
Goodhart, Arthur Lehman, 92–3
Greeley, Horace, 67, 84, 191n.28; flea in ear of, 62–63; and Lincoln letter, 135–37; support for Douglas of, 63
Green, Samuel A., 150–51, 153, 158
Greenstone, J. David, 10, 134

Hale, John, 49, 74, 76, 80
Hancock, John, 144
Harpers Ferry, 4, 70–71
Hay, John, 83
Hayne, Robert Y.: and defence of states' rights, 93; as danger to Union, 99
Herndon, William H., 3–5, 8, 18–20: as abolitionist, 22, 24, 28, 162; attends Parker sermon, 64; and biography of Lincoln, 4–5, 20, 37, 41, 47, 49, 52–53, 55–56, 59, 160–61, 163 (*see also* Weik); as bridge between Lincoln and Parker, 3, 20, 41, 58–59, 73, 90, 120, 138, 160–61; and contribution to history, 53; credits Parker, 41–42, 66–67, 165–66; credits Webster, 6, 91–92, 95, 97; and differences with Parker, 59–66, 83, 87; on Douglas, 44, 63, 66; and emphasis on secrecy, 25–26, 38–40, 45, 66; and fear of Douglas, 44–45; garrulity of, 64; on Greeley, 62–63; handwriting of, 37–38; on House Divided speech, 42–46; on John Brown, 69; obscures Parker's importance, 8, 35–37, 52, 68, 91–92, 101, 103, 160–61, 175; Parker's importance to, 18–20, 38–47, 52, 57, 66–68, 80, 160–62; and Parker's religious ideas, 18–20, 40, 54, 57; possesses Parker's writings, 3, 19–20, 22, 41, 51, 57, 162; predicts Lincoln candidacy, 53; predicts Lincoln victory, 45; and prophecy concerning House Divided speech, 42–46; "pulled" to Parker, 18, 22, 59, 91; receives Parker's speeches, 5, 19–20, 40, 44, 53–54, 91; and respect for Parker, 18–20, 22, 25, 41,

52, 56, 59, 66–68, 79; requests Parker's writings, 19, 22, 44, 53; self-importance of, 19, 41–47, 52–53, 160–61; self-proclaimed modesty of, 53; sends speeches to Parker, 43–44, 69; shares opinions and information with Parker, 39, 43–44, 66; shares Parker's works with Lincoln, 3, 5, 20, 25, 41–42, 53, 56–57, 59, 69, 138, 160; on "Spot" resolutions, 13; steadied by Parker, 66; and trip east, 48, 52, 55, 62–66, 161; underlines own reliability, 66
Herndon-Parker correspondence, 3, 5, 8, 18, 36–37, 40–41, 52–53, 59, 65–69; omissions in Newton's transcription of, 8, 37–47, 52, 188n.52, 187n.29; secrecy in, 25
Herndon-Weik Collection, 49–50, 160–67
Higginson, Thomas Wentworth, 70, 72, 82; on John Brown, 72–73, on Parker, 82–90
Histoire des Girondins (Lamartine), 154–55
Hoar, Jno, 151
"House divided" phrase, 7–8, 23, 42, 92, 100, 102, 112, 120, 122–23, 130, 166, 178, 192n.12; Lincoln's earliest use of, 100–101; Parker's use of, 112, 122–23; Webster's use of, 6, 100–101, 166. *See also* Douglas
House Divided speech (Lincoln), 5–7, 28, 42–44, 52–53, 69, 72, 90–93, 95–125, 129, 186n.28; on Basler text of, 191n.6; creation of, 6, 120–21; as leading to Lincoln defeat, 45–46; on origins of, 111; Parker and, 3–7, 10, 25, 35, 52, 91–93, 112–25, 138, 166–67, 175, 177–78; sent to Parker, 43–44; Webster and, 91–104, 166, 178. *See also* Douglas
Howe, Samuel Gridley, 76
Hudson, Anne, 152–53
Hurt, James, 32
Illinois Republican State Convention (1858), 44, 111
Illinois State Legislature, 32

Jackson, Andrew, and "Proclamation against Nullification," 46
Jaffa, Harry V., 109, 117, 142
Jayne, William, 43
Jefferson, Thomas, 9–11; on colonization of slaves, 9, 22, 130; and dream of equality, 177; on emancipation and expatriation of slaves, 103, 180n.15; and "idea of freedom," 142; and states' rights, 96. *See also* amalgamation

Kansas-Nebraska Act, 10, 21, 24–25, 104, 107, 124–26; opposed by Lincoln, 22, 24, 103–04, 107–11, 124–26, 128–29; Douglas and, 22, 24, 107–11, 124; Parker and, 10, 18, 118
Kansas-Nebraska Bill, 6, 18, 20–22, 28, 35, 74, 77, 124–25; Douglas and, 20–22, 91, 103–112 111, 124; and House Divided speech, 103–112; passage of, 21, 118; Seward and, 74, 77, 91
Kelley, Augustus M., Publishers, 150
Know-Nothing faction, 127

Lafayette, Marquis de, 166
Lamartine, Alphonse de, 153–55
Lamon, Ward H., 53, 126; report of, 153–54
Lecompton Constitution: Douglas and, 107–9
"Letter to the People of the United States Touching the Matter of Slavery" (Parker), 186n.24
Library of Congress, 49, 152, 160
Lincoln, Abraham: as "abolition leader," 22, 175–76; admires Webster, 100, 175; as "America's prophet of democracy," 149; and Ashmun amendment, 12, 13; avoids naming Douglas, 107; on blacks as property, 18, 23–24, 110, 119; and borrowing of ideas and phrasing, 7, 11, 24, 92–93; as candidate for U.S. Senate, 7, 45, 62, 100, 104, 110–11, 126; as closet

abolitionist, 26, 126–27; on colonization of slaves, 8–9, 22, 35, 130–31, 134, 136–38 (*see also* Clay; Jefferson); on conspiracy, 102, 117–18; on death of Lovejoy, 27–28; and death of son, 200n.4; and delegation of Christian ministers, 59; and delegation of free blacks, 136–37; detachment of, 82–83; distance from abolitionists and abolitionism of, 3–4, 8, 14, 22, 25–28, 31–32, 59, 68–69, 71–72, 126–30, 132–33; and D. C. Emancipation Act, 34, 136 (*see also* Stone); on Douglas and Declaration of Independence, 106; and Emerson, 57; eulogizes Clay, 9; and gradual emancipation, 22, 34–35; on House Divided speech, 46, 116; in House of Representatives, 12, 33; and "idea of democracy," 142; on immorality of slavery, 9, 33, 129, 131, 133–34, 138, 192n.22; influence on (*see* Parker; Webster; specific speeches); and Jefferson, 18; and John Brown, 4, 71; and joint parallels with Webster and Parker, 166–73, 175; and law cases involving slaves, 33; and 1858 letter to Owen Lovejoy, 26–28, 35, 126; and links to abolitionists and abolitionism, 3, 5, 10, 26–28, 31–35, 59, 123–27, 132, 176, 194n.6; and marking of Parker's speeches, 47–51; and Mexican War, 12–14, 17, 20, 122; opposes extremism, 31–32, 71, 126; opposes revolution, 96, 106 (*see also* Lyceum speech); opposes slavery, 9, 14, 18, 22, 32, 34–35, 104–12, 124, 127–30, 134–5, 175; and parallels with Parker, 5, 10, 82–90, 115–16, 119, 121–22, 175; and Parker's religious writings, 20, 56–59, 178; and protest with Daniel Stone (*see* Stone); racial views of, 131–32, 137, 196n.17; on respect for law, 31–32, 106, 126, 130, 134 (*see also* Lyceum speech); and shift toward abolitionism, 34–35, 59; and silence on Parker, 3, 92–93; slavery not paramount with, 14, 95, 131–32, 136; and "Spot" resolutions, 12–13, 122, 181n.4; and support for Taylor, 12; and tensions with wife, 200n.4; as "transparent," 174–75; "under God" phrase of, 197n.41; and use of biblical cadences, language and metaphors, 88, 135; writing style of, 83–84, 87–89. *See also* Douglas; Kansas-Nebraska Act; Kansas-Nebraska Bill; Lincoln-Douglas debates; specific speeches

Lincoln, Mary Todd (wife), 200n.4

Lincoln, William Wallace (son), 200n.4

Lincoln-Douglas debates, 54, 95, 134; at Alton, 102–3, 130; at Charleston, 132, 134; at Chicago, 132; at Freeport, 132; at Jonesboro, 132; at Ottawa, 54, 95, 131. *See also* Douglas

Lincoln at Gettysburg: The Words that Remade America (Wills), 5

Lincoln and Herndon (Newton), 36; defects in, 37–38, 52, 187n.29, 187n.31; *See also* Herndon-Parker correspondence

"Lincoln the Writer" (Barzun), 82

Lindberg, Conrad, 153

Louisville *Journal,* 26

Lovejoy, Elijah P.: murder of, 28, 30–32, 34. *See also* Lyceum speech

Lovejoy, Owen, 26–28, 34–35, 123, 125–28, 132; death of, 27–28; "for Lincoln," 27

Lowell, James Russell, 37

Luther, Martin, 85, 88

Lyceum speech (Lincoln), 28–32, 35, 96, 126, 133, 170–72

Mann, Horace, 74

Marshall, John, 156–58

Mason, James, 78

Massachusetts Historical Society, 150

Maury, Matthew Fontaine, 153, 155–56

May, Samuel J., 47, 51

McClellan, George B., 82

McCulloch v. Maryland, 157–58

McIntosh (a mulatto): burning of, 29

Mclean, John, 109
Mencken, H. L., 87
Mexican War, 12–17, 20; opposed by Sumner and Parker, 76. *See also* Lincoln; Parker; slavery
Minutemen, 172
Missouri Compromise, 10, 20, 103, 111; Douglas and, 117; Lincoln and, 20, 124–26, 128, 131, 134; opposed by Jefferson, 103. *See also* Clay
Monroe, James, 156
Mott, Lucretia, 16

National Era, 41
Newton, Joseph Fort, 8, 26, 36, 39–40, 60; and Gettysburg Phrase, 37, 47–48, 51; and Herndon's error, 36–37; obscures Parker's importance, 8, 37–40, 52, 175, 187n.29, 187n.31, 188n.52. *See also* Herndon-Parker correspondence
New York Public Library, 152
"New York speech" (Parker). *See* "A Speech Before the New York Anti-Slavery Society"
New York *Tribune,* 24, 41, 63, 135
nullification, 46; Webster and, 5–6, 97–98, 101

The Outlook, 159
The Oxford Dictionary of the Christian Church, 152

Parker, Theodore: and abolition, 5, 7–10, 14, 21–22, 25, 35, 69–82, 112–15, 123, 138, 141–45, 174–77; and access to Lincoln, 59; admired by Herndon, 18–19; and Anglo-Saxons of America, 113, 140; and Anthony Burns, 21; attacks Douglas, 120; on blacks as property, 18, 23–24, 119; and Christianity, 7, 57–58, 77; compared to Douglas, 39; conceals role, 68–71; as conscious of influence, 54, 73–82; on conspiracy, 70, 117–18, 120, 194n.33; and contact with Herndon, 3–4, 18–19, 59–71, 82; and contact with Lincoln, 69, 180n.11; criticizes Webster, 165, 175; death of, 25, 68, 79, 176; debt to Webster of, 8, 165–73, 175; on Douglas, 44; and "equilibrium," 8–9, 112–114; as "giant of learning," 7; handwriting of, 37–38; as Herndon ideal, 19; Herndon's importance to, 82; and "idea of democracy," 51, 164; and "idea of freedom," 6, 112–13, 141–42; and "idea of slavery," 112–14, 141–43; illness of, 68; influence on Lincoln of, 3–8, 10, 22, 24–25, 35, 41, 51–52, 56–59, 82, 86, 91, 115, 117, 120–24, 138, 158–59, 160–61, 165, 175–78 (*see also* specific Lincoln speeches and phrases); influence on northern politicians of, 73–82; and Jefferson, 18; and John Brown, 4, 69–73; keeps Herndon information secret, 54, 67; lecture at Springfield of, 60, 62; lecture "on the Anglo-Saxons" of, 85; and letters to Weik, 59; as link between Lincoln and Webster, 165–73; and Mexican War, 14–17, 76; opposes slavery, 5, 9–10, 14, 16–18, 21, 55, 72, 77, 112–15, 117–18, 139–45; ordination of, 16; predicts civil war, 76; promises money for defence, 79; and publication of works, 48–49; rejected by Unitarians, 7; and respect for Webster, 165, 200n.41; and "restrain bonds," 81–82; role of obscured by Herndon, 8, 25–26, 35–36, 52, 68, 91–92, 101, 103, 160–61; role of concealed by Lincoln, 3; and Secret Six, 70, 189n.76; as social activist, 16; tie to Herndon and Lincoln of, 71; and Vigilance Committee, 21; and women's rights, 16; writing style of, 84–89; writings of in Lincoln-Herndon law office, 3, 41, 57, 162. *See also* specific speeches and sermons
Parker, Joel, 153, 156
Parker, Lydia (wife), 66
Peoria speech of 1854 (Lincoln), 23–24, 91, 124–25, 129, 131, 135

Pericles of Athens, 153
"The Pharisees" (Parker), 48
Phillips, Wendell, 22, 41, 59, 62–63, 78, 162; and murder of Elijah Lovejoy, 28
The Physical Geography of the Sea (Maury), 155
Pierce, Franklin, 108–9, 117–18; as pro-slavery, 105, 194n.33
Polk, James K.: and Mexican War, 12, 16–17
Porter, Ebenezer, 158
Post, Herbert, 60
Prentice, George D., 26
"The Present Aspect of the Anti-Slavery Enterprise" (Parker), 81
"The Present Aspect of Slavery in America" (Parker), 119–20
"The Present Crisis in American Affairs" (Parker), 112, 114
"Primitive Christianity" (Parker), 48

Quasi-War with France, 151, 197n.3

Rantoul, Robert, 77
Reeder, Andrew H., 118
"The Relation of Slavery to a Republican Form of Government" (Parker), 159, 162
Remond, Charles Lennox, 39
Reply to Hayne (Webster), 5–6, 11, 36, 46, 91–104, 115, 154, 175; Lincoln and, 6, 11, 91–97, 99, 101–4, 120–21, 165–66; Parker and, 6, 36, 93, 121–22, 165–66; Wills on, 6, 92
"Reply to Webster" (Parker), 200n.41
Republican National Convention, 133
Republican Party Convention (Springfield, 1854): Lincoln and, 127, 194n.6
Revolutionaries of 1776, 30–31, 170
Richmond *Enquirer,* 24, 41
Richmond *Examiner,* 23–24
"Rights of Man" sermon (Parker). *See* "A Sermon of the Dangers Which Threaten the Rights of Man in America"
Robertson, George, 129
Roman Catholic Church, 141

Sanborn, Franklin B., 70, 72–73
Schinz, (Swiss judge), 153–54
Scott, Dred, and U.S. Supreme Court, 21
Scriptures: Lincoln and, 58, 188n.42
Second Inaugural Address (Lincoln), 18; Parker and, 41–42, 46
"Second Speech on Foot's Resolution" (Webster), 180n.8. *See also* Reply to Hayne
Secret Six, 70, 189n.76
"A Sermon of the Dangers Which Threaten the Rights of Man in America" (Parker), 5–7, 10–11, 91, 93; and House Divided speech, 112–24; and Gettysburg Address, 138–42, 144–49, 166–73, 178
"A Sermon of Old Age" (Parker), 19
"A Sermon of Slavery" (Parker), 48
Sewall, Samuel, 151
Seward, William, 22, 41, 62, 67, 74–76, 80–81, 176; and Civil War, 75–76; Parker and, 74–76; possible nomination of, 45, 67; praises Parker, 75
Sherwin, Oscar, 21
Sims, Thomas: rendition of, 76
slavery: on abolishing of in District of Columbia, 33–34; "agitation" against, 104; as basis for Civil War, 137; on conspiracy to make national, 117; and "horses and hogs" comparison, 23–24; "idea of" (*see* Parker); on justifying "scientifically," 22–23; and Mexican War, 12–13; reluctance of Lincoln to interfere with, 127–28, 130–32; and revival of slave trade, 118–19; "tendency" regarding, 102, 108–9, 112–13, 115–16, 144; "ultimate extinction" of, 34–35, 104, 130, 134–35; versus freedom, 115; word omitted from Constitution, 102–3
Smith, Seba, 16
Some Information Respecting America, Collected by Thomas Cooper (Cooper), 150
South Carolina legislature, 97
"A Speech Before the New York

Anti-Slavery Society" (Parker), 19, 22–24, 91
Speed, Joshua, 127–28, 176
Springfield speech of 1854 (Lincoln), 23, 91
Springfield speech of 1857 (Lincoln), 105, 107
Stanton, Edwin M., 82
Stearns, George L., 70, 72
Stone, Daniel: on abolishing slavery in the District of Columbia, 33–34; and protest concerning abolition societies, 32–33
Stuart, John Todd, 34
Sumner, Charles, 22, 41, 62, 74, 80–81, 83, 162, 176; attacked by Brooks, 78; condemns Mexican War, 76; elected to Webster's senate seat, 76; Parker's influence on, 76–79; as proponent of abolition, 78, 138; reelection of, 79; respected by Parker, 190n.20
Supreme Court, U.S.: attacked by Lincoln, 108–9; as controlled by Slave Power, 117; and Dred Scott decision, 105; and Webster, 157–58
Swett, Leonard, 115–16, 125

Taney, Roger: 107, 117; and Dred Scott decision, 105, 108–9
Taylor, Zachary, 12, 14
Thackeray, William Makepeace, 191n.28
"Theodore Parker" (Higginson), 82
Thompson, George, 159
"The Transient and Permanent in Christianity" (Parker), 16, 48, 57–58
"The True Grandeur of Nations" (Sumner), 76
Trumbull, Lyman, 62; speech sent to Parker, 69
Twenty-Eighth Congregational Society, 16

Underground Railroad: Parker and, 7
The Union: and Compromise of 1850, 20; Douglas as danger to, 99; Parker on, 113–14; saving of, 20; supported by Lincoln, 102–3, 125, 136, 138; supported by Webster, 9–10, 95–100, 102–3; threats to, 10
The United States as "political experiment," 140, 142

Vigilance Committee, 21
Von Frank, Albert J., and "Rights of Man," 180n.14

Warren, Joseph, 166–67
Washington, George, 144
Webster, Daniel, 5–6, 10–11, 84, 156; attacked by Parker, 165; death of, 8, 10, 104, 165; influence on Lincoln of, 6, 8, 11, 91–104, 124, 165–73, 175 (*see also* specific Lincoln speeches); influence on Parker of, 165–73; and *McCulloch v. Maryland,* 157; as pariah, 123; speech heard by Parker, 165. *See also* Constitution; nullification; specific speeches; Union
Weed, Thurlow, 67
Weik, Jesse W.: and biography of Lincoln, 4–5, 20, 47, 53, 59; and claim of study with Lincoln, 163; contradicts Herndon account, 160–61; credits Parker, 159–64; and Herndon prediction, 42–43; and taking of credit, 163–64; and two Parker sermons, 159–64
Weiss, John, 48
Wells, E. T., 60
Wilder, Daniel W., 164–65
Wills, Garry: on conspiracy to make slavery national, 117–18, 194n.33; and Gettysburg Phrase, 4–5, 47; on Lincoln's "evasions and silences," 92; and neglect of Parker, 11; on "preparing the public mind," 193n.31, 194n.33
Wilmot Proviso, 14, 33, 127
Wilson, Henry, 62, 74: influenced by Parker, 79–80; requests defence money, 79–80
Wycliffe, John, 152–53
Wycliffe Bible, 151–53

Yerrinton, James, M. W., 48

Zarefsky, David, 43